Walking the Way

A Journey in Pakistan—with a Difference!

AND THINE EARS SHALL HEAR A WORD
BEHIND THEE, SAYING,
THIS IS THE WAY, WALK YE IN IT,
WHEN YE TURN TO THE RIGHT HAND,
AND WHEN YE TURN TO THE LEFT.
ISAIAH 30:21

KENNETH G. OLD

TATE PUBLISHING, LLC

Poetry excerpts are from
Footprints in the Dust
by Kenneth G. Old

Royalties received by the author from the sale of this book are dedicated to the education of poor children who live in the Land of the Five Rivers in Pakistan.

The divine design
Purposes that I be
Different than I am.
The differences lie
Not in circumstances
But in choices I've made.

Dedicated to two wonderful women
whom God chose
to walk along part of the Way with me—

Marie, who shared the journey
the book describes,
and
Patty, without whom this book
would never have seen the light of day.

CONTENTS

Foreword

My college New Testament teacher, an ardent Lutheran, recommended that the class read Martin Luther's *Here I Stand,* but read it as if it were entitled *Here We Go.* Luther said, "Walking the Way is the record of one Christian practicing what he preaches."

My dear friend Kenneth Old is a retired civil engineer. He has produced this unusual volume on the same theme, an olio of prose and poetry, to share what he has learned about God in the course of his faith journey.

The raw material for these memories was largely obtained during his assignment as a member of the Sialkot Mission of the United Presbyterian Church of North America. This mission was located in the Punjab, a northerly province of India, but later, after East Pakistan seceded to form Bangladesh, a province of West, then finally just, Pakistan.

"God," says Ken, "puts us on the Way to make a difference not only to the person one is, but to others met along the way." Reflection on the nature (love) and the character (holy) of God induces a sense of awe and wonder. It gives rise to a conviction that we are meant to live on an ever-higher spiritual plane above mediocrity and legalism. God desires that we live to fulfill His Plan and His Purposes for us. This action is much more than a spiritual "fire insurance policy." It must be for God's glory.

Walking The Way is not in chronological sequence but draws illustrations from a period of more than 40 years. It hops where it will, imparting a sense of wonder and awe.

Ken comments in his preface, "My faith journey took me to Pakistan, where I spent most of my working life. It was a journey with God setting the signposts." He concludes optimistically, "There's still something more ahead."

May we all grow in the grace and knowledge of our Savior, Jesus Christ.

Robert Tebbe,
Principal, Forman Christian College, Lahore (retired)
Representative in Pakistan, Presbyterian Church, U.S.A. (retired)

PREFACE

For I know the thoughts
that I think toward you,
saith the Lord,
thoughts of peace, and not of evil,
to give you an expected end.
Then shall ye call upon me,
and ye shall go and pray unto me,
and I will hearken unto you.
And ye shall seek me, and find me,
when ye shall search for me
with all your heart.
And I will be found of you,
saith the Lord:
Jeremiah 29:11–14a

Iam a civil engineer who studied in Plymouth, Devon, England, more than 50 years ago. Something happened to me there that changed the course of my life and governed the way I spent it. It was a night encounter with a voice that told me something about myself. You will read about it.

Over the intervening proving years, I came to believe in a God without limits, a God eternal and perfect and patient and completely reliable. Strangely, although there is no need, He uses men and women, yes and children too, to effect His purposes. The years had to flow past before looking back revealed what had always been there, the inerrant hand of a forward-looking God. So often the obvious is only revealed in retrospect.

The mechanics of this process of the intervention of the Infinite into temporal affairs continues to intrigue me. Some imagine God as a light or a blur; I imagine Him in terms of a combination of the latest computers.

Over the years, I grew also to wonder at the mediocre level that most of us, who believe in the rudiments of faith as I do, choose to live our lives. Are there alternatives of Christian living beyond and above the option of merely living a worldly life moderated by our Christian morals and standards and attendance in church on Sundays?

Can Matthew 7:13–14 be paraphrased to read

Enter ye in at the strait gate:
for wide is the gate and broad is the way

that leadeth to the Christian life most of us are satisfied with,
and many there be which go in thereat:
because strait is the gate and narrow is the way
which leadeth unto life as He intended,
and few there be that find it.

I have spent much of my life marveling at what I call, for want of a better name, *Strangers*. These are people who live at a different and higher level of spiritual and religious experience from the rest of us. I have been acquainted with them and envied them, and I have sought to understand the differences between us. I have written poetry about them and I have written of some I have known. Without doubt, there will be some that have crossed your path.

Although we may be well content where we are, I have become convinced that God intends us to live at a higher level than comes naturally to us. Some years ago I decided that, if I could discover what that was, I wanted to walk my life in the Way He intended.

I learned it required qualities I didn't possess and a readiness not only to be vulnerable, but also to be expendable. I needed to trust far beyond the boundaries to which common sense might take me.

Closeness to the Father requires the ardent pursuit of personal holiness.

It also means being content not to know—rather than wanting, even needing, to know what is going on before committing to a course of action. Somehow, it involves passivity. The energy it needs is responsive, not creative—an ability to listen and hear before doing.

Obeying His Will
Is less doing His Will
Than allowing His Will
To be done unto you.
To obey God
Is less active than passive,
Less to achieve than to allow
To be achieved,
Less to lead than to allow
Oneself to be led.

This book is not a "How to . . ." manual. It is not full of doctrine. There may be a few principles to glean, but His way for you is like His way for me—unique—and, it's yours for the seeking and finding, if you care enough to do so.

Listen to what God is saying in Isaiah; listen carefully in terms of our personal journey and the voice behind us:

> *For my thoughts are not your thoughts*
> *neither are your ways my ways, saith the Lord.*
> *For as the heavens are higher than the earth,*
> *so are my ways higher than your ways,*
> *and my thoughts than your thoughts.*
> *For as the rain cometh down, and the snow from heaven,*
> *and returneth not thither, but watereth the earth, . . .*
> *So shall my word be that goeth forth out of my mouth:*
> *it shall not return unto me void,*
> *but it shall accomplish that which I please,*
> *and it shall prosper in the thing whereto I sent it.*
> **Isaiah 55:8–11**

This book tells what I discovered about God, the way He communicates, and the way He works. It shares some experiences along the Way.

He doesn't want us on the way Isaiah talks about in order to make sure we do not err by straying to the left or to the right. He puts us on the way to make a difference. That's at the heart of it. He knows the end from the beginning and what's at the end of your journey and mine. He expects us to be able to look back and see that our journey made a difference, not only to our own person, but also to others whom we met along the way.

For me, it was a journey that took me to Pakistan, where I spent most of my working life. It was a journey with Him setting the signposts. The last 20 years were in a kind of "Boy's Town" in Gujranwala. The story that follows is not in a chronological sequence, but hops where it will. Something like my life.

I have, whatever else happens, gained a sense of wonder and awe that will never leave me.

I have also learned that there is a God in the darkness as well as in the light.

> *Darkness is the depth*
> *Of Him who is all light.*
> *Clear water darkens with depth*
> *Into obscurity.*
> *In the darkness we*
> *Discover deep beneath*
> *The shimmering surface play*

The heart and soul of God.

Down through the surface
Of awareness
And early shallows
Of faith's proving
To the depths where
Obedience in the darkness
Forces the reluctant step
Toward the abyss,
Where suffering strains
The soul's acceptance,
Where tragedy and pain
Orchestrate a clamour
Of discord, e'en there,
In the very depth of darkness
God passes by and we
Know that He is closer
Than before although
We do not see Him.

I still long to get into the deeps from the shallows of faith's proving. There's still something more ahead.

GOD'S PURPOSES

Make the unproven assumption (for the time being) that God exists. He is omnipotent and He has not only created the universe, but also our own home, little planet earth, tied by unseen reins to a tiny star, the sun.

Why? Why did He bother? Just because He didn't like an untidy shambles, but preferred order to chaos?

We don't have to reflect on the mystery of Creation too long for we are not going to get far doing that. However, the mystery that captivates us is that somehow this unique and eternal God who lies beyond man's capacities to describe has some kind of love affair with humankind. It goes deeper than His love for all His other creation, no matter how far that extends.

After trying other ways that failed because of man's perversity, He sent Jesus Christ specifically to clear our way back to Him. The holy kingdom was relaunched.

His continuing purpose is the creation, or re-creation, of His domain on earth where men and women walk in the light and experience the freedom of the relationship with Him that Adam, once, and then Jesus enjoyed.

There is a Higher Way that He wants us to walk:

> *There is a Higher Way*
> *But dare we risk it?*
> *Jesus did—and look*
> *What happened to Him!*

And walking according to God's purposes might lead us in a circle back to where we started:

> *Ready to die,*
> *they have thrown themselves*
> *Into the caring arms of God*
> *And awakened—*
> *to find themselves*
> *Back among the twisted faces*
> *Of a crying world*
> *Lit only by the tiny candle*
> *They carry in their hands.*

It means inevitably His purposes are locked in struggle with the forces of evil determined to bring men captive into the darkness of the soul from which there is no release. We have little idea, in our modern sophistication, of the capacities or range or determination of these forces. There are many subtleties of disguise, and we are confused.

In this struggle to overcome evil, the resources of Creation are His, all the time in the world is His. His eyes are restless for those ready to be used in the task, and He is still at work among us. He has a plan for each one of us. His heart desires that we become the vessels of His hand as well as the supplicants at His feet.

This means that one of His initial activities is simply to communicate to us what needs doing and then await our responses. How on earth does the Infinite talk to the finite?

Before we look at one or two of the more unusual ways He communicates with us, let's take a look at His resources available to achieve His purposes.

OMNIPOTENCE

The other side of prayer
The silent listener waits,
One who can see me
As well as hear me,
Who catches my thoughts
Thrown into the empty air,
Who reads my heart
And understands my mind,
Who knows the value of my word
Long before its sound is heard,
Who measures out the universe
To give the inch I ask
And matches my mere morsel
Against the plenitude of paradise
And is not slow to give.

His Resources—Material . . .

THE CATTLE ON A THOUSAND HILLS

Afghanistan
August 1965

For every beast of the forest is mine,
and the cattle upon a thousand hills.
If I were hungry,
I would not tell thee:
for the world is mine,
and the fulness thereof.
Psalm 50:10,12

Seymour Lytton and I are walking up one of the main streets on the Darul Aman side of Kabul in Afghanistan. It is a bright, clear, late summer morning. We are on our way to the Ministry of the Interior. Under my arm is a rolled blueprint, a plan for a hospital.

Seymour is a doctor with a lifetime love affair with Central Asia, with Pathans and Tajiks, and with Uzbeks and Hazaras. I am not sure whether it was he or whether it was Christy Wilson, the pastor of the international congregation in Kabul, who asked me if I would prepare outline plans for a hospital specializing in ophthalmology.

I can only find time to help at the inception of the project. If it were to go ahead, then obviously the preparation of plans would call for the full-time involvement of a number of people. However, I'll do what I can to help.

On a previous visit, I have walked over the proposed site adjacent to the Darul Aman road. It is perfect—dry, completely level, pleasant location, good access, more than adequate space and water and power supplies—no problem. Now I have returned to Kabul to show the outline plans to whomever might be interested.

There is a suitable model, on which to base any drawings, in Taxila Hospital in the north of Pakistan. In a village setting not far from Islamabad the capital, it is already flourishing and very successful. The Kabul scheme, the Noor Eye Hospital, needs to be adjusted for different social conditions and the fact that it is in a city and not in a village. Eye disease is prevalent in Afghanistan, and there is no doubt that such a hospital could be immensely useful.

It occurs to me as we make our way to our appointment that no one

I have shown the plans to so far has talked about what it will cost, or more importantly, where the money is going to come from to build and operate it. I have a fair idea of what it is likely to cost to bring it to life in terms of Pakistani rupees or U. S. dollars, but I have little idea what a dollar will buy in Afghanistan.

I raise this with my companion.

"Seymour, when they ask us where the money is going to come from to build and operate this hospital, if they should give permission for it to be built, what are we going to say?"

As far as I can tell this is a fairly new thought to Seymour. He doesn't seem to think in money terms. We walk along in silence for a while. Then he turns to me with a lilt to his voice and absolutely no concern that the approval of the whole proposal may founder upon an incorrect answer.

"We shall tell them, my friend, that the cattle on a thousand hills are mine, saith the Lord."

He is quoting from Psalm 50, but it occurs to me that it is hardly convincing. Although we believe that to be true, it is unlikely to persuade some reluctant, bearded bureaucrat from a different faith and culture that the plans we offer merit serious consideration.

We are ushered into the great office, and we explain why we feel we should be given planning permission. We go through the plans, explaining traffic flow, treatment of women, partial segregation of women, residential care and day clinics, staffing by nurses and doctors, residences for staff, treatment of sewage, waste incineration, and a score of other legitimate topics for discussion.

I am waiting for the $64,000 question, but the shoe never drops! We have covered everything; we are about to leave, and still the matter of how the hospital is to be paid for has not been raised. What is happening? He has to ask this question—he just has to! *He doesn't.*

I return to Pakistan. I never do find out how the hospital is paid for or which donor country or organization picks up the tab. Neither do I ever see the Noor Eye Hospital, although I often hear talk of its ministry to the blind and to the poor in Kabul throughout the Russian occupation. What happened to the hospital when the Taliban arrived . . . I also do not know.

February 1999

A letter arrives from Seymour Lytton in Ulan Bator, Mongolia. It outlines opportunities right now for a civil engineer in places in Central Asia and comments on the story just told:

"Fancy your memory reaching back that far!

"I have never thought so much about money as about the possibilities that emerge for the Lord from such ventures. Molly always says that I think far too much about property and yet that is how the Lord has used me over the years.

"I am sure that what you remember is correct and that I never knew exactly how the Lord would provide in Kabul but He did in a very generous way!

"It was still the most beautiful and best eye clinic in central Asia as far as facilities were concerned. It was . . . who also martyred Zaid who finally sought to destroy it, even to pulling up the plumbing out of the floor! However he could not destroy the solid building and if peace returns to Afghanistan this could be rebuilt if it would again serve."

THE GARDEN I GAVE YOU

The gardener,
Pulling weeds
Upon His knees
Before the gate
Will turn and look
And make no move
To clear the way
For me to pass.

He'll simply sigh
And then He'll ask
"What did you do
With the garden
I gave you to tend?"
And wait to hear
My answer but
What shall I say?

His Resources—People . . .
"Whatchadoin'? I'll help you."

Titch is my grandniece. She is four and lives near us. The farm is her world, which she runs with great determination! She is on speaking terms with every creature on the farm, big and small, including me. As I kneel before a patch of weeds, with my tools set out beside me and with fruitful hours ahead, I hear a voice behind me that abruptly disturbs my intentions. "Whatchadoin'? I'll help you."

In one swift, instinctive movement, I hide the tools with which she could hurt herself. I direct her fingers away from the flowers towards the weeds. The tools I am using always seem to be the ones she wants. I need eyes in the back of my head to see where she is dispersing them! Before long, I am completely engrossed in protecting my patch from a little pair of hands that appear to be everywhere and endowed with limitless energy to 'help'. Because I love her so much, I let her do whatever I can to channel her energies. She is sure she is helping me, but her presence is worth it all. I know I can always tidy up the mess afterwards.

Now put God and yourself into that picture.

Have you ever wondered why or even whether God needs us to help implement his purposes? After all, He is all-powerful. Why should we bother to pray and labor? He knows it all. Why can't He just command and let it all be done?

When Titch helps me in the garden, I set aside my adult abilities and operate at her level. I avoid long words and speak simply. I talk to her in ways she can understand and give her tasks that she can do. I am patient when she pulls up my daffodil bulbs. I don't overload her. I remove difficulties ahead of her. I let her do things her way, all thumbs.

Why do I do this? Quite simply, because I love her and enjoy her. Her company refreshes and pleases me, even though she slows my gardening efforts.

So we are "all thumbs," but God chooses to set aside His powers and work at our level with fumbling human beings like us anyway. He chooses partnership with us over speedy progress.

BIRDSONG

Tomorrow,
Or perhaps today,
God is likely
To take an initiative
To move your life
More in line with His.
The odds are
That in the clashing
Of the storms around you
You will not even know
A bird has tried to sing

—or maybe
the storm is itself the song.

He communicates with His children . . .

THE NIGHT VISITOR

Plymouth
December 11, 1949

There are certain points in a person's life that become unforgettable marks along its course.

Birth and death mark the two extremities of individual experience. Within them, other peaks stand out from the broad plain of individual human existence. Changing schools, falling in love, marriage, becoming a parent, illness, scholastic achievement, death of loved ones, leaving home, fortuitous or disastrous career choices, these are some of them.

There are other peaks too. Among them are emotional and spiritual peaks. Not all of them are positive. Some turn into troughs but are also indelibly etched upon the memory.

Rejecting God, finding God, conversion, repentance, commitment, despair, and triumph. Some mark disasters, failures of circumstances, failure of character and bad judgment. Some such experiences are shared by others, some are shared with others and some are carried privately within a person's psyche throughout life. They become, whatever they are, in Shakespeare's words, *the star to every wandering barque*, affecting or explaining subsequent events.

Such an event occurred to me in Devon, in England, on December 11, 1949. At most, the experience lasted for a quarter of an hour, yet the next 40 years of my life were slowly to unfold in the way the voice of an unseen speaker told me.

I was in lodgings in Addison Road near the center of Plymouth, sharing a large front bedroom on the second floor with Keith Draper, a bus driver from Barnstaple. We had become good friends.

It was probably about 2:30 am. I was suddenly awake, alertly awake. I listened intently. What had wakened me?

I could hear Keith, the bus driver, breathing heavily in sleep in the other bed. I could see the moonlight coming through the window, but my portion of the room was in shadow. Someone, someone unseen, was standing at the right hand side of my bed, two or three feet away. I could see nothing of or about the visitor. I just knew he was there.

A voice spoke, a man's voice, a normal voice, no dialect to notice, but positive and firm in tone. Loud enough to hear easily. It was a statement, not a question.

"Ken, God has a purpose for your life.

"He is going to put you to work in a land that is not your own land, amongst people of a different color and race and culture and creed. He is going to put you to work amongst boys, and *He* is going to bring it to pass."

My mind raced. I believed in God, so it was in His Hands to have a purpose for my life BUT . . .

The voice continued. It seemed afterwards the messenger had been speaking for about a quarter of an hour, but I recall nothing else of the conversation except my own reply.

I answered, and I have to think that I answered audibly because I was awake and highly alert and the unseen messenger was still standing beside the bed.

"Give me three years first, and God can have the rest of my life."

I said it, I meant it, and I never swerved from it.

I was the oldest of a large family of children, and it would take me three years to ensure that the family was in a house big enough for its future needs. When that was done, God could have the rest of my life. It was a bargain I offered, and I knew it was a bargain accepted for suddenly the presence was gone. Keith Draper stirred noisily in his sleep.

Whom had I made my bargain with?

My belief in and understanding of God was continually evolving. It is a process that has never stopped.

I argued with Him, I often disagreed with Him, yet I never doubted His existence or His personal interest in the affairs of individuals.

I believed He intervened in human affairs through His messengers, His angels—when He felt like it. I believed He answered prayers, sometimes. Other times, even when they were very urgent and important, He seemed to ignore them. Then in my heart, I argued with Him.

I thought about Him a great deal. I knew that He existed outside time, but I observed that occasionally we, on our side, seemed to slip the bonds of time that required us to remain in a strict chronological sequence and could and did experience 'time jumps'.

I believed He was omniscient, omnipotent, and omnipresent, but often He chose to behave as though He experienced the same limitations ordinary men and women had. I believed in the power of healing by prayer or the laying on of hands.

I believed that there were lines of communication with God or, more likely, His angels (there had to be some system of delegation up there) experienced by men and women. I called them "awarenesses." The Bible described some of them: dreams, visions, voices, but not all of them. It was possible, by cultivating these senses of awareness, to sometimes hear or understand conveyed the voice of God. Each individual would, by his own searching, learn to recognize those linkages that affected his own awareness of God.

It was possible, even though it might be very difficult, for an ordinary man or woman to live in tune with the Infinite; a harmony *was* possible even though there might be lapses in the relationship.

I counted myself religious. I read the Bible, I prayed, I worshipped in church once or twice each Sunday, but I did not count myself a Christian.

My problem was Jesus. I had absolutely no doubts about his sinless life, his ministry of miracles and healings, and his teaching. I would agree he was the finest spiritual teacher who had ever lived. I didn't doubt the virgin birth, although I would have been just as comfortable, maybe even more comfortable, had his birth been a normal birth to a traditionally married Jewish couple. I had few questions about the Resurrection or even the Ascension. If God was indeed omnipotent, He was quite capable of engineering all these things, and for that matter, equally capable of protecting the ensuing record about those events.

BUT, and this was my BUT, accepting these events in the Biblical record did not require me to stop using my mind and the common sense He had given me. How could I believe that he, Jesus, a man born of woman, was the unique son of God, the earthly representation of the Ineffable Godhead, co-Creator of the universe out of nothing, set down once and for all in history? That just went too far.

I was not at all wedded to consistency in my belief structure and was quite comfortable living with apparent anomalies. If you committed yourself to the search for truth, you would sometimes see opposites, but ultimately you must come out of the fog at a destination where you would find God playing solitaire or the guitar while He waited for you to get there.

Considering my heretical views, it was somewhat of a puzzle that He even had a purpose for my life.

I did not understand at all the implications of this bargain with God that I was making. I was totally ill-equipped to be of any use to Him. I would go through years of testing, honing, shaping, preparing, purging, whittling away at the flaws in my character and the deficiencies in my beliefs until eventually the door would open that God intended for me to pass through. I didn't know He purposed, before He set me to work, a very different "me" than the one in Addison Road.

Before I could be useful to God, I would be taken like a blind man holding the hand of a sighted companion for more than 20 years along a route that would sometimes appear to lead backwards. I would have to learn to trust implicitly in my guide, step forward into apparent emptiness, trusting that solid ground would be underfoot by the time my foot landed. I would have to learn to listen as well as argue.

I would learn the truth of the Chinese proverb "When the pupil is ready the teacher arrives."

At this time of striking a bargain with God, I was as a block of rough marble; the possible man within the block was only in God's mind. It would take decades of removing the chips to uncover what was hidden there underneath and to discover whether it was of any value.

But God had all the time in the world.

In August 1952, almost three years later, the Old family moved from Days Lane, Sidcup in Kent, to a house twice the size in Wheathill Road, Anerley, a few miles away. From it, five marriages took place, with the young couples living in the house with the parents until they could get accommodations elsewhere.

The first part of the bargain had almost ticked away. What was to follow?

He communicates with His children . . .

COMMUNICATION THROUGH DREAMS

*But while he thought on these things, behold, the angel of the Lord appeared unto him **in a dream**, saying Joseph, thou son of David, fear not to take unto thee Mary thy wife: for that which is conceived in her is of the Holy Ghost. And she shall bring forth a son, and thou shalt call his name JESUS: for he shall save his people from their sins.*
Matthew 1:20–21

*And being warned of God **in a dream** that they should not return to Herod, they departed into their own country another way.*
Matthew 2:12

*And when they were departed, behold, the angel of the Lord appeareth to Joseph **in a dream**, saying, Arise, and take the young child and his mother, and flee into Egypt . . .*
Matthew 2:13

*But when Herod was dead, behold, an angel of the Lord appeareth **in a dream** to Joseph in Egypt, Saying, Arise, and take the young child and his mother, and go into the land of Israel:*
Matthew 2:19–20a

*. . . notwithstanding, being warned of God **in a dream**, he turned aside into the parts of Galilee:*
Matthew 2:22b

Intimations

We have a haunting awareness
Of infinite forces of grace
Pure past conceiving, transcendent,
Breaking like stars in the heavens
Through holes in the perforate shell
Of the sensible universe.

He communicates with His children . . .

DREAMS AND VOICES

Before we go much further, we need to reflect on how God communicates with these frequently mono-language creatures He chooses to allow to help Him.

There will be at least a score of ways by which God communicates with us, His children—during prayer, by response to prayer (or non-response), by placing a strange desire within our hearts and minds, by inner reflection and guidance, by Scripture (even by highlighting certain portions as we read), through preaching and teaching, through Bible studies, through the counsel of friends and even of strangers, by doors opened or closed, by congruence of events, by bringing together people in one place, through circumstances around us, by response to a fleece, through nature and through natural events, through the disciplines of devotion and through regular reading aids and helps like Daily Light, through hymns that we sing or songs that we hear sung, through the inner impress of the Holy Spirit who directs our words, through the nurture and guidance of right habits, during occasions of great joy or sadness such as bereavement, even through silence. There are some less frequent ways, such as by lights or colors that we see and by touches of affirmation or restraint without anyone nearby.

During this narrative, there will be a number of references to dreams and voices. There will be a little curiosity about these two communication channels that I might try to satisfy.

To many people visions are perhaps the most significant and penetrating of their individual experiences of God. I have had little personal experience of visions.

With voices and dreams it is different. I used to think that both perceptive dreams (dreams that had something more than the run-of-the-mill subconscious fantasy content) and voices were commonplace and that most of us could, by dint of cultivating a 'listening' mind, experience them.

I have come to think that probably this is not so, and that it is a gift experienced by only a few.

To my recollection, Marie, my first wife, never had any of the 'higher content' type dreams and never heard any voices. (She was also far more spiritual than I was.) At the same time, she accepted without question that occasionally her husband did have such experiences, and I shared them with her when they happened.

They were never experiences I had any capacity to predict or create. They happened out of the blue, and they happened infrequently. They were, however, always significant and sometimes important.

Strangely, where prediction of the future became involved, the details were sometimes wrong as though there was an inevitable blurriness in the connection. I think more likely, it is as if the future was even yet remoldable, not set in stone.

When I 'hear' voices, without a person present to utter the words I hear, it is sometimes literally that. I turn around, wondering who has spoken, and there is no one there. The voice is for me always a man's voice, never a woman's.

At other times, I know the voice is an *inner* voice, inserted into my mind from somewhere outside or above and bypassing my hearing organs.

I was recently asked whether the 'voices' had ever given me wrong information or had ever tried to lead me astray. After all, how does anyone distinguish between the spurious and the true? I could only answer that in the dozen or so instances I had heard 'voices' that I had usually been helped and not once been misled.

Asked whose voice it was that I might have heard with either the 'inner' or the 'outer' ear, I have little idea. I cannot say that the voices had any identifying characteristic or similarity. I do not attach the voice to any concept I have of the person of the Father, the Son or the Holy Spirit. My assumption is that each voice belonged to one of those intermediate beings that the Bible refers to as angels. I have speculated little about that.

I have, however, often wondered about the mysterious mechanics by which prayers are answered and events brought into an ordered congruence. I do believe there exists some divine network of organization that eventually I may understand more clearly than I do now.

I will instruct thee
And teach thee
In the way which thou shalt go:
I will guide thee with mine eye.
Psalm 32:8

And thine ears shall hear
a word behind thee, saying,
This is the way,
Walk ye in it,

When ye turn to the right hand,
and when ye turn to the left.
Isaiah 30:21

Dreams as well as voices have been significant in my life, sometimes very significant.

They are channels of communication well referenced and demonstrated in Scripture. My own experience has been that dreams that have a deeper significance than the wanderings of the subliminal mind have a different quality. They are impressed more clearly, like an original typescript as against a carbon copy. There is a stronger clarity of recollection. The timing in my own case has usually been about 2:30 A.M. with my waking up immediately afterwards.

This is not a book about dreams and voices. Where it has seemed appropriate I have just given the narrative of events as truthfully as my recollection allows. The reader is free to draw his or her own conclusions.

Soon after we moved south from the Punjab to Karachi in Pakistan, I asked Marie at breakfast who 'Jacob' was.

I explained. In a dream that night, Mac, her first husband, whom I had never met, had appeared. It is the only dream of Mac I can recall.

Mac, I knew him immediately, had leaned over towards me. It seemed as though we were in a cabin on a ship and he said with urgency, "Tell Jacob I'm sorry I was unable to repay the debt I owe him." I think he repeated that once more, and then was gone; the dream was over.

Marie smiled, not seeming at all surprised. "Oh, that would be Jacob Bakker. He was one of Mac's closest friends."

Later I was to be able to tell Jacob this when we met in New Jersey. Undoubtedly, both financially and spiritually, Jacob had been a great support and encourager to his friend. But Jacob, if he knew the debt to which Mac referred, chose to keep such knowledge to himself.

DUSTY ROAD

And so, O Man, I took you at your word—
You said to knock and sure I would be heard,
You said to seek and sure I'd be to find
The kingdom's door though mine eye be blind,
You said to ask and sure I'd be to get—
Well, Man, I've knocked, I've sought, I've asked—
—and yet!

Then next, O Man, I took you at your word—
For my very troubled soul (O Lord)
You said to come and surely I'd have rest
You said to trust like any child would trust
And such a faith could move the highest hill—
Well, Man, I've trusted like a child—
—and still!

And so, O Man, I took you at your word
Once more. Do you remember what you said?
Except a man deny upon the rack
Himself and put a cross upon his back
Instead and follow where you first had trod—
Well, Man, I've got the load—
—so help me, God!

And now, O Man, don't get ahead, that's all—
The mist is in my eyes and I shall fall.
I don't know where or how, you know the way.
Just share the road and ever with me stay.
I'll walk, I'll stumble just where you have trod—
Trudging in your dust, Man who could be God!

He communicates with His children . . .
BILQUIS HAS DREAMS

As we are looking at the way God communicates with His children, we will pause for a while to see what happened to a very unusual Muslim woman in Pakistan.

When we first became acquainted with Bilquis Sheikh (pronounced Bill Keece Shake), she was already very well known in Pakistan as a high-born woman of the Wah family of the Punjab, child of a Government minister, and wife of one. She was eminent in her own right for her Army service and for her concern for the rights of women.

The story of her fateful encounter that changed her life and made her an outcast for a while is told in her book *I Dared to call Him Father*.

She shared with us some of her dream experiences that were so significant.

Normally, she did not dream, and she was not given to fantasizing. One night, at the beginning of her spiritual migration in October 1966, she dreamed.

The dream had a quality and depth of impression, stronger, more distinct than any dream she had previously experienced. It was unforgettable, clearer by far than any of yesterday's memories.

I was having supper, in my own house, with Jesus. I just knew it was Jesus. He had stayed with me for two days. He sat across the table from me, and we were enjoying each other's company.

Then the dream changed.

I was walking alone along a path and approaching a junction, a Y junction where the path divided. At the junction a man dressed in white was standing.

It was not Jesus; I knew him already.

He said to me, "Are you sure you know which way you are going?"

I answered, "Oh, yes, I am following after Jesus and I have to find Him. Do you know where He is?"

"When I awoke, imprinted upon my mind were the three words without specific meaning, *John the Baptist*. Who was John the Baptist? I needed to find out.

"I looked in the index to the Bible. There were four books attributed to John. The three shorter ones were letters, very good letters for certain, but they didn't appear to have been written by John the Baptist. The fourth book in the New Testament was also called John. Although John the Baptist was not mentioned by name, there was a man called John who was baptizing. That was probably who John the Baptist was, but I would need some help to understand what my dream meant.

"Now I had another dream, my perfume dream."

A perfume salesman called at the house, one of the pre-Partition perfume salesmen who traveled around the country on foot with a variety of perfumes to sell village by village. He wore a black achkan (frock-coat) and displayed his stock from his valise. He took a golden jar, removed its cap. It was the most wonderful perfume I had ever experienced! I was about to put a drop onto the back of my hand when he took the jar from me and put it on my bedside table. "This perfume" he said "will spread throughout the world."

When Bilquis awoke, on the table where the dream had placed the golden jar of perfume was the Bible she had been reading, open to the Gospel of John.

The room, strangely, still carried the fragrance of the perfume.

Something was happening inside too. Her heart was carrying its own strange fragrance of peace, as though all striving was done and she had at last come home. That afternoon, walking in the garden, again she caught traces of the same beautifully delicate and haunting perfume of the night.

Several days later, she tells, "I had read right through the New Testament and was now into the last book. Suddenly a verse caught my attention.

Here I stand knocking at the door;
if anyone hears my voice and opens the door,
I will come in and sit down to supper with him and he with me.
Revelation 3:20 NEB

"This was my dream! Jesus was standing at the door. Now I had choices to make. He would not force his company upon me. The dream was from God, and it was directed to me.

"I had a choice to make. I made it."

_____

Interesting dream experiences were now occurring. We had given to Bilquis a framed copy of Salman's *Head of Christ*. It was not a picture I particularly enjoyed. I felt it made Jesus look older than his thirty-odd years.

However, when Marie had been given it as a gift, she had been told the artist had a vision of Christ and had painted this picture as an immediate response to that vision.

Bilquis was pleased. While we were there at her home, she removed another picture and hung it in her bedroom where she could see it from her bed.

Nur Jan was Bilquis' Muslim maidservant. She came into her mistress' bedroom the following morning as usual, stopped dead in her tracks in front of the picture, and in awed tones gasped, "Begum Sahiba, who's that?"

"Why, Nur Jan, that is Jesus. Do you like that picture?"

Nur Jan, her eyes large, drew in a long, long breath. "Begum Sahiba, HE is the man I dreamed about the other night. That is HIM. I told you about my dream. That is the man in my dream! Begum Sahiba, that is his picture! What does it mean?"

Bilquis was also having dreams that sometimes in a strange way interlocked with dreams I was having in Taxila, seven miles away. In the mornings when she drove down, we would compare dreams, laugh over their connections and relationships, and try to fathom what they meant. Most interesting of all were what she called her "floats." She appeared to float out of her body while sleeping, float out through the window, and wander strange places where she had never been before. The first time it happened she was frightened, but as time passed and the experiences recurred, she became accustomed to these apparent nocturnal adventures. Often the float experiences seemed to repeat themselves. She would tour towns and western cities, where there seemed to be just hundreds of churches and very modern buildings. She had no explanation for what was happening or why it was happening.

There were few records of something like this to go to, although there are a couple of references in the New Testament. The apostle Paul wrote, speaking presumably of himself, *I knew a man in Christ above fourteen years ago, (whether in the body, I cannot tell; or whether out of the body, I cannot tell: God knoweth;) . . . caught up to the third heaven. II Corinthians 12:2*

Bilquis was confused as to what was reality and what was dream state about these floats.

We were observing how God was keeping this woman on the Way He intended for her. Bilquis was more dependent on her relationship with Him than she was upon food and drink. She was completely focused on maintaining a right and close relationship with God.

An analogy might be the tuning to a radio station. You get the signal full and clear, each note of music at its correct and sharp pitch, and in the right place within the harmony, when you are correctly tuned. Even just a shade off the absolute correct tuning and the music blurs a little, the notes become less clear, and fuzziness can be detected. If you mistune far enough, you have lost the signal completely.

Bilquis was fine-tuned to God. She knew, as few others might know, what a correct tuning sounded like. As soon as she detected a slight blurring or fuzziness, then the alarm bells were ringing, and she was chasing back in her memory to the last time the tuning was perfect. What had she done that marred the tuning?

If Marie or I were around, she would go over things with us, checking where she had wandered away from God. She would worry her memory incessantly until eventually it gave her the answer to what had happened. She would identify unerringly where she had self-chosen, by an unkind or careless act, word, or thought, lost Him and the sense of His nearness.

Immediately she would be down on her knees. Tears would stream down her face. She had hurt Him who loved her so much! "Please forgive me, Jesus. I love you so much! I'm sorry. I'm only a child, you know. I'm learning; I'll try harder. Please, Jesus, be patient with me; I'm sorry, Jesus." Then suddenly, she would know with relief, know with certainty, that she had been heard. She was forgiven and the connection was once again perfectly restored.

Helplessness

God incites us to rebel
Against the well regarded
And the comfortable,
Against the certainties
And suppositions of our time
And the clichés
That point to Him
Throwing us instead,
Stripped bare,
Upon some wave lashed rock
With barely a toehold
To be slashed by the spume
And know our helplessness.

He communicates with His children . . .
BILQUIS AND BAPTISM

Pakistan
January 24, 1967

At some point, every new convert begins to face the question of baptism. Is it an irreducible part of the process or an option within the Scriptures that would allow the conversion of the heart to proceed and mature without the glare of publicity and family and social opposition?

Very soon, this question began to claim Bilquis' attention. She had little doubt Jesus expected her to go through all the way, including baptism, and for her there was no question.

We, her friends, were fearful for the possible consequences. We looked at it together in the light of Scriptures. There were places where baptism took place in the early church as an outward expression of an inner work, a declaration to the world and to oneself that a transaction had been accomplished, and this was the receipt as evidence. The consequences appeared to place the individual amongst the group of persecuted Christians, but not necessarily to single them out for specific brutal treatment, worse by far than the treatment their new companions received or were receiving.

However, if the consequence of baptism were to be not just persecution, but death, then surely that negated the value of the act for what good was a dead Christian?

Marie held the orthodox position that the New Testament rules that baptism is an inevitable part of the process of accepting Christ as Savior and Lord. There was certainly good Scripture to support that view.

I myself was not so certain. Islam was a post-Christian development. The reaction was not to baptism of itself. The Muslim had little concern should a Hindu neighbor choose to be baptized. He might even have found himself approving such an action as a halfway step. The concern Muslims felt, and felt very strongly, was resentment that a person who had already received the ultimate revelation of God given by the angel Gabriel to the last prophet Mohammed should thereafter turn the back on that impeccable gift by choosing allegiance instead, and that by public demonstration, to a prophet less ultimate. It was the implied public rejection of the Prophet Mohammed that stuck in the craw and brought often swift and violent reaction. It involved an indelible stain on a family's honor.

We read together in our Bible Studies at her house the various records of baptism in the Gospels and Acts and the references within the Epistles. None of us, except Bilquis, had ever had to face the question of consequences to baptism on any scale. Our lives were not at stake. All of us had been born into Christian families. For some of us, our recent forebears had had to make similar choices, but they had been out of Hinduism and not out of Islam.

Bilquis was urging me to make arrangements for her baptism. As a Presbyterian layman, I myself could not baptize her, and the thought did not occur to me. I wrote to a missionary in Peshawar, but received no reply. He was away. This would have been risky anyway, since Peshawar was a volatile city.

Bilquis was becoming more and more urgent. She had a feeling time was running out on her. It probably was.

One night in January, it was made very clear to me that delay must end, and that the consequences of Bilquis' baptism were not our business, but God's.

I woke suddenly. Marie lay sleeping beside me, but something had awakened me. What was it? The night was dark; little moonlight eased the darkness. A voice, a man's voice, spoke, and spoke in a commanding tone. "Turn to page 456 in your Bible," That was all. I turned on the light. Marie stirred, awakened, and found me reading the Bible. Page 456 opened at Job 13 and 14.

It was the only time I ever received a Bible reference by page number!

These verses shone out at me:

> *Hold your peace, let me alone, that I may speak,*
> *and let come on me what will.*
> *Wherefore do I take my flesh in my teeth,*
> *and put my life in mine hand?*
> *Though He slay me, yet will I trust in him:*
> *but I will maintain mine own ways before him.*
> ***Job 13:13–15***

> *Behold now, I have ordered my cause;*
> *I know that I shall be justified.*
> ***Job 13:18***

> *Only do not two things unto me:*
> *then will I not hide myself from thee.*
> *Withdraw thine hand far from me:*
> *and let not thy dread make me afraid.*

Then call thou, and I will answer:
or let me speak, and answer thou me.
Job 13:20–22

For there is hope of a tree, if it be cut down,
that it will sprout again,
and that the tender branch thereof will not cease.
Though the root thereof wax old in the earth,
and the stock thereof die in the ground;
Yet through the scent of water it will bud,
and bring forth boughs like a plant.
Job 14:7–9

Thou shalt call, and I will answer thee:
Thou wilt have a desire to the work of thine hands.
For now thou numberest my steps:
Dost thou not watch over my sin?
My transgression is sealed up in a bag,
And thou sewest up mine iniquity.
Job 14:15–17

For me this was enough. What I was reading was a conversation between Bilquis and God. Who was I to have hesitations? It was her life, and she was ready, even anxious, to commit it. Let happen what would, the baptism must take place without delay. As soon as we could contact Bilquis, we must tell her so.

(Later that day, she was baptized twice, but that is another story.)

HOMELAND

There is a land beyond our seeing
Filled with a most aweful splendour
As though the Sun itself
Were here upon the earth
Moving round among us
Daring darkness into the distance
And yet, at the same time,
Breaking through
Into our perceptions
With the softness of a butterfly
Lighting on a petal
Telling us that love and hope
And gentleness and holiness
Are keys into that Kingdom
And that we have a birthright there.

He communicates with His children . . .

THE FLEECE AT THE TREE

Pakistan
September 1955

God not only communicates with His children by His own initiative, but also as a response to a question or questions He is asked. That response is often by a straight answer to prayer. Do you ever wonder how your individual prayer makes its way through the crowded airwaves surrounding Heaven long enough to get even a nanosecond of consideration up there?

There is one particular type of communication that became famous because of a story in the Bible (in Judges 6). The bewildered questioner asks God to confirm that He intends to save Israel by his hand (Who, me?) by showing him the perverse effect of dew upon a fleece.

The questioner sets the conditions for the answer, and God responds (or not). This has led to the practice being termed 'putting out a fleece'.

I have used a fleece only twice as I recall. The second time, whether to return to work in Pakistan or go to Tajikistan after my retirement, was an answer, quite correctly as events turned out, not to do either.

Here is the first occasion:

It had been a long, hard, hot summer. Little of the very heavy, late Punjab monsoon had spilled over into the Hyderabad desert to the south, and the tender shades of early green prompted by showers did not mature across the desert this year.

Expatriate help had come through the summer. There were four of us now working on the cement factory project, sometimes five. It was going well. We had caught up with the backlog and were frequently waiting for drawings. The men, about 1500 of them, most of them Pathans, organized into tribal gangs with their own gang leaders (jemadars), were working flat-out. Some concrete pours were 30 hours without stopping. Hagen the Dane was setting and aligning the supports for the long kilns. The machinery was being removed from packing cases and positioned.

It was nearing mid-September.

A phone call came from my employers in Karachi. It was Managing Director Ian Hibble, the Australian. The company had received a contract for the construction of the Dry Dock in Karachi. I was being transferred there. Yes, he knew the work in Hyderabad wasn't finished; I should hand over within the week and get on down to Karachi. Oh yes, he knew I was pretty well exhausted. I could fly home to England for a couple of weeks rest as soon as the accounts were all sorted out. When could that be? Oh, probably about a month or so.

A month seemed to me at that time about as long as a century. "Oh," I groaned, "I can't wait that long; I'm done in. I'll hand over to Bob and go on up to the Punjab for a break before I come down to Karachi."

I reckoned later that I must have been suffering from heat-stroke to turn down an offer of a flight home to England, because I wasn't willing to wait for a month. Much more likely, I was unknowingly keeping a divine appointment and going on a tour that would show me in the next couple of weeks almost all the places that would fill the next 35 years of my life.

I sent a telegram and a letter to Taxila, asking if they could accommodate an exhausted engineer from Hyderabad for a couple of weeks. I would be arriving on the Khyber Mail on the 21st. I was sure Marie would be happy to arrange return hospitality, if it were possible. If it wasn't convenient, I could always move into Flashman's in Rawalpindi.

I had spent little time with any missionaries, apart from the previous Christmas when Marie and her friends of the Laubach Literacy team had visited and stayed at our shack in the desert when other arrangements for their housing collapsed. Oh, yes, there had earlier been the inauspicious occasion when I went over the edge of the ravine at Nicholson's monument.

I had, however, worshiped and socialized with them at Taxila. Even before going down to Hyderabad, I had recognized in those I had met the qualities of love, friendship, openness, service, hospitality, and trust that were missing in the cut and thrust world in which I lived. Yes, qualities of faith, too, although you would expect that. They had a completeness of faith that seemed to give them an inner calm and repose. They did not require the constant picking at the uncertain edges that tantalized me and kept my mind exploring the ranges of God.

I had seen this strange serenity in Marie last Christmas. God had treated her most brutally, stealing her husband Mac from her at the prime of his life. Was this the way to treat faithful servants? What were the qualities within that enabled her, without question or resentment, to respond to this harsh divine treatment with resilience and love and loyalty and acceptance? How did such qualities emerge and grow?

The train journey of 24 hours from Hyderabad to Taxila was refreshing. I felt the tensions and pressures that had been with me almost constantly for the past 16 months beginning to relax and unknot. I carried no incomplete work with me. I was just going to enjoy the Punjab, perhaps go up into the hills to Murree, perhaps have a few games of chess with OA Brown, tell the Christy children some stories if they were back from furlough, and yes, I was looking forward to seeing Marie again and pushing my irreverent questions into her immovable, unshakable faith.

Marie met me at Taxila station. She had a little 500cc Fiat Popolino. Into it, we dumped the luggage and then maneuvered ourselves.

I was surprised to have been met and to see how pleased she was to see me. I had not remembered what a lovely smile she had that seemed to light up her whole face. She had news. Oh, no, of course my visit was not inconvenient. I would be staying at the Browns. I was aware she had spent the summer in Murree as a supervisor at the missionary language school. She, herself, had only just come down from the hills. However, she would only be here for one of my two weeks. There were problems in the nursing school at Sialkot Hospital, and she had been asked to transfer there as nursing matron.

She didn't want to go. Taxila was home, but she would go. She would be going at the end of the week. She had handed over her work prior to going to the hills so she was free until she went, except for packing things away and things to take. She would take me places I might wish to go; maybe one day we might go back up to Murree. She had friends at Sandes Home, who had been ill. She'd like to see them before leaving. How was she going to Sialkot, by rail? Oh no, she would take the car. Who would be traveling with her? No one at this point. Then—before we had finished waiting at the level crossing gates—I had arranged to travel with her as escort to Sialkot. It wouldn't be safe for a woman to be traveling alone on a journey of close to 200 miles, and besides, I'd never seen Sialkot. Marie seemed pleased with the arrangement.

The days passed pleasantly; I had been warmly welcomed by the Browns. The Christys were not yet back from furlough. Marie drove me out to the building sites where I had worked in Wah. She also took me to her literacy groups of women to complete her farewells.

Something was happening to us that we had not planned on or even dreamt of when we met at the station. I was realizing that Marie was a beautiful woman, and it was not just her smile. She had further an inner radiance and strength that previously somehow I'd missed. We were falling in love. Love enhances beauty. There were so many good reasons why it should not have been so. There was an age difference of almost 11 years. My theology was very suspect, to put a gloss on it. I definitely was not a missionary 'type' and had little desire to be one, and Marie was committed to her missionary life in Pakistan. My language usage was clearly not Twentieth-Century American Conservative Evangelical. In addition, I was English and Marie was American. We were still laughing over differences between us 40 years later.

The Browns would have been uneasy. They must have noticed something was happening. I had shared my critical views on the exclusiveness of

Christian teaching with OA on more than one occasion. He particularly would have been nervous for Marie.

It was Marie's last day in Taxila. The manager of the cement factory, an Irishman, had invited Marie to a farewell dinner and graciously included her guest.

That afternoon, I knelt down in my room at the Browns on my own and talked to God about the strange thing that was happening to me. I needed to get it straight.

"God, I don't know what's happening. All I know is that I have promised You can have the rest of my life. I meant that and I mean it still. The rest of my life is Yours. If it fits within Your will for me that I ask Marie to marry me, **I want You to stop the car tonight just in front of the shisham tree that's 30 yards short of Gilani's garage** so that I'll know. I need to know for sure, God. Amen."

If Gideon could put out a fleece on the threshing floor beneath the oak tree at Ophrah in order to make sure he understood God's will, then I could put out my fleece at the shisham tree in Taxila.

It was a late dinner. It was dark when we left the hospital. We were driving in the Popolino. If Marie had measured with a tape, she could not have stopped suddenly, more accurately, in front of the shisham tree, 30 yards short of Gilani's garage, as we went towards Sarai Kala. "I have a strange feeling the rear lights aren't working." I got out to check, but I knew I didn't need to. The lights were okay, and I could sense God was smiling.

Between Jhelum and Kharian, on the way to Sialkot, there was a stretch of winding road at the last set of hills before leaving the Potwar plateau for the very flat flood prone plains of the alluvial Punjab.

Marie was driving. I told her I had a question for her. Would she marry me? For a moment or so, there was no answer. Her eyes were fixed on the twisting hill-road.

I reached over, touched her hand, and repeated my question to her. "I am asking you whether you will marry me."

She flashed a smile at me. Were there not others I should check with first?

"I have already checked, and besides, I am of age," I answered.

Another moment or so of silence and then that lovely smile and the answer. "Yes."

Marie pulled off the road and stopped the car. We let the traffic clear, and then, for the first time, we kissed.

A TOUCH

Behind, and far beyond
Our reason
our memory
our intelligence
And our comprehending
Lies remote,
Almost too far for us to know it's even there
A Touch with something other than ourselves.
A touch, faint and transient,
Emerging for a moment through the meshes of our minds
Like wavedrops from a net dipt into the ocean face.

It is this emergence, hardly grasped or sensed
That gives significance to what and why we are
And qualifies our words and actions as worthy.

The Way He Works . . .
THE OPEN DOOR

I know thy works:
Behold, I have set before thee an open door,
and no man can shut it:
for thou hast a little strength,
and hast kept my word,
and hast not denied my name
Revelation 3:8

It was in the late sixties. We were on furlough and en route to Washington State. Marie and the two boys were following later. It was Sunday in New York. I found a church in which to worship. The sermon text was on part of Revelation 3:8.

. . . behold, I have set before thee an open door . . .

I hadn't ever noticed that particular verse previously.

On Monday morning, before I headed for the airport, my devotional book for Monday meditated on the same verse. Curious.

The magazine I read on the plane opened at an article where the writer exposited on the message to the church in Philadelphia, particularly the meaning of the passage

. . . behold, I have set before thee an open door. . . .

By the time I reached Denver, I had accepted that God was trying to tell me something. Something I didn't want to hear. He would soon be setting before me an Open Door.

Sure enough, a move was on the way.

I have used for years, as an illustration of God's purposes, the idea that the open door that God places before us leads to a corridor without doors on either side. It leads to a tee junction with another corridor. We need to go through that Open Door and down to the junction without knowing what lies around the corners. Only when we get to the junction can we look either way and see what doors are there and which of them are open and which of them are closed. An essential prerequisite to finding and doing God's will is to go through that initial door having no idea what lies ahead.

I now feel that perception is inadequate. God's open door to each of us leads rather to an immense scape, like a desert or seascape, open wherever we look and offering an immense and limitless perspective and the wonderful stimulating freedom associated with that openness. The freedom lies in the richness of being associated with God's power and purposes and in cooperating with them.

I carry a candle
It's not very bright
The softest of breezes
Can extinguish my light.

Now, old man, you are wise,
Tell me where I shall go
So that the flick'ring light
Of my candle may show?

Not into the city
Now so flooded with light
Go far from the city,
My child, into the night.

There your candle so bright
Will glow forth like the sun
For there's no other light
In the dark but your own.

The Way He Works . . .
LOOKING BACK

Pakistan
April 1990

We have looked briefly at the resources God has and some of the ways He communicates. The next section is, if we can, within the context of a personal story, to observe how God implements His purposes by using His resources of people and material and the forces of nature through the managing frame of time viewed from eternity.

He has purposes. How does He go about implementing them?

I am quite clear that His concern for the nurture of the Pakistani Punjabi Church was what caused Him to involve me in His plans and processes. I happened to be a civil engineer with training as a mechanical engineer and as an electrical engineer. I also had some experience of India. He needed someone with that kind of a background. As for the man's faith, well, definitely not up to the mark, but He'd sort that out in due course—no hurry, no worry.

Before we look at the process, let's look back from this side of the task completed.

It is more than 40 years since I heard a voice in Plymouth that told me of God's purpose for my life. In 1970, God brought Marie and me, both reluctant and struggling, to Gujranwala in the Punjab where He had intended. There He set us to work amongst boys. We were assigned to work there three years.

Now 20 years later we were retiring from Gujranwala. Marie was 75; there were younger people in place to carry things forward. We had been unable to achieve many of our dreams—the new suburb town of Kanaya, a bank for the poor, a college for Christians, a hostel for girls, a cooperative, small industries, a catering school, and a beauty school for girls to learn the cosmetic and beauty industry. It had never been lack of resources, always lack of time, sometimes lack of energy.

Yet some things had been achieved.

What had been a small faltering institution of 60 students, near to closure, was now one of the pre-eminent educational institutions available to the Punjabi Christian community. The Government had nationalized other Christian colleges and schools. That situation still held. We, almost alone, were still independent. Our various schools each had a high reputation for excellence. We were well accepted by and important to the Muslim community. There was a revitalized campus, with many new structures and new institutions and no debt. Endowment funds were adequate. Three thousand students on and off campus were being educated, although for two thirds of them it was no higher than primary level.

We had been privileged not only to see God working, but also to be a part of that working.

It was an experience both enervating and humbling.

Here are some of the lessons the years taught us.

Lesson 1
Whatever, wherever the open door is for you, REMEMBER, Jesus set that door in place, and He has already gone through it ahead of you.

Lesson 2
When you give your life over to obey God, you do not enter into a Master/ Servant relationship but a Father/Child relationship.

Lesson 3
You are not inadequate. God will equip you in His own training school. Just relax!

Lesson 4
The greatest opposition to the spiritual life of the church comes from within or through the church/Christian community, not from outside it. (This was so in Gujranwala and probably elsewhere also.)

Lesson 5
If you want God's blessing, then you MUST first deal with the sin that stands in the way.

Lesson 6
The plans are God's, but He works through individuals. He needs us to be there too. Don't try to fathom out why, just be there!

Lesson 7
Don't wait until everything is in place and ready. Start in with what you have.

Lesson 8
God knows what He is doing and there are no limits.

Lesson 9
Live expectantly . . . and be prepared to be caught up into great enterprises.

The Way He Works . . .

YOU ARE IMPORTANT TO HIM

The very heart of Christianity is that it is individual in nature.

In other matters, we can act as a family, as a congregation, as a community, as a society, or even as a state or nation, but Christianity is essentially an encounter between the individual man or woman and Christ Himself.

For most who go beyond the vestments of an inherited faith to explore and find reality, it is not an encounter with God, remote, impersonal, and omniscient, or even with a Loving Heavenly Father painted in human terms and perceptions. Rather, it is an encounter with the enduring *One who is like as we are, who suffered under the same temptations but who was yet without sin.* It is the most significant person-to-person encounter anyone can experience—simply between Jesus and oneself.

There is always a sense that this is a mystical encounter, even though it may not set itself forth in such terms. There is ever-present an instinct that . . .

> *Only*
> *By walking*
> *Across the snow waste*
> *Alone*
> *Into the face*
> *Of the blizzard*
> *Shall I emerge*
> *Into the sunlight.*

When you really think about it, it is incredible that you, the reader, are important to Him as a person. He authored all of Creation and you—well, who are you after all? A breath for a while and then gone in a last puff!

Yet you have to pull in your breath with surprise because you are important to Him!

The eternal silence
Of star strewn space
Is full of the call
Of the Father to us
Singing so softly,
So softly—

    I love you, my child,
    I love you so much
    I would die for you
    If I could
    So I did.

        And it hurt!

It is so easy for us to work with stereotypes, group people together, and forget they have individual home addresses, faces that are unique, and unfathomable complexity of character. Each man and woman's faith-walk has some subtle, unique difference from the jostling neighbor standing alongside.

What does God see as He looks down on a surging struggling mass of more than six billion people knocking His world around?

Quite simply, He is focused on you and sees your face and your hands holding a name tag giving all your details. He has you all marked out, your achievements, your capacities, your merits, and your demerits. He knows what you can do when He taps you on the shoulder, but He leaves to you the way you respond. That's your business. It's known as free will. The odds are that He has already tapped you on the shoulder, and you already know how you have answered.

No more than you expect you'll get
From each experience on your way,
Each moment of the day,
From self, from love, from life's array.

Expect little, get no more than that.
Expect much—some will leave you flat,
Others give a tithe and some a little more
But always sure there'll be a few
Who give everything that's asked
To see a job go through.

A man from strangers little can expect
But from the children of his flesh

He must not ask for little lest
That's all he shall receive and thus
Diminish their capacity to give.

None expects as much from us as God.
From His only gentle Son
He asked and then received
E'en the very breath He breathed.
From us of later time and line
Who claim of Him his holy kin
He asks the same in terms divine
And standing silent at the gates
Just waits
and waits
and waits.

Here follow several stories . . . the first is about a young Scotsman and the next about two young Americans. The three of them, each an individual important to God, felt that the answer to the great questions of faith lay with the Eastern religions.

The Way He Works—Individuals are
important to Him . . .
JAMIE

Pakistan
October 1986

We were not quite sure what to expect when Jamie arrived. The initial letter came from Scotland, from Edinburgh. I think we were rather expecting a young man wearing earrings and his hair tied at the nape of his neck with a black ribbon in a big bow.

How he had heard of us, I do not know.

There was nothing unusual in his letter until the last sentence. He explained, how in previous years, he had been mountain climbing in India and in Pakistan. He was planning another visit to the subcontinent. He wanted this trip to be more than just mountain climbing. He wanted not only to gain good experiences for himself, but he wanted to give something back. The people he had met had been consistently kind and helpful to him, even though most of them had been very poor. Would we have a place where he could give some service? He didn't mind what he would be asked to do; he'd be happy to do it. He had a strong desire to respond in some way to the generosity he had experienced.

He gave us dates when he expected he could be available. The last sentence was the intriguing one. He realized that perhaps it might not be possible or convenient for him to come to a missionary-run institution because he was a Buddhist, but we needed to know that before responding to his request.

Marie wrote back to tell him that we would be expecting him. We were rather surprised that a Buddhist would even want to come to a missionary-run institution.

In the early stages of my own spiritual journey, I myself had looked at Buddhism as a possible faith to live by. I had read several books about it. Its emphasis on peace I appreciated, but I had felt it failed to express the nature of the involved and intervening God that I did not doubt existed.

We liked Jamie the moment we saw him, a tall, slightly built Scot in his late teens or early twenties. He was quiet and diffident. When he was ready, we were pretty sure he would be telling us about his conversion to Buddhism. He obviously hadn't been born a Buddhist.

However, that was not what happened. He started telling us instead about his conversion to Christianity. It had happened just before he came to us, totally unexpectedly, in the mountains of north Pakistan, while he had been alone.

Jamie had given us dates at the end of his climbing tour that he planned for the summer. He had flown into Rawalpindi and then gone on to Peshawar.

Later he recalled:

"I flew out to Pakistan with my climbing partner to climb an unclimbed route on the Hispar Wall. On the Syrian Arab Airlines flight to Karachi were a couple of British nurses going to spend a year working in a hospital. The brother of one of them had been killed in the mountains the previous year. The waste of a young life was a sobering thought as we were heading for the mountains ourselves. It made me feel very selfish, all this expense of flying to Pakistan just for adventure. I was climbing with a friend, Roger, from Yorkshire. We climbed Sphinx peak on the Hispar Wall—including a bivvy in a storm when neither of us felt we would survive. The storm suddenly blew over in the night, and we descended in the dawn light. We both felt we had been given a new lease of life and an opportunity to start again. Roger returned to England, and I went solo climbing in the Shimshal area."

Jamie enjoyed mountaineering by himself and did not miss company. He bivouacked at night on the hillside in the sleeping bag he had brought. He had plenty of rupees to buy bread, milk, tea, curry, and biscuits. Often people refused to accept any kind of payment. In a hard country you share with each other or you don't survive.

One night Jamie was sitting up in his sleeping bag, leaning against a rock, high up on the hillside. The air was still. He could almost feel the stillness. The night sky was a canopy of sparkling light. Only in the mountains, devoid of artificial light and at high altitude, did you get such skies. The great constellations struggled with thousands, millions, of other stars suddenly bright and vying for attention.

He was alone. No one knew where he was, not his family, not his friends, no one. And then almost suddenly, it dawned upon him that Someone, Someone Out There, did know where he was. Somehow that was important, very important. Just the two of them knew where he was. And the Other cared about him, loved him, touched him, and above all wanted him, Jamie, to acknowledge His presence. Later it was hard to determine how long this sense of the Presence, the communion, the conversation with (Was it? It must have been . . .) God persisted. All Jamie knew was that his life would never be the same again. The questions were gone; only the certainty remained. The answer was in Christ after all. He was laughing to himself on the hillside. They had—

his friends, his family—tried to argue him back into the faith of his childhood, and they had failed. Now without a word, it had happened anyway.

Jamie reflected later on what had happened to him.

"The experience in the mountains of Pakistan was very strong and has never left me. It changed my priorities in life. I still enjoyed being in the mountains, but there were more important things than just climbing mountains. I stopped climbing at a high level, while my friend Roger carried on climbing the hardest routes. Roger was killed in the Alps a few years later. It was a tragedy; he was my best friend, and it still hurts to remember. I feel there may have been something I could have said to stop Roger from trying harder and harder routes, but one route inevitably led to a harder and more dangerous one.

"My baby daughter is being baptized tomorrow in the Catholic Cathedral in Edinburgh (his wife, Joanne, is an Irish Catholic). It is a big responsibility bringing up a child in the world these days. I still enjoy the peace and the quiet of the mountains. You come away refreshed, knowing what really is important."

Once I wrote:

> *I reach my half inch*
> *Through the dark sky*
> *Where clouds roll,*
> *Brush with my tips*
> *Fingers of God*
> *Searching the sky*
> *For the one touch*
> *That is mine.*
>
> *He is the Seeker,*
> *He the wild star*
> *Ranging the sky*
> *Searching for me,*
> *Ready to grasp*
> *Whenever I lift*
> *Hesitant hands*
> *To the sky.*

EASY WAY

Easier by far to ignore
The wrongs we do not wish to see
By choosing blindness
Than by sight to seek
To set aright what hurts
A distant stranger.

The Way He Works—Individuals are

important to Him . . .

TOM AND GUY

Pakistan
November 1973

The two young men on our front porch had a note of introduction from John Wilder in Lyallpur. He wondered whether we might have anything they could do. We smiled at each other. We always had something young men could do. Marie particularly was quite prepared to invest much time and energy into caring for these young foreigners that God was bringing to our door. She had a deep sense that He would one day, and probably in some other place, unfold His purposes through these young people's lives to His glory. Her role was to facilitate their encounter with Him, though she might never see or hear of them again after they left Gujranwala. They were never a burden to her, although they should have been. Instead, she enjoyed their youth, their freshness, their brashness, and their questions and never sought to assert her own certainties into their thinking.

They brought in their backpacks. We looked them over. They were Americans; they were well educated. Tom, the taller one, looked Jewish. He was bearded. They were clean and alert and did not look as though they might be on drugs.

Over tea, in bone china cups, they told us about themselves.

They had become friends at Stanford University in California and had graduated together. They were disenchanted with what their own culture had to offer them. The idea of slipping smoothly into the niches their parents dreamed for them was unpalatable. They rejected the premises of both prosperous Christianity and prosperous Judaism. They rejected, too, the hippie culture as spurious and introspective. They had a common interest, to discover the *real* truth, to discover the reasons why they were living, and to discover something to live for. In the fraternity house they had long, long sessions. The Jew and the Presbyterian argued with the others and with each other. The truth did not lie in their traditional faiths; they were not going to be encumbered or misguided by the undue influence of their inherited environment.

It must lie elsewhere.

Possibly, the truth lay in Communism, not Soviet Communism with its excesses of brutality, but perhaps in the Chinese form, where Marxism was moderated by the inherited traditions of a strong familial society. More likely though, the truth, the essential essence of life and living, of belief and action, would be found in Hinduism or Buddhism. To them both, this was the essential quest—discovering a meaning for life. If India failed, then China must provide the answer to their search.

They were on their way to finding out, and we were along the trail that they took.

The Senator from K——- had asked us to build a number of our dwellings (prefabricated, concrete, flood-relief dwellings) in two lines on either side of the mosque at Rannmal. Each simple home would be similar to the initial house that we had built.

The village would provide all the manual labor that was needed.

We sent out Munir, Sain Ahmed, and Caleb John. Caleb was one of our Christian students who had graduated as an auto-mechanic. He was now working with us on the flood relief housing project. Munir was Muslim, Sain Ahmed . . . now a Muslim, but out of Sikhism when caught in the chaos of Partition.

There is a quite spurious general view that the Muslims and Christians are at each other's throats in Pakistan. This is not so. Many close friendships between Christians and Muslims exist. Most of the time, the two communities coexist peacefully and cooperatively.

When the three men arrive in Rannmal with the first load of foundations, they are faced with an unexpected snag. The villagers will, of course, feed Munir and Sain Ahmed, but Caleb is a different matter. He is a Christian. They don't have any Christians in the village with whom he can eat. In the circumstances, presumably he will cater for himself.

Munir and Sain Ahmed acknowledge their problem with nods of assent. Yes, of course, they understand. They beg their host's indulgence. They are grateful for the offer to feed them, but you see, Caleb is their friend. You know what friendship is. You can't eat a meal when your friend doesn't have a meal; you have to share your meal with him. After all, this is the custom. The villagers would forgive them if, in these difficult circumstances, they can not accept the generous and appreciated offer of food. They will find some other way to manage. Now let's get on with setting out the positions of the foundations.

Only a few minutes pass before the village delegation is back. They are very sorry. There has been a misunderstanding. Of course, all three of the men will have meals with them. Are they not here, far from their own homes to help them? Is it not their duty, and privilege, to offer them hospitality? This is their custom; they can accept no demur.

Guy and Tom were quite willing to work at Rannmal. I took them out, backpacks and all, checked the work, and left them there. They could speak nothing but English. Among the others only Caleb could speak a little English.

Every week or ten days, one or both of them would come in by bus. By this time, both of them were bearded. Their first stop after tea would be Marie's bathtub. They would be so glad to talk English again and tell their stories. It wasn't just the building work. They were learning about people who lived in villages, people with virtually nothing, people that had been hit by a devastating flood, people who were poor, people of a different faith than their own, people who did not complain, people who were happy, people who were rebuilding their lives and homes, and people sharing each other's pains and sorrows.

Add then to the initial three who went out: an American Presbyterian and an American Jew. Quite a mix. They were to learn about the immense generosity of the poor and that poverty has no capacity to limit laughter or kindness. They were seeing how people could love each other across the divides that normally separate rather than unite. They were learning especially to love and respect Munir and Sain Ahmed and Caleb.

The work inevitably was tiring; it involved heavy manual work. Guy and Tom loved it. They were doing something worthwhile that they would never get paid for—and never forget.

They loved the rhythm of village life, dawn, dogs barking, cockerels crowing, women bustling, women squatting in front of the twigs under the cooking pots blowing and coaxing a flame, children playing tag, little girls wearing their red shawls around them strung out on the paths between the fields to the school in the next village, little boys playing games with sticks and wooden pegs, men squatting in a circle passing the mouthpiece of the water-pipe around to each other, the steady patting of the women's hands fashioning flat breads out of the ball of dough, the call for the meal, and the rich buffalo milk in the metal drinking vessel.

They loved, too, the quiet evenings before bed as the light faded quickly, and they were left with only the softness of the kerosene lantern. The village then became an island under a canopy of stars brighter and more numerous than they had ever observed back home.

They had thought they would never get to know the names of the people. They knew them all. The seeming absolute similarities of appearance that limited identification had quickly been lost in the dissimilarities of each individual that permitted no confusion. They knew who was related to whom, so they understood the chemistry of community activity. Caleb translated some of the stories the villagers told about each other. They watched the practice of Islam in a rural village setting. They saw how even the littlest ones were nurtured in their faith from an early age.

Tom and Guy left for India at the end of April in 1974. They had been with us for half a year. After Rannmal, they went out to Pipeen on a similar assignment. Two of the few letters that have survived from those days are from Tom. He wrote as he left:

Dear Ken and Marie,

And here we are, our last days in Pakistan and our very last day in Gujranwala. After so many postponements we are on our way again. Each of those postponements was worthwhile.

Many thoughts about how our experience here has meant so much to me and, I'm sure, in a different way to Guy.

I came to Pakistan a tourist, a footloose lackluster traveler. Something happened, back in November, when we decided to try and DO something for the people of Pakistan.

I never would have guessed. . . .

I wish I could think I had done more here. We contributed so little and took such rich experiences and insights for ourselves.

Thank you both for giving me the opportunity to live here with you, to try my hand at helping others, to get to know so many good Punjabi people and to share your burdens, frustrations, hopes and dreams.

I appreciate greatly your gift of The Book. That aspect of my experience here, my exposure to Christianity, through truly good Christians, has certainly been the most unexpected fruit of the last five months. I often have reflected: Me, a Jew (by birth if nothing else) in a Christian community in a strictly Muslim country. One might think I would have felt threatened, ill at ease in such a milieu of beliefs so contrary to that of my family's faith. But not in the least.

I've felt more welcome than I usually do in my own home in the States.

Guy and I have indeed at times felt a bit intimidated by some of the 'preaching' we have heard—Guy more than I, I'm sure, on this account. He seems to have made the firm decision that Christianity is not for him—particularly some of the after-dinner devotions.

Now and then I have felt there was nothing you would like more than to see Guy and me accept Jesus. You know better than I that this is a decision that one makes by himself. It comes from within.

I am at a point very close now to making such a decision. Day-by-day the feeling within me grows stronger telling me that I really can't get on with the serious business of my life until I have the strength of a spiritual (or anti-spiritual, as the case may eventually be) commitment as a foundation for my thoughts and deeds.

What it comes down to is a choice between Christianity or Communism. The choice must seem to you outrageously obvious but to me it is a difficult one. I have yet a lot of thinking on and weighing the alternatives to do. I know one thing, an uncommitted person is bound to be useless and the day of commitment draws near.

Now we must catch the train to Lahore. You have enriched our experience in Pakistan, enriched the remainder of our travels and enriched the remainder of our lives more than any of us can now know. We shall draw strength from your perseverance and, in our good times, remember the best of times.

Love
Tom

Tom also wrote a Christmas letter in 1976.

My experience with you and the housing at Rannmal and the UP Mission was far and away the most profoundly determining of my life. I cannot express what an effect those months, our interactions, your teaching and the plight of the Pakistani people had on my world view, my goals and my attitudes towards my fellow people and the value and potential of a life.

I arrived in Gujranwala with little care for the human condition as a realistic focus for one's life energy. The suffering I had seen up to that point seemed too immense for any one person to take on and try to affect. But then I saw how you people seemed unfettered by the possible hopelessness of your task. You plug on. You do as much—sometimes it seems like more—as one person can do and rest in the knowledge that the abilities of one person are limited as well as, in another way, unlimited.

From you I learned, among other things, that this planet is not so utterly corrupt that a single person cannot try to do and succeed in doing good works in an effort to lighten the loads of others. That may seem banal and mundane, one of the givens on which your lives are founded but you should know that there are millions of people here at home who believe the future of human life on this planet is hopeless and that the best thing we all can do is not step on each other's toes, withdraw from the mainstream and just get by.

I was close to entering into such a life when I was traveling in Asia but you showed me another way. From you I also learned what Christianity is really about in terms of relations between people and the endeavors of one's life. The spiritual side of your Christianity I still respect and admire but could never accept as my own for fear of the bondage of dogma. You two are towering figures in my life.

I hope that some day I may influence some wandering soul as you influenced me.

Much love,

Tom

PS How do you reconcile the murder of Brend with your belief in a merciful God?

After their return to America and completion of their further studies, Guy became a doctor and worked in Africa. Tom became a geneticist working to develop improved seeds for use in third world countries. He married a lovely Catholic girl, but I don't know how they sorted out their ultimate questions.

The Way He Works—Individuals are important to Him . . .
BILQUIS' BROTHER MAHMUD

Pakistan
March 1967

This story about a quiet Muslim gentleman may not fit easily with a particular theology. However, we are attempting to understand how God works and this is, I think, part of that story.

Bilquis was already drinking tea with Marie on the lawn when I came across from the building site at the hospital operating block. I had seen her white Toyota come in and make its way across to the house.

After we greeted each other, I asked her a question. "Bilquis, what were you doing at 2:30 A.M. this morning?"

She looked rather surprised at the question, smiled, and then replied, "Well, you know, Ken, I wasn't sleeping. I had been lying in bed thinking about Mahmud, my brother." Her eyes filled with tears. I knew Mahmud had died not long previously and that the siblings had been close.

"I was thinking how undeserving I am, and yet Jesus has blessed me so much with His presence. Why did He choose me? He gave me a chance of knowing Him, and I am happier now than I have ever been in my life. But Mahmud had no chance. Now he will never get a chance. He will spend the whole of eternity without knowing Jesus. That must be all that hell is—the whole of time, and beyond that, spent without knowing the love of Jesus. He didn't have a chance. I was just pouring my heart out to my loving Father, praying that somehow He would give Mahmud the same chance He gave me, even though it is too late."

About seven years previously in the summer of 1960, Marie and I decided that she and Tim, our baby, would spend the summer in Murree, rather than stay down in the village at Wah Cottage with me, while I was building a memorial church to Mac nearby. Tim had had severe malaria the previous year when they had stayed down, and because of our proximity to water, there were many mosquitoes. I would come up for weekends and for the month of August.

Mahmud and his family had come up from Lahore to the home village for a break from the oppressive heat and humidity when the monsoons broke. They dropped in to see us.

Mahmud was our landlord. He was a cultured, kindly man, slim, tall, and courteous with a lovely wife and several daughters. He asked our summer plans, and we quickly agreed that during our month away he and his family should use the house. We would not put anything away, and the family should use whatever supplies they found in the house.

Mahmud grinned as he turned back the house to us. They had a wonderful rest and enjoyed their family in the village. He had time to read. He had read everything in our library, including, he remarked pointedly, *How to Lead Muslims to Christ*. That was one of Mac's books that we still retained.

I responded to Bilquis' quizzical look. She was wondering why I had asked that particular question.

"This morning, Bilquis, at about 2.30, I had a dream.

I was looking out over a rough stony plain littered with small boulders. It wasn't sand but rather plain earth and stones and entirely without vegetation. It stretched as far as the eye could see.

Approaching me on foot from the left center of this plain were two people. As they grew nearer I saw that they were both Pakistanis. The man was tall and slim and wearing a black ankle length achkan (a frock coat worn by upper class Muslim men). The woman was much younger, looking like and dressed as a college girl wearing white shalwarqamiz.

They came up close to me and stopped. I had seen the man before but although I racked my brains his name eluded me. He spoke to me in a cultured voice, in English. "Do you know who I am?" I had rather been hoping that he would lead in with his name but now I had to apologize profusely. "I'm sorry, I know you, we have met before but I am terribly sorry, your name has just slipped from my memory." "No matter, I'm Mahmud." "Oh yes, of course, how could I have forgotten."

We chatted in casual conversation, exchanging news of which I have no recollection. The girl said nothing and was silent throughout our encounter. Finally, as the conversation drew to an end Mahmud, with a twinkle to his eyes, said "I suppose you'll be wondering what I am doing now."

By way of answer without words he put both hands up to the stiff straight collar of his frock coat and with his thumbs pushed out for display metal badges at each end of the collar. Each was a cross. He smiled at me again and the dream faded and I awoke.

"Bilquis, I think that was an answer to your prayer but I am puzzled over one thing. Why was there a woman in the dream? She said nothing throughout."

Bilquis looked at me with surprise. "Why, don't you know? That was his daughter. She was a college girl in Lahore and was killed in a car accident. That's who she was!"

No, I had not known.

What are we to make of this story?

First, we recognize that the primary character is not Mahmud but Bilquis. This is a woman who has just taken a hazardous leap from the faith of her fathers into the arms of a newly-discovered spiritual Father. He is listening to her anguished prayers. She is filled with love for Him and grieves for her family members who do not yet know Him. She can hope to share with those who are still with her in her family circle in the days to come, and they must then make choices for themselves similar to the one she has faced. But Mahmud! It is too late for him. If only, if only she had been able to share with him before he died . . .

And I can imagine the Holy Listener smiling and saying quietly, "Relax, Bilquis; it's all taken care of. I'll let him answer for himself."

Second, let us recognize how this responds to the question, *Does God really answer prayer?* To imagine that there is some empathetic thought/dream correspondence between two friends seven miles distance from each other at the same instant without the intervention of a third higher party is even more far-fetched than the strange cycle of events that has actually occurred. The dream I experienced answered her prayer more fully than she could ever have imagined at the time she was making it.

I am fascinated by the strangeness of His ways as He brings things He purposes to pass. How on earth does He do it, or perhaps we should be asking, "How in Heaven does He do it?"

What of the dream itself? We do not know the details of Mahmud's spiritual journey or the extent of it. We do know that by reading Mac's book in our library he had been faced clearly with Jesus' challenging words that the only way to the Father is through Him. How that worked its way through in his life, we have no way of knowing. We do know from the dream that somehow the connection was made.

Paul says, *Now we see in a glass darkly but then face to face.* I am content to leave many of the spiritual mysteries unsolved and place them securely under the benevolent blanket of God's sovereign will. It's just the way He works. We don't have to understand everything.

The Way He Works—Individuals are important to Him . . .
MARGARET

England
1998

This story is different from the three previous ones; its setting is in England, but its theme is similar. Individual people are important. This is a simple low-key story of a woman's need for help when far from home and the way that need was answered. It gives us a glimpse of the compassionate heart of God reaching between continents and over seas. It is just the way He works.

It is surely wrong to affirm there is no such a thing as coincidence, but it is right to affirm that alongside coincidences are deliberate concurrences and congruencies brought about by God's interventionist hand to bring desired consequences to pass. Walking His Way must mean moving beyond the personal act of supplication to Him to the prompted act of response to an unknown other's supplication. This is where the holy partnership begins to fulfill itself.

Ester Mortimer lives in Tieton, Washington, in a fertile land taking irrigation water from the eastern foothills of the Cascades. It is a land of fruit orchards, and the whole valley extending through the Gap as far as Richland is profuse with orchards and vineyards. Her husband Herb and she had apple orchards on the side of a gentle hill.

In the 30s before she married Herb, she had trained to be a nurse at St. Elizabeth's Hospital in Yakima. In her class was Marie Johnson who had gone to Pakistan as a missionary and eventually married an Englishman. Their friendship persisted, and they had kept in touch. She had been saddened when Marie had died in England of cancer in 1997—another friend to cross off the mailing list.

Ester is ill, but she nurses a lifelong dream. It is a cruise. Ever since she was a girl she has wanted to visit the Mediterranean and see the isles of the Aegean, Malta where the Apostle Paul has been wrecked, Cyprus and Crete, and the coasts of Turkey and Greece. She had wanted to go with Herb, but although they had often talked about it, there isn't that much money in apples, and he had died before they could actually make it. Now she has a terminal illness, and it is never going to happen.

Margaret, her younger sister, isn't so sure. She is staying at the orchard with her husband, Pat, helping to take care of Ester. If she's going to do anything for her sister, it has to be soon. She makes enquiries, checks costs, and finds what cruises are available and when. She checks with her nephew Brian who lives in a trailer home further towards the road in the orchard. She sees new life come back into Ester's pale cheeks, a new vitality, a new hope, and a new determination. Her sister has something to live for.

The two sisters take off at Yakima airport. From that moment, the prayers of the family and the local community and the Presbyterian congregation with which Ester has worshiped through the decades surround them. All wonder whether they will ever see Ester again.

They will not. Cruising the Mediterranean, on the way back from the eastern end towards the Straits of Gibraltar, Ester dies in her sleep.

Margaret, coping with her own grief, now has to face difficult problems alone. How does she get Ester's body back home? What does she do next? The purser and members of the crew are as helpful as they can be. There is a chaplain on board, but Margaret does not want a burial at sea. It will need to be soon after the ship docks at a port where a cremation can be arranged.

The ship is on its way to Dover in England. That is the first feasible stopping point for a funeral service. Cables are sent. When the ship docks, and after the passengers are disembarked, a hearse draws alongside the ship and takes the coffin with Ester's body.

Margaret is in a hotel, in a strange town, in a foreign country, waiting until the cremation service is over, and she can receive her sister's ashes and go home. If only she knew someone, anyone—but she doesn't.

It is about eight o'clock this lovely, fair June morning. I check on the e-mails that have come in. There is one from a Brian Mortimer. Who is he? It is a general letter that seems to have been intended for the community of his mother's friends back in and around Tieton. His mother, Ester Mortimer, has died while on a Mediterranean cruise and is to be cremated in Dover, England, at nine A.M. local time this very day. He asks that those who knew and loved his mother remember her in prayer.

I look at the clock. Eight o'clock. There is going to be no one there to receive her ashes! I need to do something, quickly. She has been Marie's friend. We have visited her home. I have to find out where the cremation is taking place and be there. There is a strange urgency. I search the yellow pages of the telephone directory. Dover is 18 miles away. I have never heard of a crematorium in Dover. There is one at Hawkinge, near Folkestone. People haven't started work. I try funeral homes in Dover out of the book, one after another. Eventually, I get a response from Hawkinge. No, there is no cremation of an Ester Mortimer scheduled. Back to the phone. I dislike phones at the best of times. Why don't people get to work earlier?

Eventually, I get an answer from a funeral home. At last, somebody who knows something. Yes, the lady is being cremated at Denton crematorium between Dover and Canterbury at nine o'clock. The map! Where is Denton? Eight miles as the crow flies, sixteen miles by country lanes.

It's a funeral service I'm going to, I have to wear the right clothes. I hurry to the car. As the clock at the crematorium shows nine o'clock, I hurry in. The music is playing softly. A solitary woman sits in the front row. The room otherwise is empty. I whisper that I am a friend of Ester's. Introductions can wait until later. Seven thousand miles from home, she is no longer alone, and He is answering someone's prayer.

THE WIND

Hold on!
Keep holding on!

He knows what is to come
And intervenes
    Beyond the reach of dreams.

Beyond the Plan He has for you,
Further far than you can see
    He sings His future song.

Demands compliance with His Holy Will.
Commands the massing clouds be gone
    The future winds be still.

Beyond your grasp or deepest sense
All things random and by chance
    He captures into congruence.

While trickles back so far behind
To the Now wherein you stand
    Only a whisper on the wind
        To say the Years are in His hand

        *—Or **is** it just the wind?*

The Way He Works . . .

THE TIMING IS ALWAYS PERFECT

Think about it. God, if He exists, dwells beyond the reach of time. He dwells in eternity, where time is not. Yet He also intervenes in history. It is not only that Jesus was an historical figure who lived and died about 2000 years ago. His Father is having a constant and continuing interaction with time. If we believe He answers prayer, then nine times out of ten there is a time element to that answer.

It is not difficult to understand that God, presuming He exists, is going to be vastly superior to any human mind in dealing with time. We might know the beginning when something starts to happen, we may be clear about what is happening around us at this very moment, but go heading off into the future and there are a dozen directions to take. We humans are distinctly second-rate when it comes to the future.

God, on the other hand, knows the end as well as the beginning. He can back-step from the future into our present, and he can do so the other way and know pretty well how things are going to end up. If He wants something to develop in a certain way in 1970, He can easily start in 1949 to set the ball rolling to bring that event about. Once it is moving, all it needs are gentle little nudges or occasionally a sharp hard push to ensure all things work out to the required end. The same for a hundred years earlier or later.

If He knows that a catastrophe is likely to occur in 1972, He can set the ball rolling with countermeasures so far ahead that no one will link one with the other or even think the two are remotely related.

But He knows and this is the way He works. Walk with me a little further along the Way.

FLYER

'Climb a little higher'
He said.
Higher yet?

'Draw a little closer'
He said.
Closer still?

'On the limb further'
He said.
Still further?

'But it's about to break!'
He said
'No matter.'

'Time for you to fly'
He said
And pushed.

The Way He Works—The timing

is always perfect . . .

Return to Pakistan

January—August 1953

After graduation as a civil engineer, I had initially been working with a contractor in Southend, on the north side of the Thames estuary in Essex, England. I changed my job after a year or so to work in the office of the Borough Engineer.

At the end of January in 1953 heavy storms and gales coincided with very high tides in the North Sea leading to severe flooding around its coasts, the sinking of a large ferry, and much loss of life in England and Holland. It was as though, propelled by adverse winds, a tidal bore sitting on top of already high tides swept up the river Thames towards London. Islands in the estuary were flooded. River embankments upstream were breached. Damage was considerable.

Initially all the engineers available in the office were engaged on the simple task of draining the islands and helping repair the breaches to the sea walls with sandbags. One by one, as the walls were raised above tide levels, trapped seawater was drained and only drying out remained to be accomplished. I was now sent as resident engineer further toward London where sheet steel piling was being driven on the north bank of the river. The river wall had been breached just upstream of the projected tunnel crossing of the Thames at Dartford and the repairs were urgent.

In the middle of May in the resident engineer's office, I picked up a daily newspaper that **in normal circumstances** I would not have had access to. I opened it automatically without paying any conscious attention to the front or back pages. It was as though, subconsciously, I was searching for something in the newspaper that I had previously seen. I went immediately to the third page from the back as though I knew I would find it there. Printed in one of the many columns, in small print, but shining out at me **as though it alone on the page were printed in red ink** was a small classified advertisement of a job for a civil engineer in Pakistan. Curious that my eyes should light so immediately on that particular advertisement! It stirred many memories of my Army service in that land. I looked at it a long time, and then closed the paper and set about my work.

My brother Geoff worked in the British Museum in London. I used to say we had a regular correspondence, a letter about every 20 years. The following morning there was a brief note.

I saw this advertisement in the newspaper today, and I think it may be for you. ~ Geoff

The enclosure was the same advertisement.

Unknown to me, in Pakistan, the husband of my future wife had just died of bulbar poliomyelitis, infantile paralysis. As far as I could later estimate, it was about this very same time.

Two months later I arrived in Karachi. The company headquarters was there. After I had become acquainted with various principals in the company, I was told I would be working in Wah in the north on underground explosive magazines for a new ordnance factory. I should fly to Rawalpindi, buy myself a motorcycle, and settle in at Flashman's Hotel. The district engineer would contact me as soon as he returned north. He would get me started.

I received some sage advice from the managing director, an Australian. He deflated my self-importance by reminding me that I had not been employed for my engineering ability. "If we wanted that, we could have employed locally. There are many fine engineers here. No, we have employed you for your integrity. That's why we are paying you a high salary.

"We can employ honest men locally too. They are almost always fools who can achieve nothing. The alternative is to employ crooks who are smart and can achieve the results we need. We always work against deadlines. We can't afford to be late.

"Guard your back!"

I was on my way.

On the anniversary of Independence Day, I moved out to Wah from Rawalpindi and was given a comfortable room in the Junior officers mess . . . utilized by British employees of the contractors building the ordnance factory.

For our own Christian worship, it was fortunately not necessary to go into Rawalpindi. Those who wished to attend an English language service at a nearby mission hospital at Taxila on Sunday evenings were able to do so. The ordnance factory authorities provided a bus.

The great mosque in Wah was under construction, but not yet complete.

It was now six years since those first proud beginnings of Pakistan. I well remembered the occasion of that first Partition Day, for it had put me out of a job I enjoyed.

What had happened during the intervening years to those bright hopes and starry eyes?

Now that I was settled, there would be opportunity to find out what had happened to the country since, and I was ready to learn.

The Way He Works—The timing is always perfect . . .

MOTHER MARIE

Karachi
August 1956

M arie and I have married in Taxila, in Pakistan, at the end of 1955. My intention is that, as soon as my contract with my employer is over, we will return to England, remind God of the night encounter in Plymouth, tell Him we are ready, and ask Him what it is He wants us to do and where does He want us to do it.

I have no idea that the journey is already well under way. It is much further on than asking for or receiving starting instructions. As far as He is concerned, it is time for some different instruction.

Our way, His way. There is a distinct observable difference in process of teaching and learning. When we study to learn, it requires hard thinking, intensive memorizing, extended time, and often homework. God's lessons are rarely that. They are short, sharp, and unforgettable, and as always, the timing is perfect.

It was early evening in late August. The steady, hot, moist wind off the sea seemed never to tire. The monsoon had brought a recent torrential rain and local flooding, but it made the humidity even worse. My prickly heat was healing up after the trip to Quetta; I had nearly 150 boils all over my back from infected prickly heat and had also discovered I was allergic to penicillin. I was beginning to feel better.

We had done our shopping in Elphinstone Street and there was opportunity to visit Marian at the orphanage before returning to Mauripur.

Marian would always find us a cup of tea, but this time she was preoccupied and puzzled. We walked in the garden. The children were having their devotions with Janebai. It had been time for Marian's furlough back to New Zealand in the spring but there was no one available to take the work over. She had been waiting for God's timing to provide her a substitute.

Just this morning she has had a letter from home. She showed us. Her widower father was seriously ill, no longer able to care for himself . . . could she not come immediately? What was she going to do? She was the only child. She was just going to ask all her friends to pray. God would have an answer out there somewhere. Meanwhile, trusting Him to provide, she has been doing her packing and has been down to Cox and Kings to see about shipping luggage. She herself would fly as soon as she could.

So would we pray earnestly about this need? She couldn't leave the children without having arranged for them, and not everyone who might be willing to help would be suitable.

One of the lessons I had already learned was not to ask God in prayer for things that you were perfectly able to supply yourself. That was just making a convenience of God.

Prayer needed to follow self-examination, not precede it. I looked over at Marie, quizzically. She, standing slightly behind Marian, gave what I thought was just the slightest hint of an affirmative nod.

"Marian," I said, "we'll come. You need to get on home."

Marian looked at me in amazement, and then her eyes filled with tears. She turned to Marie, questioning, almost not daring to hope. An answer, so soon!

Marie held her tight. "That's right, Marian. You need to get on home. Your father needs you, now. We'll come. We can come right away. I can come in tomorrow and get started, and we'll bring the luggage over later."

With these few words, on the spur of a moment, Marie, without regrets, accepted immediate disruption of her life, exchanged a lovely home for a large single bedroom with an attached bathroom above classrooms in an orphanage school, across the street from a noisy late-night, open-air cinema.

There would be no going back, ever.

She had launched her career as mother with a family of more than 50 daughters and her first son, Shamim. Although she bore no children herself, there were scores, even hundreds, who over the years were to consider themselves her children.

Marian disengaged herself from Marie and turned to us both. Her eyes were shining with tears but her face was aglow. She took both our hands. For a while, her heart was just too full to allow her to speak, and then she said, "You know, Ken, you will be the first man ever to live here. Now the children will have a father! How wonderful for them. You'll love them, and they will love you. We must go over and tell them because they have just been praying for someone to come. They couldn't have dreamed God would give them a father as well as a mother!"

Before we went over, I took opportunity to try to sort out a few details. This might well be the last opportunity to discuss things with Marian before she was on her way.

"We can do it this way, Marian. Marie will run the school (the school had over 200 other students besides our own children) and look after the girls. You'll need to show her what to do. I'll still continue with my work. (I was wondering what would happen if my next job was away from Karachi.) I'll take care of the accounts in the evenings."

Now I was getting down to brass tacks.

"Do you have any endowment funds?"

Marian's answer was a little disconcerting. After a pause for a moment or so, she answers somewhat hesitantly (her eyes seemed to flicker skywards)."Well, y e . . . s, in a way." Maybe she didn't understand my question.

I put it a little more plainly.

"Do you have any bank accounts?"

Strange, her response was exactly the same. "Well, y e . . . s, in a way."

I obviously needed to be forthright. Marian somehow wasn't understanding, or else I wasn't. A little unease began worrying my mind.

"Marian, do you have any money?"

"Why, yes, here it is. You may as well have it now because you'll be dealing with things from now on."

From her purse, Marian extracted and gave me a white envelope, an ominously small white envelope. This was both her bank and her endowment fund! I removed the rupee notes and counted them.

My stomach seemed to drop into my shoes. Inwardly, I was saying to myself, "You fool, Old. Why don't you keep your mouth shut; look what you've done. Every rupee you earn as an engineer is going to have to go into keeping this orphanage going. Well, this time you really HAVE put your foot in it!"

There were 600 rupees. In those days, when the rupee was worth more, it would have been about 40 pounds or maybe 100 dollars.

And we had committed ourselves for the length of Marian's furlough, a full year!

As Marian led us over to Janebai's room to meet the children and introduce their new Momma and Poppa, she turned to me reassuringly and said gently, "Don't worry about the money, Ken. The children know what to do!"

The *children* know what to do!!

The Way He Works—The timing is always perfect . . .
THE ORPHANAGE

Karachi
August 1956

M arie had done her best to make the bedroom look like home. There were flowers and frilly feminine things, but it was a difficult task to make that dingy room upstairs, with its high ceilings and dark woodwork, attractive. She had no complaints.

Marie had a composure and a confidence that radiated similar response. Few would have known she was totally new to the job of running a school, supervising the teachers, or running an orphanage. There were already experienced Pakistani women there, outstanding women, and they accepted direction from Marie as though there had been no break in continuity from Marian.

It was different with me. This was my first experience of living within a religious environment. I loved the children. They were so excited to have a Poppa. They were waiting at the gate, pressed up against it, waiting for the first sight of Poppa coming home to play with them.

BUT I was watching that little bundle of notes disappearing rapidly.

It was evening devotions in Janebai's room. As the custom was, the children had squeezed in and were seated on the floor. Their shoes had been left outside for this was devotions time. The littlest ones had their usual tussle as to which of them should sit on Poppa's lap. Marie held the youngest of all, not even a toddler. We sang some choruses. Some were in Urdu . . ."Shad, shad, shad (Joy, joy, joy)." Others were in English–"In my heart there rings a melody . . . Now I lay me down to sleep . . . Fishers of men." Janebai read from the Bible and explained a Bible story.

For prayers, Janebai turned to me.

The children also turned in my direction. I was about to learn the most important lessons I ever learned in my life, but I wasn't aware of that. I just knew the envelope was empty.

"Children, I want to tell you that all our money that Missahiba left behind is now gone, and we don't have any more money for food tomorrow."

Parveen jumped to her feet. She said simply, in Urdu, "It doesn't matter, Poppa. We'll tell Jesus." And she proceeded to do so.

The children closed their eyes, even the littlest ones who were now off my lap and on the floor with the others. They inclined their heads down. The older girls, there were some approaching marriageable age, pulled their dopattas (chiffon scarves) over their heads.

My eyes were half-open watching this little girl. She was about eight, possibly a little older. She was wearing the simple, blue one-piece dress that all the children wore over the usual white baggy trousers (shalwars). She wasn't old enough for a dopatta. She was bareheaded with her hair gathered into two tightly tied braids.

"Piyara Yisu Masih (Dear Jesus), Poppa says that we don't have any money to buy food for us tomorrow, but we are your children, and you know we get hungry. Amin"

That was all.

For Parveen and for the other children too, that particular matter had now been dealt with. She sat down while the other girls continued in turn and prayed for Hubboo, the grandmother of them all who lived with them and Piyari and Janebai and Poppa and Momma and Jhaggoo and the various girls upstairs in the sick room.

Not really that much of a prayer!

The U.S. Army Corps of Engineers truck that took me to work at the concrete laboratory at Mauripur would pick me up at seven o'clock each morning outside the orphanage gate. To the American engineers who traveled in with me I was a strange oddity, the father of many Pakistani children.

The truck was unusually late that following morning. While I was waiting at the roadside, two men crossed the street and came towards me. One was a Pakistani and the other a foreigner. They were strangers, perhaps wanting directions to somewhere in the locality.

"Excuse me," the Pakistani began. "Are you Mr. Old?"

"Yes, I am. Can I help you?" *How did they know my name?*

"We hope so," the foreigner broke in, speaking with an American accent. "Do you have a few moments?"

I looked along the street. The truck was not even in sight. Until the truck came, I was available and would help if I could.

"We are from CARE," the American went on.

I wasn't quite sure what the initials meant, but I thought it was something like 'Christian Aid for Relief Everywhere.'

"We are very concerned about the considerable malnutrition of children in southern Asia, and we are planning to start a major program of food aid. However, we need to make sure we are sending the right kind of food, and we are looking for a monitor group that we can try out a pilot food project on. It was suggested you might be able to help."

I looked up the road, thoughts—deep thoughts, thoughts about God—whirling in my head. In the far distance, I could see the truck on its way.

"My wife's inside," I said. "Do come in. I am sure we'll be able to help you, and she will have time to discuss it with you."

The Way He Works—The timing is always perfect . . .
THREE LESSONS

Karachi
August 1956

God was taking me through His academy of practical life. It went on for more than 40 years, but it took half that time for me to reach a point where I was even remotely usable.

After five years, He probably saw I'd never make it without help, and so He brought Marie into my life and then things began to happen. Marie, of course, was wise and relaxed. She already had things sorted out. She wasn't forcing things; she just stayed on her own consistent course and allowed things to happen to me. When they did, I changed and each time my course became more parallel to hers.

When Parveen prayed at the orphanage; the little girl knew God would answer her prayer. She knew because He always had before. She didn't know how, but for her that was not relevant. The following morning CARE was on the doorstep.

That simple event changed my life, or at least, my understanding of life.

The three lessons I learned, summarized, were these:

1. God is UTTERLY reliable.
2. His timing is ALWAYS perfect.
3. Jesus is more than mere Man.

Lesson 1: I believed in God. Yes, no problems there, but I needed to take that belief further. It is just not enough to believe; there has to be more than that. The great lesson Jesus had for the men and women of His time was that they needed to treat Jehovah as their Father. The Old Testament occasionally used that term to describe Him, but Jesus gave the term substance and credibility and reality.

IF your father is sitting with his feet up on the sofa reading the End Times, and you, his child, have a chicken bone in your throat in the next room, there is no way he is going to continue reading while you are in trouble. He is going to be there for you, not once or twice, but every time you need him. You fool, can't you see? He loves you! There is no way he can't be there. He is locked into his relationship with you. He would do it for any stranger, slap him on the back, give him water, give him bread, whatever was needed to dislodge the impediment. Can you imagine he wouldn't be there for YOU, his child? Of course not!

Even while your father goes about his business in other parts of the house and you are messing around with your toys in the basement or making cookies in the kitchen, one of his ears is half tuned to 'noises off' that might suggest you need help. If he hears something, or perhaps more ominously, nothing, he might come noiselessly to the head of the stairs and take a peek at the mess you are making. You've got the toaster to bits on the kitchen table and no idea what to do next. He'll smile to himself and tiptoe away. You won't even know he has looked in on you. But he has, and he keeps doing so.

A father like that had a son, so the story goes, who left home and went to a far-off land and wasted his money in riotous living. He fell on hard times and became a swineherd. Eventually, you know the story, he went back home. Have you ever wondered what happened meanwhile? Remember, it wasn't his uncle back home; it was his father. Every chance Dad had, he'd make enquiries about his son. Neighboring farmers, merchants going there for business, wedding parties traveling, people coming, people going, even strangers passing through on journeys, Dad was full of requests for those going, enquiries for those coming. The boy might have broken away, but Dad needed to know how he was making out. Occasionally, when visitors were few coming and going, he'd find an excuse for a servant to go and make discreet enquiries. He could have bailed the boy out, of course, but he withheld his hand. Meanwhile, he just needed to know. Just before the boy came over the far hill, he'd had a servant go down to the travel agent and find out when the next camel caravan was about to leave, but as you know, he didn't need to make the long journey. Instead, he went for a short run.

I wrote:

Do not shout so loud, my child,
He hears you call,
He hears the echoes of the dumb,
He hears you call.

Do not weep so loud, my child,
He hears you cry,
He hears the whimper of the worm,
He hears you cry.

Do not pray so hard, my child,
He knows your need,

He feeds the sparrow's hungry young,
He knows your need.

Why do you call 'Lord, O Lord'?
You are His child.
Call to Him softly 'Father dear',
He'll wrap you round.

Why do you so strive, my child,
To reach to Him?
He's standing right where you are now,
You're in His arms.

Now tie that love into something else you already know. God is omnipotent, God is omniscient and God is omnipresent; you have uncovered a mystery and have a grasp upon the answer. IF you place yourself squarely in the center of God's Will, then He MUST provide the resources to fulfill His Will. Otherwise, quite simply, He is not God.

God IS able to bring to completion anything He sets His mind to simply because He has all the resources of Creation to achieve it. This is the reason for our impotence, we haven't yet discovered this stupendous truth. It is also the reason why physical or financial resources, money or otherwise, are NEVER the real problem in religious work.

Either that work itself is not within the center of His will, or you have not discovered where the center is and you are standing in the wrong place!

Lesson 2: His timing is always perfect. He must keep whole legions of angels busy coordinating things here on earth because sometimes the timing is almost down to the second.

This is really a corollary to lesson 1.

If you recognize that we can only know two of the three dimensions of time, the past and the present, then it follows as the night follows day, anyone who can see the future, not in an intermittent flash but laid out as clearly as is the past, has a distinct advantage in planning events. It is beyond human understanding to conceive of a God and time relationship whereby God is both outside of time and at the same time, operates within it. Yet I believe it to be true. My observation also is that the future, no matter how certain it may seem, is still subject to the vagaries of chance or accident or to the divine response to the urgency of prayer.

The meaning of this lesson for us is simple: *Rest in the Lord; wait patiently for Him* (to act). He is in possession of more knowledge likely to affect any purposed action than we are, so the timing of our actions is a considered judgment whereas His timing is always perfect.

Of course, it also helps that He is wiser than we are.

Lesson 3. Jesus is more than man?

This is simply the fundamental question that we all face as part of the human race.

If we do not believe it, it is perhaps not fundamental. If we do believe it, then, of course, it is fundamental.

Those that do not believe that Jesus is more than simply man, however high on the pedestal of humanity he may be placed, are on one side. They are by far the large majority.

Not even all Christians, although the nominal appendage of Christian applies to them, believe in and accept unreservedly the divinity of Christ. In the desire to affirm our solidarity with Islam or other non-Christian faiths in the struggle against secularism, humanism, hedonism, and materialism, I believe that we shall see over the next few decades an increasingly expressed desire for a restatement of the position of Jesus Christ as less than divine.

Until Parveen's little prayer, I was with the majority. I recognized the significance of the question but thought that I already had the answer.

***He** is the question*
That disturbs the world
And gives no rest
When we would only
Wish to sleep.
He
Not people,
Not famine
Not frontiers
Not war
Not peace
Not hate
Not love
But a person
Spread-eagled
And slain.
*It is **He***
Who speaks out
Demanding an answer
From men
And from women

And children
Crying 'Speak,
Who am I?
There's no rest
To your soul
Or your land
Or your nation
Or world
Till answer is made
And beware!
The answer divides
And breaks free
One from another,
Nation against nation,
And friend against friend,
Father against son
And son against father,
Sister against brother
and brother against sister.
I came with a sword,
Not a sprig of green myrtle.
I came with a question
Demanding an answer
Who am I?
Answer me,
Now. '

Parveen had prayed to "Piyara Yisu". "Dear Jesus." Simply that. The prayer had been answered. I saw that myself. Not only that, but prayers to Jesus for the past 60 years had been similarly answered. Does a mere prophet answer prayers?

Suddenly, I was seeing from a new perspective. It wasn't a rational analytical perspective, but the kind of perspective that Paul talks about in his letter to the followers of the Way in Ephesus:

But God, rich in mercy, for the great love he bore us, brought us to life with Christ even when we were dead in our sins; it is by his grace you are saved. And in union with Christ Jesus he raised us up and enthroned us with him in the heavenly realms . . . For we are God's handiwork, created in Christ Jesus to devote ourselves to the good deeds for which God has designed us.
Ephesians 2:4–6, 10 NEB

For a short while I seemed to see, from a heavenly perspective, the anguish of God at the waywardness of mankind, the persistent failure of the children of Israel under His guiding then chiding hand, and the divine omnipotent logic of the eventual response in Christ Jesus. A famous editor of the *Daily Express* admonished his reporters never to try to tell a story except through a person. People are interested in people. God knew that first.

God's timing is always perfect, and in the fullness of time, it came to pass that . . . Christmas happened.

Suddenly, the fantasy of a man-God, or more correctly, God become man, seemed to me no longer irrational, but absolute Ultimate common sense—not human common sense, certainly, but divine common sense, yes. I no longer had to argue against Scripture, but could accept it as the divinely inspired and protected record of God's intentions for men and women. It had taken a little girl to show me that.

I wrote, totally refreshed in my amazement:

> *One face become my universe,*
> *Yes, before me and behind,*
> *Above, below, within, without,*
> *The stirrings of the soul,*
> *The mirrors of the mind,*
> *The startpoint and the goal*
> *Are full of that one face*
> *Which does not vanish,*
> *Rather grows hour by hour.*
> *It feels and knows*
> *My heartache and my ease.*
> *It fades, then, bright once more,*
> *It grows upon the sight*
> *And always somewhere near*
> *In sun and shadow, pain or peace,*
> *Waits for me to raise my head*
> *And join my gaze with His.*

Nearly 50 years have passed since then. The truth of these three lessons has been confirmed to me time and time again, and I have never had cause to doubt them.

Working His Purposes Out . . .

THE DOOR OPENS

Pakistan
1970

In 1949 I had received a voice message that "He is going to put you to work in a land that is not your own land, amongst people of a different color and race and culture and creed, and He is going to put you to work amongst boys, and *He* is going to bring it to pass."

For 21 years since then I had been on the road, His road, and now He is ready (or is it I that am ready) to bring what He purposes to pass.

The operating block at Taxila was still a long way from completion when, in the spring of 1970, two missionaries of the Dutch Reformed Churches came up to Taxila to see us. Marie, who was very much a reluctant participant in the consequences of that visit, maintained she was not present at that particular meeting. Both men were friends of the Sialkot days, for they were professors at Murray College, and I had been helping them with building work at the college.

We sat together on the managing board of the Christian Technical School in Gujranwala, and for this reason, we continued to meet each other once or twice a year after we left Sialkot.

The town of Gujranwala, where the school was located, was 31 miles from Sialkot and 45 miles northwest of the center of Lahore. It was an old, walled city with narrow alleys and crowded bazaars. The school, the other side of the railway tracks from the city, was small and struggling and quite dilapidated. It had started in 1900 as a response to famine in Rajputana. Orphan boys from the famine were brought by train to Gujranwala and inducted into an industrial home established for them where they were given training in soap-making, tailoring, shoemaking, and carpentry.

The two visitors reminded us that the Dutch Mission had supplied financing to the school and, in January of '67, a missionary family. They had now decided to pull this family out and to cease their financial support. They saw no hope for the institution as it was, so why prolong the commitment and the agony? They accepted with regret that their withdrawal might lead to the closure of the school.

However, they would defer their action for a year and then reconsider it, provided that I would go and take over as principal.

I laughed. I outlined reasons for my refusal. I knew nothing about education. I had never worked in an institution nor did I desire to do so. You need a particular type of person to work in an institution. I wasn't that kind of a person. My work in Taxila was incomplete. Men were dependent on me there. I was doing drawings as I went along. I couldn't leave. I also knew some of the problems in Gujranwala; only a fool would get involved in them. There were missionary relationship problems. I didn't want to lose my friends.

The two listened. They agreed with everything that I said. Marie would have been pleased at the way I was so clearly turning down the idea. They did not argue. They accepted my response, although they were disappointed by it.

This was the Open Door. "Ken, there is a job for you to do in Gujranwala."

I was refusing to go through it.

As they left, remembering past experiences, I hedged my refusal. "I don't want to go, but really it doesn't matter what I want, or even what Marie wants. If God wants us there, He will put us there anyway."

Going through the Open Door for us was best likened to two children being taken to the dentist by a determined father.

At the end of July, I took over as principal. The Mission had assigned us for three years to Gujranwala.

Two months later, early in October, we were loading our luggage into two gaily-painted open trucks that had too recently been carrying water buffaloes. We would meet the drivers at their destination. Marie was still in tears and stamping her feet and saying, "I won't go! I won't go!"

––––––––––––––––––

For both Marie and for me, this is the end of a journey. We are going to go no further. Although we do not know it, 20 years later we will see our time out in Gujranwala.

For Marie, the journey has started two years after she had come home from the war, when she sees, pinned onto the notice board at North Park College in Chicago, an appeal for help. It is for trained medical staff to volunteer a short stint of service among the refugees on the Indo-Pakistan border during the Partition days of 1947.

During her journey, she is to fall in love with a country strange to her and in love with its people. She is to find, and lose at an early age, a husband and then acquire another and adopt two sons. In the orphanage, she is to become mother to half-a-hundred surrogate daughters. Ahead of her, as yet unmet, are many surrogate sons.

For me the journey started in Devon, not quite as long ago, but still more than 20 years previously. I have lived with those nocturnal words imprinted on my mind and watched them come true.

I now live in a land other than my own. I live amongst people of another race and culture, color and creed. For the first time, the final piece of the assignment is facing me, to work amongst boys. My training days in God's workshop on the road are over. I know nothing about working with boys, and I know precious little about education. From now on, it will be a case of learning on the job. Neither of us have any idea we are being thrown headlong into a fight.

We both hope He knows what He's doing!

THE PROMPTER

He is the prompter
Not the possessor
Of our souls.
He is the hope
For us of glory
Not the glory
Reached and claimed.
His the voice
But not the jailer,
His the bright
Beyond within us
Bringing to us
The higher way
We must walk in
But ours the nerves
That guide the feet
Into His way,
They are our own.

Working His Purposes Out . . .

INTO THE FRAY

Gujranwala
1970

A ll that had preceded the move to Gujranwala proved merely preparation. That which followed after 1975 was largely blessing, but the heart of Marie's and my time together in Pakistan was the first half of the 1970s.

There is a common belief that the primary struggle that takes place within missionary endeavor lies in the resistance to the Gospel from the indigenous non-Christian faiths. I do not dispute that this can be so.

This is, however, but the initial phase of the struggle in planting a church. Inevitably, as time passes, it becomes supplanted by the struggle for the purity of the church and its life and structures.

We tend to think of the church community as a saved society, a community of grace.

In most practical instances, we have only to have our eyes half open to see it just is not so. It is not cynical to describe things as they are. In purely experiential terms, it is a secular society within a religious context. We are surprised by the weaknesses and corruption within the church, newly planted or other, which we discover but we should not be so.

We should expect to meet corruption, fraud, vice, greed, simony (preferment) and nepotism, hypocrisy, superstition, and manipulation of persons, and we do. It is, after all, just human nature at work within a particularly comfortable and safe haven that can usually be relied upon to deal more leniently than outside with discovered sin.

Rather, our surprises are those little cells of light, those agglomerations of spiritually tempered minds within the church that we do discover, or think that we discover, even as we also find them to our similar surprise outside the church in society itself.

These are the great and wonderful unexpected gifts God indeed bestows upon us—encounters with Strangers or near-Strangers working individually, independently, or in community, congregationally or otherwise, working actively and in silent splendor to dissipate darkness and spread good.

Love, a spark,
Becomes a radiance
When fanned

By sacrifice
And action.

This is the great surprise He has for us. Not the surprise of darkness in the church, but good fighting evil within it without regard for end.

The primary struggle then may well not be against forces and ideas inimical to the Christian faith, but against the corruption, driven by personal desire and greed, within a particular element of that faith organization we call the church.

In some form or other, it usually involves sex, power and influence or money, common enough and easily recognizable sources of corruption.

I take time to describe it, for it was, we felt, the purpose of our, or at least my, being in Pakistan. Our experiences fell largely within the life and work and witness of the Presbyterian Church of Pakistan, as we were to observe it in the Punjab.

The Sialkot Mission no longer actively existed, although its personnel were to remain on the field in various capacities for another two decades. The rundown of its work followed a classic pattern of devolution to indigenous bodies increasingly controlled by nationals. Slowly, but steadily, the controlling missionary influence on decisions faded. With it, a significant change occurred that was to set at jeopardy the carefully balanced structures established in an earlier era.

The change, an inevitable and unavoidable one, was simply the loss of the missionary ethos. It would have occurred anywhere and was not the consequence of its particular cultural and geographical location.

The true missionary is a strange creature. He (or she) is not ambitious. He is happy to be treated on a par with his peers, but desires not one jot of preference. He does not desire pay higher than his fellows, and he is more likely to complain at a rise in pay than a cut in pay. He wants no extra consideration over others for achievements, proven ability, position, added qualifications, or breadth of experience. He seeks no laurels or recognition. He is long suffering; you can abuse him totally and continually, and he is still there when you have tired of abusing him. He will then invite you in to tea.

His perspective is a lifetime, not a contract term of a few years. He does not pay lip service to obedience to God. He has been called out and has responded. He stands committed and does not give up when the going gets hard and the way steep. He will be here until he dies or he retires. He is here because he has had no choice but to come. Frequently, it has been costly, but the costs are back in the home country and are not known where he serves, and he draws no attention to them.

He makes his decisions pragmatically without rules of order and manuals of procedure. Instead he relies upon a few basic and simple principles. He is loyal to his friends, even to a fault, yet treats his enemies with consideration and charity. He can be relied on to tell the truth at all times, no matter what the consequences. He seeks, whatever his position of authority, to practice a leadership of servanthood. He passes everything beneath the searching screen of 'What would Jesus do?' He strives to see both sides and make decisions based on merit and not bias, prejudice, or self-interest. He will agree with you when you point out his imperfections.

His aim is to hand his job over as quickly as possible to someone likely less well-equipped than himself to handle it, and he is more anxious to play second fiddle than first violin.

The individuals of the Sialkot Mission were a band of Christian brothers and sisters, exemplars of a fast-vanishing style of living discredited by both organizational experts and opportunists as unsuited for the rapidly moving events of the later years of the twentieth century. They did not work easily under the constraints of a carefully developed organization structure.

Understandably, such bodies of people are rare. They are not unique. War or commitment to high causes will occasionally throw up such bodies of people, but they, wherever found, are unusual.

They were replaced by national men and women who had grown up under their tutelage. Often by prodigious individual effort, these replacements had struggled up from poor and illiterate families to positions of relative eminence in their community. Inevitably, for the first time, appointments and promotions, transfers and scholarships were becoming subject to family pressures and also simple human greed.

A corollary was that the various boards and governing committees that managed the college, the various high and middle schools, and the hospitals had their disciplinary teeth pulled. Similarly, the Synod of the Punjab moved out from under the disciplining sanction of the home church in the States. Which national member of a governing body was not vulnerable through his relatives, if not through his own culpability? Remove discipline for infraction, and you remove or reduce incentive to morality.

The struggle for the soul of this young church and its institutions was unavoidable. Although it was to range from the early sixties to the late seventies (and still goes on), it developed most fiercely in the early seventies.

The first national appointment to the linchpin activity of district missionary proved an unmitigated disaster and delayed further appointments.

Throughout the church, the pastors found themselves organized into two parties of almost equal strength to vie for supremacy. The democratic forms of government on which Presbyterians pride themselves became chicken feed for rapacious and astute church politicians interested only to subvert them.

The primary institutional focus for the struggle was the Gujranwala Theological Seminary, neighbor to the technical school, where pastors were trained for the Protestant ministry. This was the heart battleground. The first two leadership appointments were disastrous and the seminary nearly went under.

In the other institutions, the medical work was best equipped to fight absorption by and corruption by the organized church structure. Doctors in the mission hospitals, well educated and able, saw the dangers, organized themselves to resist, and did well. Missionary doctors were still there to support and give assistance to good against evil, even after they had handed over authority to others.

The schools were less well equipped to fight. The headmasters and headmistresses were part of the new administrative boards. They had relatives, their own interests, and other matters to consider.

Hajipura Girls' Boarding School and, more focally, Pasrur Girls' Boarding School came under spiritual attack. Among the boys schools, the Christian Training Institute in Sialkot was safe and stable while Lall held power, but in September 1972, almost as a judgment on what was going on the Christian community was collectively brought to its knees. The Government of Pakistan nationalized all privately operated schools and colleges. This was almost total catastrophe.

The narratives that follow should not detract from the admiration we felt for Punjabi Christians and Punjabi Presbyterians. Our people were growing up and moving forward. As a community, we had come from one environment, and our journey into another was by no means finished. Each generation marked a further step forward. We were not yet a hundred years old. Naturally, we had a great deal to learn and much yet to accomplish.

If we study the letters of Paul in the New Testament, we find he spends little time on the non-Christian environment surrounding his young churches, but much concern and effort to identify wrongdoing within those churches and to counsel and admonish against it. His struggle primarily was not for roots, but for purity. We were to find, or think we found, in our Punjab, many similarities with New Testament times.

The early and tragic death of Brend Kuyvenhoven, vice principal and chief instructor, was to leave us bereft of one of the architects of our survival as an institution. The experience of pruning was to test our resolve at the Christian Technical School, now renamed as the Christian Technical Training Center. At the same time, it left us able to look forward to a buoyant and challenging future. It was an experience bringing much pain, yet it was also wonderfully, in the end, rewarding.

God and Evil . . .
THE ULTIMATE STRUGGLE

The practice of the Kingdom of God
Is not piety but passion,
Not separation but struggle—
Confronting evil with good
With all of our strength.

We will pause here to give thought to this reality, that there is an ultimate struggle that God is engaged in, in a context beyond our comprehension. It is a struggle against evil.

How does it happen that if God created everything and He is totally good that evil even exists? This leads on to the first great lie, it doesn't exist. It is just mankind's own deceitful human nature (the devil within) that we fight against.

The story of Adam can be looked at in this way. The serpent in Eden is a myth, a concoction. What happened was within the couple themselves, an inner, innate deceitfulness and greed that wanted what they weren't supposed to have. After all, aren't all children born with these instincts?

Yet evil is clearly more than this. What brought Jesus to the cross and destroyed him there? It wasn't His good words or works, the preaching and the teaching, the healing and the expulsion of demons; it was that He went further, into what Satan considered *his* territory. Satan had earlier offered Him a deal, under his dominion Jesus could have his territory too, but it had been turned down.

Jesus attacked particularly the powers on earth that Satan used, the powers of control of the mind and of the emotion. In His own context, this was not the occupying power of Rome, but the encrusted religious vehicle that had subverted the love of people for a holy God to structures designed to maintain, within a facade of piety, a power group that ran things to serve their own and the Devil's purposes.

To Jesus, the Devil was a spiritual reality, not merely the internal trampling roughshod over the human conscience. How does the Devil become a spiritual reality for us? Until that happens, we are fighting on the wrong battleground.

A part of the power of evil is the cloudiness, the obfuscation that prevents identification of the specifics that make up the different aspects of evil.

What we need is not a new theology of God, most of us are fairly clear about God, but a new understanding of the nature and reality of evil. Until we have that, we are merely beating the air. Evil is surrounded by its own miasma, and we either doubt it exists or can't, in its more subtle forms, seem to identify it, particularly in our own environment.

In our human terms, evil needs to be broken down to its component parts before we are able to deal with it. Go beyond the clear proscriptions of the Ten Commandments; they are not a limiting definition and were not intended to be so.

Recognize evil where you live, the way in which, through radio and television, newspaper and magazine, and nowadays the Internet, it enters your home. Recognize the falsehood, explicit or implied, of advertisers, the blandishments to get hold of your money, the promises of hedonistic pleasures, the false and unattainable promises of politicians hoping to rule you, calls to your own covetousness, the constant promotion and attraction of ever lowering standards of morality and behavior. Recognize the ways you join in, your own greed, the manipulation of people to your own ends, the readiness to cheat the big faceless organizations, either of business or your own government—anything that persuades you down to the level where it will be enough, to fulfill what God has purposed for you, to live like the others around you live.

Preachers rarely seem to focus on specific sin, they prefer to mill around in the more muddy but indistinct fields of general sin. In our Pakistan setting, you never disturbed any members of your congregation if you inveighed against general sin, and your congregation would affirm its warm approval of your presentation.

Specific sin was a different matter, a very sticky wicket indeed. Everyone in the congregation knew everyone else's business including the sins, general and specific, which each neighbor was engaged in. They knew in a moment who was being attacked from the pulpit, and as long as it wasn't themselves being singled out, they sat back and awaited the counter attack.

When God engages with us in the ultimate struggle against Evil, He will use us to attack specifics, people we know and are neighbors to, people with faces and families our kids play with. We shall find ourselves opposing the familiar, even the friendly, rather than the distant evil it is so much easier to face. We shall be challenged to stand apart from others, upset the status quo, threaten the entrenched, stand for truth, identify and then hold on to meticulous integrity. We shall risk becoming islands.

It will require us not only to be totally vulnerable, but even, if need be, like Jesus, expendable. That recognition strangely gives a wonderful freedom. It is a leap into the enemy trenches. It is a freedom where we can expect to see God at work.

God and Evil—the ultimate struggle . . .
BILQUIS STRUGGLES WITH EVIL

Pakistan
January 23, 1967

Bilquis told us of a frightening struggle she had the previous night with supernatural dark and evil powers. She had awakened into the darkness with an overpowering sense of evil in her room. Fear gripped her. There were dark and evil presences there that weren't human. They permeated the atmosphere and filled it with foreboding. She felt herself seized and lifted physically above her bed. This wasn't imagination! It wasn't dream state but real, going on about her, in her own room; she was desperately, frighteningly awake. Her soul screamed inside her. Some struggle was going on, both physical and spiritual, and it was going on for her. She was being torn somehow between Heaven and hell, and hell was gaining the upper hand. She was being tossed and violently thrown about. Fear was now close to becoming terror. What on earth or in Heaven or in hell was going on? It was as though she was in the midst of a mighty storm of unlimited and horrible dimensions. She was in the center of it, but there was no calm there—only utterly terrifying turmoil.

She cried out, at the top of her voice, "Let me go! In the name of Jesus let me go! In the name of Jesus let me go!!"

She turned to us in awe. "You know, Marie, I wasn't dropped. I was thrown! Thrown with force back on to the bed! I bounced up and down on the bed and almost fell off. As the turmoil, the darkness, the uncanny sense of wind and movement vanished, I just pulled the quilt about me and over my head and waited for a while to be sure it was really ended. Then I reached out and turned on my light, and thanked my Lord Jesus for saving me. It was an awful experience!"

Devil's Kiss

Who prefers the lie to the truth,
And chooses it instead of the truth—
Though it be ever so small—
With that act takes the devil's kiss
And intervenes adversely
At the front rank of the struggle
For the hearts of men, for the world
And for all creation.

God and Evil—the ultimate struggle . . .
ENCOUNTERING EVIL

Gujranwala
Fall 1970

This is an excerpt from Bill Milton's letter. Bill is pastor of a Baptist church in Kilmarnock, Scotland. I had asked him to clarify a recollection.

The event you mention took place when we were teaching at the Lahore Bible Institute, Sheikhupura.

One of the first year students, Munir, from an ARP (Associate Reformed Presbyterian) village, gave us cause for concern from the first. His presence was oppressive and in times of prayer he would shout out and pray in the name of Satan.

There were times of great spiritual conflict, especially prayer times. We were convinced the young man was demon possessed. The staff and the student body prayed much for and with him.

One evening we battled in prayer for hours. There were about 12 or 15 of us present. His face changed into the appearance of a lion and he died spitting blood which landed on some of those gathered round. This blood wiped off their clothes without leaving a stain.

I was asked to drive down to his village to inform his family of what had happened.

This was in the Sahiwal area if I remember correctly.

On arrival in this 'Christian' village (meaning a village with a goodly number of Christian families) there was an evil atmosphere but it took me by surprise when the family told me his brother had died in the same way.

I remember coming home thinking 'What darkness!' and in a 'Christian village.'

I never heard any more from his family but I did learn never to underestimate our enemy.

Bill

The letter above is shocking. I have no doubt as to its veracity.

We have previously discussed the nature of evil, but let us look a little more. Although it appears that the matters that divide us are largely our different views of God, particularly if you are to live in a non-Christian culture, yet in fact, no less divisive is the view we have of evil. We are not divided on religious grounds as much as we are divided on the matter of whether an external evil exists beyond us. The way we live and the ultimate division between us both depend upon our response to this question. If we believe or we are persuaded that evil is the result of a losing battle of personal conscience with God, then evil is internalized. We then can be led into a sense of individual failure when the rigors of personal right conduct fail.

It will not be long before we are convinced with good conscience that the best way to fight evil is with the weapons of evil. They are so effective! Yet, in fact, the only weapons available to us are truth and integrity, faith in God, and right perspective of God and Satan.

That is true for both Muslim and Christian.

It is appropriate to look at this matter closely at this stage in our story. We had just been transferred to a Christian Mission compound in Gujranwala. To our surprise, this would mean that for several years we were to live in an atmosphere dominated, not by the light of Christians in active Christian service, but by the darkness and immediacy of evil.

At times, for months on end, I would walk home from the school office wondering whether the cloud would ever lift, longing just to sleep yet knowing that tomorrow would bring more of the same. The cloud of darkness that seemed to rest constantly on my head and shoulders never seemed to lighten, only to increase.

I wrote wearily:

> *Come early, night,*
> *Let the shades fall soon.*
> *Darkness is the shroud that covers me*
> *And brings its transient death to comfort me.*

> *Fades for a while the angriness*
> *That man in concert orchestrates*
> *The bitter world rolls on and all*
> *Its fretful temper spends elsewhere.*
> *Thoughts held captive in the mind*
> *And burning bitter words no longer hurt.*
> *Life's chain of bitterness that holds in thrall*
> *And captivates the brighter hopes of men*
> *Is trailed in vain past where I lie*
> *And only sweet oblivion sits upon the air.*

The sweetness of sleep, but like Hamlet, there was the rub, to wake again.

Browning had written, "God gives us a little light to rise by, and we rise." In this instance, Browning was wrong! There was not even a little light; it was black, black unrelieved darkness.

There was nothing I or anyone else could do to relieve that blackness. Others felt it also. Marie was one with me. We strengthened each other. Brend and Marjet had this for years. Some of the other missionaries were aware of what was going on, others apparently not so aware of it.

In the Christian community around us were many who had been experiencing this darkness long before us. Often their support had to be discreet and prayerful rather than overt. The wickedness lay within their own community and amongst their neighbors. My fine, young missionary predecessor had gone home ill, not to return. We knew that a spiritual conflict was going on for this place to which we had just been sent. It continued to look as though we were losing the fight. The form that struggle took was devious and unrelenting. So many smiles we received hid deep malice within.

The few Muslims who were aware of what was happening, there were not many, were totally supportive and loyal to us. This was a struggle within the Protestant Christian community and for the heart of a part of that community. All were nominally Christian. The neighbor to the Christian Technical Training Center was the Theological Seminary. Two of the men who worked there in the highest positions were overshadowed by spiritual darkness. Another neighbor was the women's Bible Training Center that had experienced its own attacks of darkness and vanquished them. The staff there was well aware of what was happening across the road at the Technical Training Center and constant in prayer and encouragement.

The evil I write about had many elements and manifestations. It was a conspiracy of deceit to create an illusion of health in an organism sick almost to death. There was the overarching sense of darkness and present evil.

There was the indication I was observing on the faces of several men, four of them in particular, of a frightful supernatural darkness of countenance quite unrelated to their natural complexion. All were very active in church life; all proved to be evil men. St. Paul had talked about the spiritual gift of discernment. Was this what he had been referring to?

There was sexual deviance. There was widespread dishonesty and theft and embezzlement. There were threats of and plans for violence. There was manipulation of people. There were indications of occult practices.

My first awareness of demons in Pakistan had come soon after I arrived back in 1953 and had joined the junior officer's mess at the Wah cantonment. I sat at table with a young Englishman who gave me a running diary of events as they happened to a work colleague and his wife

Alongside the Grand Trunk Road, near the Mess, was the old brick elephant well that was reputedly used for water by the Emperor Akbar and his court followers en route to Kashmir. In late evening, the coolest part of the day, a Pakistani engineer and his wife had been walking past the well when, in the full moonlight, they saw what appeared to be something like a large black dog run from the trees to the left toward them.

Instantaneously, two things happened. The dog (if it was a dog) disappeared in the middle of the road and the wife fell to the ground writhing, shaking, and frothing at the mouth. The husband called a passer by, and together they were able to get the wife home and get help. The woman, still conscious, tried to speak and eventually was able to articulate, gruffly with a strange, deeper voice than her natural one, a torrent of words in some foreign language. Eventually (by now more and more neighbors had gathered), she lapsed into sleep.

The saga of this unfortunate woman continued over weeks. Sometimes she was normal. At other times she behaved irrationally and spoke in a foreign language, identified as Old Persian, of which she personally had no knowledge. The voice purported to come from the trapped spirit of a man from an earlier period who was seeking rest. Attempts at exorcism were made. The local Muslim priest, and then another, failed in their efforts. Desperate, the family asked a Roman Catholic priest for help. He too failed. Finally, to my best recollection, she was taken to the Pir Sah'b of Golra Sharif, a renowned Muslim pir (holy man) who succeeded with the exorcism.

Bilquis, too, had asked me for help with a young acquaintance who behaved abnormally and appeared to be using Hindu temple vocabulary, although the Muslim girl had been born after Partition and had no opportunity to acquire such a vocabulary.

Both the Christianity and Islam practiced in Pakistan have within them elements of folk religion and practice inherited from many centuries of a dominant stratified Hindu culture. Any discussion of religious practice or even community practice must recognize this. Particularly for the Christian community in northern India, its origins lay in the accrued cultural inheritance of the lower levels of the outcaste Hindu community. It was here that the work of the Holy Spirit, during the decades on either side of the turn of the century, flowered gloriously in what became known as the Mass Movement.

Out of the Mass Movement had come the church with which we were privileged to work.

I will close with a quotation of St. Paul from his general letter addressed initially to the church in Ephesus. This became so pertinent to us in the early years of our Gujranwala life:

Finally then, find your strength in the Lord,
in his mighty power.
Put on all the armour which God provides,
so that
you may be able to stand firm
against the devices of the devil.
For our fight is not against human foes,
but against cosmic powers,
against the authorities and potentates
of this dark world,
against the superhuman forces of evil
in the heavens.
Therefore,
take up God's armour;
then you will be able to stand your ground
when things are at their worst,
to complete every task
and still to stand.
Stand firm, I say.
Fasten on the belt of truth;
for coat of mail put on integrity;
let the shoes on your feet be the gospel of peace,
to give you firm footing;
and, with all these, take up the great shield of faith,
with which you will be able to quench
all the flaming arrows of the evil one.
Take salvation for helmet;
for sword take that which the Spirit gives you—
the words that come from God.
Give yourselves wholly to prayer and entreaty.
Ephesians 6:10–18a NEB

Repairing the Walls of Jerusalem . . .
THE THRIFT SOCIETY

Gujranwala
November 1970

Iqbal was the accountant, and it was the end of my first month on the job as principal. When he came for the money to pay out the wages to the staff, I told him it was my custom to pay wages myself. It helped me get in touch and keep in touch with what was going on.

As a young army officer in South Waziristan, I had been amazed at how happy, even delighted, the red turbaned Pathan road repair coolies had been to get their pay the first time I had gone out to pay them. It had not taken long to work out why. For the very first time, they were getting the pay to which they were entitled with nothing by way of commission being deducted for the perquisites of the sub-divisional officer and the overseer who were paying them.

If you wanted to pick up fraud, the first place to look was the wage sheet. I was an experienced wage sheet scrutineer. I took the pay sheet from Iqbal and was puzzled. I looked up at him. He was quick to explain. He was only the accountant. He didn't make policy. A custom had grown up that members of the staff were allowed to have advances on their pay in cases of severe necessity—illness for instance. I waited for him to continue. Initially, permission had to be sought from the missionary in charge. However, everybody had been so busy. In recent months, he had been using his own discretion. He knew everyone's circumstances, of course, so they couldn't pull anything over him. Yes, he agreed a number of the staff were overdrawn several months ahead of the pay they were due. Yes, it was true that he himself was four months early in taking his pay, but his wife had almost died in the Civil Hospital, and it had been a crisis arrangement that he was paying off.

I asked him to bring the past monthly wage sheets.

It seemed to me that he was not succeeding in paying off his advances of pay very well; when had his wife become sick? He knew I could check this with others, so he was cautious. He ventured May. Then why had he taken another month's pay in advance last month? His daughter had given birth to his first grandson.

I asked the staff to gather. I explained that almost all were receiving pay before they had earned it. Some were a number of months in advance. I told them that I considered men had an absolute right to receive their wages on time. The Bible taught this. They would, as long as I was principal, receive their wages on the last working day of the month. They could hold me accountable for this.

Equally, they had no right to receive pay in advance of their earning it. The Bible did not teach this. The parable of the daily wage laborers that Jesus told indicated the men were paid at the end of the day when their work was done. It was not paid in advance. Therefore, from this time forward, wages would not be paid in advance. Those who had received wages in advance had been depriving their employer of the use of that money. This money was needed to run the school. The staff would begin to receive their wages after they had earned them from this day forth. Yes, I did regret that it would mean that some of the staff would not receive any pay for several months, but after all, they had already been paid, hadn't they?

There was absolute silence. You could have heard a pin drop. They were horror-struck.

"But what are we going to do?" Afzal burst out. "Our wives need the money to buy food." The others chorused assent.

"You know," I said, "sometimes you do need to borrow money. Not always, but sometimes. You don't borrow from your employer. He needs his money to pay you your wages and buy the supplies and pay his bills. You borrow from each other, and you pay each other for the use of the money you borrow. That's the right way to go about it."

Few of them would trust each other enough to lend money. Loaned money was treated as a gift. They knew that crazy idea wouldn't work.

"You come back tomorrow at the same time, and I'll explain. Furthermore, for three months, I will lend you 3,000 rupees of my own money, not the CTTC's money, but my own money, so that you can borrow from that. But I warn you, in three months, I will take the money back so you had better get saving."

By the following day, the CTTC Staff Thrift Society was born. It was a simple savings and loan society. I had no previous experience of such societies, but it was just common sense. It had a short page of rules.

I would be patron and would ensure there was good management; that was all. The staff would run their own society.

There would be an elected chairman, treasurer and secretary. There would be an annual meeting of members. There would be no membership fee and all monthly paid members of staff were eligible to join. Two other staff members must guarantee in writing any loan. The three elected officers must approve each loan. A regular monthly repayment schedule would be agreed at the time of the loan. Every loan had to be repaid within a year. There was a maximum limit on the total loan that could be taken. Interest due on loans taken would be payable at the end of each month when wages were paid, at the rate of one rupee for each 100 borrowed or outstanding. Savings investments would normally receive the same rate unless there was a surplus of invested funds over loans. Then the actual earnings from high-income bank investments would apply. The Thrift Society would have its own bank account. Two officer's signatures would be needed on checks. There would be no charges for services; CTTC would provide stationery and postage. CTTC would also allow the officers to do Thrift Society work during their paid working hours.

As soon as the rules were settled and agreed, borrowers began nibbling at the launch capital of 3,000 rupees. I was somewhat surprised at the people elected as officers. They were not the powerful people, but people who were quiet, elderly, and probably trustworthy. I was learning whom the staff thought they could trust with their money.

Suddenly, we were observing something interesting. The storekeeper who had sons and a daughter working produced money to invest. It was a good deal. Twelve percent was a higher rate of interest than he could get from the bank, and Mr. Old was making sure it didn't get stolen. If necessary, he would recover it from the wages due to a defaulter. Then the auto-mechanic helper prompted by the storekeeper produced 400 rupees to invest. A trickle in was beginning to grow.

In three months, I removed my start-up capital. It was probably just about as much savings as we had as a family, but it had never been at risk. The Thrift Society began to get on its feet. Not everybody could have loans initially; the money wasn't there, but the list of those waiting for loans slowly shortened until there was no backlog at all.

And then, crisis!!! Nawaz and Siddique, two of the senior staff, both officers of the Thrift Society, came into the office. Had I cleared Afzal Bhagash's accounts? Yes, indeed I had. He was a graduate engineer who had got a good job elsewhere. He had come from very poor beginnings, and I had encouraged him to take this promising new appointment with a quasi-government department. "Sir, you should have checked with the Thrift Society first; he owes 2,000 rupees and has left without paying." They expected me to be as concerned as they were, but I was quite relaxed.

"Well, never matter, we will take it from the wages of his guarantors. Who guaranteed his loan?"

Both men blanched simultaneously and looked desperately at each other. They nodded with dismay. "But, sir . . ."

But sir, yes indeed! I casually scribbled a note to the accountant to deduct Afzal Bhagash's loan in installments from the wages of Nawaz and Siddique until the full amount had been recovered. They both begged urgent leave for the afternoon and left in a hurry.

Afzal Bhagash lived in Wazirabad, 19 miles up the Grand Trunk Road. When Nawaz and Siddique got back, it was after dark, and they were tired and exhausted. They had cycled both ways. They came right over to see me. They had tracked Afzal down in Wazirabad. I wondered what they had threatened. He was very apologetic. He explained he had forgotten. He didn't have the money right now, but as soon as he got his first wages he would pay them. Whatever deal they reached apparently satisfied them, and Afzal must have come through with paying up.

The deductions that were to be cut from Nawaz' and Siddique's wages were made as I had asked. The Thrift Society, not just two but ALL its members, had learned one big lesson. No longer was a guarantee merely a signature on a piece of paper to help a friend. It was a tiger! It had teeth and could bite.

The staff had representatives on our governing board, but that was not where their interests lay. The meeting that had, and continued to have, the whole staff's support was their Thrift Society. There was keen lobbying for the officers' posts, and equally, the voters were determined to keep some candidates out. As far as they were concerned, they were only prepared to trust certain people.

I requested the Thrift Society to consider opening the society up to our daily paid laborers. Some of them had worked with us more than ten years. They also needed the opportunity to borrow money. The Thrift Society was reluctant. There was no security. They could always recover the loans through the wages of the monthly paid workers. They'd have no way to do so with daily paid workers.

I told them I would personally stand as guarantor for any loans they made to our laborers; it was a risk worth taking. Well, in that case . . . and now even our workers on the lowest daily wages were given the opportunity to obtain credit. They never defaulted.

Toward the end of our time in Gujranwala, I was looking toward the possibility of opening a bank for the poor. I was sure it could be made viable. I studied the example of the well-known Grameen bank in Bangladesh. It had a good record, but no better certainly than our own Thrift Society. This had loaned out over a million rupees, and although I do not recall a single default, losses certainly were much under 1%. It had absolutely no overheads, and during its operation, staff had learned to trust the system and to trust each other. They had learned how to cooperate for mutual benefit.

God and Evil—the ultimate struggle . . .
THE EVENING VISITORS

Gujranwala
July 1971

Marie is up in Murree making a home for the two boys while the hostel at their mission kids' school is closed for the summer.

It was my custom when Marie had to depart for the hills to get rid of the servants and go into virtual hibernation. The servants could return in September, two days before Marie, to frantically try to recover the situation before she returned. I would allow the dust to fall quietly for four months and try to keep my trails of footprints on the concrete floors to a few well-worn paths. Marie opened and closed doors and windows during each day to match the change of temperatures between inside and outside. She could keep a house comfortable even on the hottest or most humid days. I didn't bother. I was content to be uncomfortable. Birds and bats would get in and virtually take over the upper air space. They had nothing to fear from me. Ants emerging from the mud walls would shed wings and create trails of workers carrying off grains of sugar like miniature stevedores. I stepped over or around them. Termites made their trails of earthen tunnels wherever wood or paper was to be encountered.

It is July. The time is about 8:30 in the evening. A knock at the door. I recognize the callers, a man and wife, and invite them in.

Iqbal had been, until about a month ago, the accountant in the school. It had not taken very long to determine that Iqbal was on to a very good thing. He had been looting the school accounts for years. In some instances of fraud, he had been colluding with other senior staff, but most of what I discovered had been the results of his own entrepreneurial skills where he had been the sole beneficiary. There was also a practice of double billing customers of the auto and woodwork shops. He considered all missionaries a gift to him. They were gullible, and if they should happen to query a bill, it was easy to apologize and claim a mistake. As the sole bookkeeper and accountant, it was not difficult for him to set up a whole network of opportunities for himself, and he did so with great efficiency.

Slowly and quietly, I pursued my enquiries, calling for back ledgers that hadn't seen the light of day for years. At last, I was ready. Iqbal was a pillar of our local congregation, a very accomplished public pray-er often called upon by the pastor and a model of humility and gentleness. I didn't want to make a mistake.

When school was over for the day, and only he and I were working overtime, I spoke to him. Step-by-step, I outlined what I had discovered. He did not argue. He knew the game was up. He also knew that there was much more for me yet to find out as I pursued my investigations. I listed many thousands of rupees he had taken. I knew, too, there was virtually no chance that any of it could be recovered.

"Iqbal," I said, "you have betrayed every trust you have been given. You know you will have to face the consequences now for your actions. I can dismiss you immediately and then bring disgrace on your family and upon you by charging you with the crimes that you have committed. You know me well enough to know I will have no hesitation in pursuing that course.

"However, I shall have no pleasure in seeing you go to jail, although you fully deserve that to happen to you. The only asset we hold of yours is your Provident Fund (Pension Fund). This is only a small fraction of what you have stolen over the years. I am inclined, if you sign over to the institution your Provident Fund and any claims to it, to accept your written request to resign your post immediately, owing to pressing personal reasons. Your course of action you must decide now; tomorrow will be too late."

Hope and then relief leapt into Iqbal's eyes. This was far more generous than he might have expected. He quickly signed a document surrendering any claims to his Provident Fund, worth about 3,000 rupees, and a second requesting me to accept his resignation with immediate effect for pressing personal reasons. I took his keys, locked his office, and watched him leave the premises.

The couple, completing their usual walk around the officers' colony, has called to see me. What do they want? I seat them and ask them why they have come. Iqbal has a grim expression on his face, and Soraya has a reputation I don't want to tangle with.

"I want my Provident Fund," Iqbal begins.

Soraya joins in. "We are a very poor family. You have no right to take my husband's Provident Fund. This is our pension. It is all that we have. We need it and we must have it."

I point out that the governing board of the Center has accepted both Iqbal's resignation and the voluntary surrender of his Provident Fund. I have no intention of persuading them to any other course of action.

"If you do not do so," Iqbal says ominously, "I shall douse myself in kerosene and set myself alight in front of your office and burn myself to death.

Then everyone will know what a wicked man you are." There have recently been several suicides of this nature for political reasons, and I don't doubt for a moment that such a suicide is possible, if unlikely. Soraya joins in.

"And I will do the same, Mr. Old. I shall do exactly the same as my husband. You are a wicked man to steal my husband's Provident Fund, and I shall set myself alight also. The scandal of our deaths will show everyone, and the Government, what kind of a rascal you are."

She rises suddenly to her feet, throws aside her chiffon dopatta, and begins tearing her kamiz off, ripping it from the neck-band down to the waist and then wrenching wildly at more of her clothes. I decide discretion is the better part of valor. I am in a very vulnerable position with no witnesses except Iqbal as to what is happening. I need to be somewhere else quickly! I leave them to it, hurriedly departing by the front door, leaving them in possession of the house. It is dark. I go quickly towards the hostels to find someone, even schoolboys, who can witness to events if what is happening shall ever progress into the courts.

I come to a halt. A thought strikes me. If they are talking about kerosene, maybe they already have matches with them. There's kerosene in the kitchen. There are matches there too! Suppose they are setting alight to the furniture, the rugs. Those rugs are precious to us. Some have belonged to Marie and Mac. I turn and hurry back to the house, no idea what now to expect. I push open the door. There is silence. There is no one in the sitting room. I search the house. No one. I breathe a sigh of relief. Much better than I expected. I bolt all doors well. It is nine o'clock. Bedtime.

Iqbal and Soraya work their way up through the seminary lines, calling at the homes of the married students. Soraya is weeping hysterically. She is distraught. She is wearing Iqbal's coat around her, clutching it to herself. Iqbal talks for her. They had been making a social call. Suddenly, Mr. Old (overcome by bestial desire while Iqbal was using the toilet), had seized his wife, thrown her to the floor, and tried to rape her. Had he not returned in the nick of time and wrestled Mr. Old off, it would have been too late. Look at his wife's kamiz. The man is nothing more than a wild animal! Something must be done to control these foreigners!

After the seminary lines, then the parade through the adjacent Christian suburb of Khokherke with more of the same. What goes on during the night, what meetings and cogitations, I do not know, for I am fast asleep and quite unaware of unfolding events.

People look at me oddly the following morning. My reputation is sullied with some, but I survive. Iqbal does not get his Provident Fund, and neither he nor Soraya set themselves alight in front of my office. They move to Karachi, and other crises in Gujranwala emerge to take precedence and attention.

WIDOW'S MITE

When God offers you
The widow's mite
To use
You'd better refuse
If you fail to see
This small coin is
Dedicated,
Accepted,
Consecrated
And committed
And you realize
His eyes
Will be fixed on you.

It is holy.

It will require
Use as intended,
Complete vigilance,
Utter integrity,
Accountability
And a report
Back to the donor
With no hocus-pocus.

Working His Purposes Out . . .
A TRIP TO HOLLAND

March 1971

Two streams of activity are now developing. On the one hand is the struggle against evil that continues for a full five years in its initial phase. At the same time, God is going beyond the containment of and then victory against evil. He knows the Government of Pakistan, for its own political reasons, is going to nationalize privately owned schools and colleges. This will strike at the heart of the Christian community and it will happen less than two years down the road. In the Punjab, the struggle against this will focus on the technical school in Gujranwala. Things need to move on.

I have had the pleasure of working closely over the years with four different nationalities other than Pakistanis. For a spell in the Suez Canal Zone, in Egypt, I was O.C. of an Artisan Works Company of engineers—comprising German prisoners of war, Africa Korps veterans. The Middle East was in turmoil, as the British, reaching the end of their mandate and patience in Palestine, fought off the Irgun Zvai Leumi and the Stern Gang. The prisoners of war were waiting, almost three years after the war had ended, for repatriation to Germany. I do not know whether the shortage of troopships was the genuine reason for the delay. They had every right to be rebellious, but they were patient and cooperative. We were involved in building and maintaining military facilities and infrastructure. The Germans were well organized, had their own smooth structures of command, worked well to plans, and were highly competent and efficient. I was to observe these were national characteristics. Germans liked to have plans that were worked out in fine detail and well thought through on paper before they ever went out for site execution. Once turned over for implementation, they did not like deviations or alterations.

The British, on the other hand, were woolly minded. They didn't mind loose ends. They did not think in straight lines. They were pragmatists. The less detail, the better. The more that was left to be worked out on site by the brick mason or the carpenter the better. They were and are confused thinkers. It was really a wonder that Wellington won the Battle of Waterloo. That was a pitched battle with plans carefully drawn and fiercely executed—much more a German-type battle than an English one. Probably if Blucher had been on the other side instead of Napoleon, we would have lost! The ideal soldier for the British is not the infantryman, but the commando, venturing outnumbered into a difficult situation with insufficient information, haphazard planning, and only his wits, skill, courage, and momentum to carry him through. The great gift the British bring to any situation is not their ability, but their sense of the ridiculous. They get themselves into untenable situations, look round, guffaw at their own stupidity, and press on regardless because it looks less difficult than going back. Basically they are muddlers although, even so, history suggests a remarkable capacity to achieve goals.

The Americans were out and out achievers. They were and are linear thinkers. They thought straight from a problem through to its solution, applied the resources necessary to achieve results, and looked around for the next problem while others were still getting organized for the last one. They were never far from a coffee percolator. Their sense of humor was a snappy punch line rather than a shaggy dog story. Maybe that's why I have rarely met one that appreciated cricket.

My favorites were the Dutch. They combined the best traits of the British and Germans. They liked plans, but could cut through them. They were quick to take initiatives when they were needed, while others were not even aware of a problem or an opportunity. They were never woolly like the British, but had a capacity to tolerate the vagaries and impreciseness of others. They liked arguments and were happy with confrontations as a means of solving problems. They were energetic and industrious. Marie believed that as a result of skating on the canals in Pieter Brueghel's day, they had become addicted to speed and habitually drove faster than any rational, high speed limit would have allowed. She had to be persuaded gently into any car that Brend was driving.

I was asked if I would go to Holland to meet with representatives of Bread for the World, Germany, the Reformed Churches in the Netherlands, and the Presbyterian Church, U.S.A. It would only need a day or so, and then I could come back.

Jaap van Klinken met me at Schipol. He drove like Jehu down the fast motorway to Bunnik near Utrecht. That wasn't because we were late; that was just the way he drove when he didn't have to hurry. A conference room in a motel had been booked. Fred Wilson of the Presbyterian Church and Siegmar Bartke of Bread for the World were already there, having flown in from New York and Stuttgart. I knew all three; all had visited Gujranwala within the last year or so. There were just the four of us, four different nationalities.

Jaap started the ball rolling. "Well, Ken, we have come together to see how we might be able to help you. What do you want us to do?"

Before replying, I opened my brief case and took out two wooden models on flat board, made as large as the briefcase would allow. Placed together, they showed a plan of the campus of the technical training center in Gujranwala. Painted on the board were the existing buildings. Screwed onto the board were the dream buildings we were planning. Little blocks showing new workshops, new dormitories, and a reorientation of 90 degrees to face the campus toward the town with its entrance from Church Road. On the north side of the road to the chapel, where presently was only a field, were the model structures of a building trades training center that was just a dream for further down the road when this current development plan was out of the way.

I gave each of the men a copy of the technical training center development plan.

A verse from Exodus prefaced our booklets of those days as a challenge.

> *The Lord said unto Moses,*
> *"Why are you crying out for help?*
> *Tell the people to move forward."*
> **Exodus 14:15 GNB**

I explained briefly the goals we were pursuing. We would assist the boy with limited means or limited schooling. We would prefer the son of the peasant and the villager to the urban dweller, the failure rather than the success, the boy from a large family, and boys from the lowest strata of society. Need would be the criteria for admission. We would reverse the trend toward ever higher standards of admission, encouraging boys to come after eight rather than ten years of previous education. We would create and subsidize whatever dormitories might be necessary to accommodate boys from distant rural areas.

We would reduce course lengths to the minimum length consistent with the skills to be learned. We would teach in Urdu and Punjabi, rather than in English, wherever this was possible. We would create new vernacular texts and materials ourselves, as they were needed. We would increase enrollment to 250 boys with admissions and graduations twice annually. We would conduct quarterly examinations with high minimum pass marks that had to be achieved before moving on through the course. This would help us quickly identify the boys needing special help.

We would raise the quality of teaching and the level of skills taught to the highest possible level. We would recruit staff from our best graduates and establish a staff-training program running concurrently with our regular program. We would emphasize the acquisition of manual skills. We would eliminate from the syllabus all material not directly concerned with employable skills or human growth. We would graduate not less than 100 boys a year.

We would establish a strong religious training program of Bible teaching for Christian students and concurrently for all students, a strong sports and athletics program. We would tailor the courses we offered to job opportunities in the marketplace, dropping and initiating courses as and when appropriate. We would continually scrutinize outside job opportunities and keep track of the fortunes of our graduates.

We believed that what we were proposing was right, and it was, given the resources, eminently feasible.

The three men listened carefully. They asked questions principally for clarification rather than out of doubt concerning the basic premises of the plan. They were still waiting for the answer to Jaap's first question.

I paused. The presentation of our plans was over. Now it was up to them.

"What we need is $853,000. We want $553,000 for the buildings and the equipment and the basic changes to the campus. The bulk of the work can be completed in three years. That is all costed in the plans before you. We also need $300,000 for an endowment fund that can be managed from outside the country to give $30,000 a year income for scholarships for both hostels and school."

There was a long silence. Each man was considering his own situation and what, if anything, he could contribute. Jaap had his answer.

He asked Siegmar for his comments. Behind Siegmar was the committed desire of the German churches to help third world countries. There was a state religious tax in Germany. This provided resources to the state churches and enabled assistance to overseas projects also. Siegmar was still thinking of how the development of CTTC might mesh with the priorities of Brot Fuer Die Welt. They would mesh very well, he decided.

"This is a large amount Ken is asking for," he answered slowly, "but we can certainly assist.

"The total amount will not be given until we are satisfied that the progress he is promising is being achieved. *Bread for the World* will undertake to meet the costs of the buildings and equipment, provided that you two, Fred and Jaap, meet the scholarship fund endowment needs."

I could hardly believe my ears. What was happening! Were all the dreams suddenly about to come true?

It was Jaap's turn. He knew his limits. It was Jaap's church that had sent Brend and Marjet Kuyvenhoven out in January 1967. Since that time, it had been generous in its commitment to the technical school. For a while, a year or so previously, it had considered withdrawing, but had taken one more chance. This would determine how much further it was prepared to go. The Dutch Reformed Church was not a wealthy church, but its commitment to missions was linked to sagacity and sacrifice. It had good missions leadership.

"Thank you, Siegmar. With that assurance from you, we surely can come up with our part of the answer. If we were to split the $300,000 Ken needs between us," he said, looking at Fred now, "we would need to give $150,000. We can't quite manage that, but ADB can give $143,500. What about you, Fred? Can you make up the difference?"

Fred had been a missionary in Iran. He was an able mission administrator and had become a close friend through his visits to Gujranwala. There was no doubting his personal support of our work. He was, however, hesitant about any commitment he might be able to make on behalf of his church. The Presbyterian Church in the States had mission partners throughout much of the developing world. All were hungry for help. Every year the mission budget was stretched beyond prudent limits. The church had just had a fund raising drive; it would be years, even decades, before another could be considered.

Jaap asked whether there were funds available from the recent fundraiser. The *Fifty Million Fund*, Fred explained, was not available for scholarship endowments. It had been a desperate attempt to clear the backlog of capital needs for repairs and development both in the States and overseas and the constituency of the church had responded with immense generosity. The target of $50 million had been oversubscribed, but the funds given could only be used for capital needs.

Jaap was listening carefully and thinking hard.

"Could," he asked, "the *Fifty Million Fund* be used to build a school in Indonesia?"

"Yes," confirmed Fred, "if it fell within the criteria for approved projects. There would certainly be no difficulty there."

"We have a school we wish to build in Indonesia, Fred. Would the Presbyterian Church U.S.A. be willing to take over the funding of that school? That would be capital funds. If it would do so, it is $100,000 that is involved, then I think ADB could see its way clear to increase its contribution to Ken's endowment fund by a similar amount to $243,500. Could you make up the difference now?"

The only extra money that Fred could find was $15,000 that had already been budgeted to help fund a leadership development program for CTTC.

The horse-trading had been done. Jaap turned to me.

"Well, there you are Ken; that's all we can do for you. Do you think you can manage on a scholarship fund of $258,500?"

It would take time to build up to the 250 boys we were planning, and meanwhile, we could place the unused income excess back into the fund. We could do it. I expressed my thanks to the three men who would have to take their commitments back home and sell them to their organizations and supporters.

I, too, was soon back home in Pakistan. The whole nature of our work was now to move from the plans on the printed page to the creation of a much larger oasis for the poor, more precisely poor boys, on the edge of a Punjabi town. It would be costly and full of incident, but we were determined to make it come true.

Before all the problems were sorted out and we could get started, we would face a war with India at the end of the year, when the school would be closed and troops billeted on us. The following September would see the nationalization of privately owned and operated schools and colleges that could finish us off. For now, it was enough that the detailed designs for the buildings and the identification of the equipment we needed could go ahead.

In retrospect, most of the mistakes I made were from thinking too small, not having the heavenly vision, but only my own much smaller version, a grasshopper view instead of a giraffe view. I did not realize for instance that within a few years our enrollment would not be 250 boys, but close to 450. We would be graduating not one hundred boys a year, but more than double that number.

That would mean more than 300 boys in the hostels. All would need subsidized help.

In one of those wonderful concurrences of timing, there was the Iranian oil crisis of 1974 when the prices of oil skyrocketed and international currency exchange rates did all sorts of strange things. A consequence for us was that after the Dutch money was transferred to New York for our consolidated scholarship endowment fund, our $258,500 had become worth not $300,000, but $400,000.

What a wonderful God! Talk about the windows of heaven! And what a responsibility to ensure that every rupee was spent wisely and with integrity!

God and Evil—the ultimate struggle . . .
GRADUATION

Gujranwala

June 1971

About a week before the first graduation since I had become principal, signs of a new problem began to appear. The certificates each boy would receive needed to be prepared and signed—ready for distribution at the graduation ceremony.

I asked to see the scholastic records of each of the graduating students. They were kept in a register maintained by the Pakistani headmaster, Salim Mubarak. He brought the register for me to scrutinize and compare with the list he had prepared.

There was a clear discrepancy between the marks in the register and the marks on the list from which the certificates would be prepared.

Salim explained patiently. Yes, this was not a mistake; this was deliberate policy. No, he had not decided the policy; he was merely carrying it out. The Christian community in Pakistan was under immense pressure. It was only a tiny part of a society that was ranged solidly against it. When our boys got out to search for jobs, they would encounter a wall of discrimination against them. Because they were not Muslims, employers were reluctant to offer them jobs. Fellow workers despised them. Why, in some factories, they weren't even allowed to use the same faucets to obtain drinking water. Supervisors picked on them; foremen gave them the dirtiest and most difficult jobs to do and those with the least pay. All through their working lives, they would endure dislike and discrimination. They were the automatic recipients of blame for bad work done by others and were always the first to be laid off from work.

In an attempt to somewhat level out the imbalance against them, the school management had decided to increase the marks earned by each boy by 15%. This succeeded in lifting many boys into a much better grade evaluation and gave them a better start in their venture into a hard and angry world. There was a rationale for the upgrading. Our grading system was strict and demanding and the recording of marks was not corrupted as in most institutions.

If I checked the list, I would find that the increment to each boy's marks had been accurately calculated. Salim was correct. The calculations were a consistent 15%.

I told Salim that the school was now under new management, and in the future, boys would get on the certificates the marks they had earned and only those marks. I would also, in future, be checking the entries in the records regularly.

The students were very unhappy.

Graduation Day. In the almost full chapel sit the parents and invited guests and the students who are not yet graduating. The Secretary of the West Pakistan Christian Council is our guest speaker, and he has his speech ready. The front three rows are reserved for the new graduates. The seats are empty.

Some of the staff have urged that the graduation be postponed, but that is not an option to consider.

Outside, a procession circumambulates the chapel. Occasionally, the cries and shouts in unison break into the graduation program. The banners, in both Urdu and English, are brief and simple.

"WE WANT OUR MARKS"
"LET US GRADUATE"
"DOWN WITH Mr. OLD"
"GIVE US BACK OUR MARKS"
"DOWN WITH THE PRINCIPAL"

This is going to be a graduation without graduates. There is no thought of canceling the ceremony. If the boys do not wish to come to their own graduation then that is their choice. The graduation goes on.

William Mall makes his speech, congratulating the absent graduates on their efforts to move out of poverty into prosperity. With God's help and their own determination, they will succeed. I scribble on the back of the graduation program a few lines of poetry.

And so you're down. Ah, child
Don't cry,
Up off the knees and brace the heart
To struggle on.

—To fight, and well enough to win
Is half the battle done, no more—
To be defeated, on the knees
And in the dust yet breathless rise,
Bloodspattered, empty, done,
To fight again, the fight not o'er
While breath shall last or heart beat on
Or man's will hold—that's gain indeed!

Not in victory or defeat
Cause is lost or won
But who holds on until the end,
'til, all dust set and pain forgot,
The struggle is no more, he wins.

When wav'ring spirit's done, well spent
In victor's ease or dull despair—
It matters not which way—then all is lost
Yet while, on t'other side, the spark,
Though dim, still burns, gathers
Strength and light and blaze or merely
Holds the light it has—this is enough!

Though foe be strong and friend deride,
This blow, and others more ahead
Will temper you to finer steel
And fit you for the cause you hold.
Rise up, show now the will you had
When first the fight was joined
And let it hold whate'er befall.
Cast all your strength into the fray again.

Rise up, go down you may.
Keep on rising, give not up
And the victory that you need,
And that within, is yours indeed.

We call out one by one the names of the missing graduates. None are present, and the certificates are set to one side, uncollected. The prizes and cups for the best graduates in each shop and the best overall graduate are similarly treated. The prizes for the trainees who are continuing provide a little interest. We close with a hymn and a prayer. The processional comprises merely senior staff and important guests. On the steps of the chapel, we pause to allow our graduates opportunity to raise their slogans a few more times. Some of the boys I know and have grown to love are half-hearted, even ashamed, in some of their declamations.

The slogans accompany us across to the reception for graduates and parents. Only the parents join the reception.

Later, without fuss and with good temper and no rancor, the boys, garlanded by their parents and friends and accompanied by their parents who are so proud of their boys, come to collect their certificates from me personally. They are good boys and will make good craftsmen, and their parents are right to be proud of them.

God and Evil—the ultimate struggle . . .
YUNUS WILLIAM

Gujranwala
1974

It is Sunday afternoon. Sunday afternoons are sacrosanct. No one goes visiting on Sunday afternoon, at least before teatime at 4 o'clock. From lunch until 4 P.M. on Sunday is the missionary equivalent of the Sabbath day of the Old Testament. Keep it holy! No matter how busy you are for the rest of the hours of the week, these three hours are your time to rest with the assurance there will be no interruptions.

The best hours of each day for Marie and me are 4:30 A.M. to 7 A.M., and the best hours of each week are on Sunday afternoon.

Not this afternoon! Banging on the door! Rubbing the sleep out of my eyes, I recognize several of the boys from Whitfield Hostel. They are looking worried. "Forgive us, sir. It's Yunus William, sir. He's behosh" Behosh means literally 'without sense' and could have a number of interpretations.

I wait for Marie. We go across to the hostel together with the boys. What they explain seems to make little sense, but we are soon there, and we'll find out for ourselves. Yunus is upstairs in room 2.

His friends move back from his bedside.

The boy, maybe 18 years old, is a poor Christian boy from the Narowal area. He's never been a problem. He lies on his bed. His eyes are open, fixed on the ceiling, but there is no sign of life in them. He does not turn in any way as we come in and stand beside him. There is no sign of recognition or awareness.

"Yunus?" I ask. Nothing. "Yunus, do you hear me?" Nothing. "Yunus, sit up!" This is an order, given firmly. No response. It seems like catalepsy of some sort, suspension of sense and movement in a trance like state.

I call Xavier and another friend aside. No, something like this has never happened before. He doesn't take any kind of drugs. He is a good boy, doesn't even smoke.

I go back to the bed. "Yunus, sit up!" At my nod, his friends sit him up in bed. He does not resist. He does not even seem to blink. Marie is as puzzled as I. "Yunus, get up!" His friends help him to his feet and hold him lest he fall. He does not resist. They walk him round the room. He does not seem to have control of his limbs and his senses are certainly elsewhere.

"Xavier, three or four of you take him for a walk around the main hostel, and then bring him over to the house."

Marie is brewing a large pot of tea when they come in. The boy's condition is unchanged. We seat him on the settee opposite the fireplace. I kneel down in front of him. "Yunus, where are you?"

Again, more emphatically this time, requiring, insisting on, an answer. Yunus turns his head slowly and takes in the bookcases and Marie coming in with the tea. Around him are his friends.

"Yunus! Where are you?"

"I am home, home in the village."

I point to his friends. "Who are these?"

Slowly, with some difficulty as though trying to communicate from afar, he responds. "They live in my village with me. They are my neighbors."

I point to Marie. "Who is that?"

Again, after hesitation, the response is slow, almost mechanical without any life or inflection. "That is my mother, Ammajee."

I give Xavier Marie's Urdu New Testament written in Arabic text. Yunus sees it, and with a start, shrinks back against the wall. He has recognized it. Something like life has flickered into his eyes. It is almost like fear. "Find John 3:16, Xavier." Yunus is now clearly frightened. "Come near and read it to Yunus."

Yunus tries to push Xavier, his closest friend, and the book he holds away from him.

I motion Xavier even closer and he reads, slowly and clearly. "For God so loved the world that He gave his only begotten Son that whosoever believes in him should not perish but have everlasting life."

Yunus is looking around the room now, like a frightened animal looking for a way of escape.

I take the New Testament from Xavier and thrust it into Yunus' unwilling hands.

"Now you read it, Yunus. John 3:16, find the place. Have you got it? Now you read!" Yunus is scared to death, but there is nowhere to run. "Read it, Yunus!"

Slowly, reluctantly, Yunus begins to read. His voice is without inflection; he is reading from way inside himself and forcing his lips to make sounds in a monotone. It is as though he is at the far end of a long tunnel from his voice. The room is in total silence except for his hesitant, dragging words.

"For God so loved the world that He gave his only begotten Son that whosoever . . ."

He can go no further.

"That whosoever, that whosoever, that whosoever, that whoso-ever . . ."

As he tries to move on, his voice is changing from a slow, reluctant whisper to a voice of meaning, of wonder, of dawn out of darkness and sunrise and joy and glory!!!!!!!

"WHOSOEVER!!!!!!! WHOSOEVER!!!!!"

He is loud now; his eyes suddenly bright and alive, looking around at us with puzzled recognition as though he can't understand why he is here in the principal's living room, but knowing only that he is shouting "WHOSOEVER!! THAT MEANS ME, THAT MEANS ME!!!!!"

It is time for Marie to pour the tea.

Working His Purposes Out . . .
THE KHOKHERKE BOYS

Gujranwala
September 1971

My 1949 visitor had told me I would be working among boys. True enough. Wherever I turn, there are boys. Not a single girl student yet. We have boys coming out of our ears. Not all of them are in our boarding hostels. There are Muslim boys from the town. In order to give our Christian students their first and only taste of being in a majority environment, I am limiting our Muslim boys to a maximum of 40% of the enrollment. They are good boys. There is no attempt to push Christianity down their throats. They join us for lessons after chapel and the morning Bible Class are over. They leave early on Fridays so that they can get to the mosque for Friday prayers, if they wish to go.

There are also Christian dayboys. Many of them are from across the Sialkot road in the suburb of Gujranwala known as Khokherke. The very word usually means trouble.

The Sialkot Mission, with great foresight at the end of the First World War, had purchased 40 acres or so of land on the northeastern side of Gujranwala. The east side fronted onto the Sialkot road. On it, over the years, became housed the Mission Treasurer's office and four significant institutions.

The Theological Seminary prepared pastors for the Protestant church in the Punjab. It became a united institution with students from a variety of Protestant denominations. Its staff, principally from the Sialkot Mission and the indigenous church, also occasionally included members from Scotland, England, Ireland, Canada, New Zealand, and from South Korea.

Another institution was the Adult Basic Education Society doing sterling work from the late fifties in pursuit of the far distant goal of countrywide literacy. It became the pioneer of many new techniques and programs, focusing not only on the ability to read, but also upon the content of what was being read. This led to the successful establishment of a pioneering publishing house providing inexpensive books for new literates.

Across the road from us was the United Bible Training Center, a training center for girls and women. This was immaculately run by able and dedicated missionary women on a shoestring budget. One of the great needs of an emerging church among a largely illiterate community is good solid teaching and memorizing of the Scriptures and its principles of behavior and conduct. Trained here, a cadre of well-equipped "Bible women" spread out through the Punjab, working alongside rural and urban pastors and alongside evangelists in hospitals. Often, too, they worked independently. When they married, they became leaders of the women in their local community. They were and are a great asset to the church.

Finally, there was the technical school. This restarted in the year 1900, after an earlier attempt at the very beginning of the mission work had failed. There was a severe famine in Rajasthan; many thousands died of starvation. Two missionaries of the Sialkot Mission went down to see what they could do to help and brought back with them to Gujranwala a trainload of famine orphans. The girls went on to Sialkot, and the boys stayed here in Guj. It had some shaky times during the depression when funds from home were very short, but the appointment of an English ex-Army officer, Major Whitfield, helped immensely. He had met and married an American missionary in Egypt. During the Second World War, the Boys Industrial Home, as it was then known, trained hundreds of drivers for the Army.

As the institutions and the development of the campus had progressed, so more and more Christian employees had come to work there. Some were able to have the accommodation provided by the institutions for their own employees and the domestic servants of both local and foreign staff. More and more though, they tended to move into their own dwellings on their purchased land across the Sialkot road in Khokherke. A crowded settlement (basti) of brick-built dwellings developed. Lanes developed into roads and streets, with their own subsidiary lanes and cul-de-sacs off them. Entrepreneurs among them opened shops on the corners while some others, upon whom fortune had smiled, even opened small factories or private schools. Further up the Sialkot road was the cemetery, so most of the essentials for a community to prosper were present.

The problem, I quickly found when we arrived in Guj, was the boys.

Khokherke was congested and crowded. There were few areas where boys could play or just hang around. The girls were, by the very nature of Pakistani society, kept indoors and protected. The boys were allowed to wander. Across the road were the open expanses of the Christian institutions. These included playing fields, running track, and basketball courts. The boys regarded these as 'their' institutions. If there was anything to be plundered from them, it was their right to do so. If any thefts took place, the Khokherke boys were blamed, and frequently, rightly so. There was a virtual war of attrition going on. The boys regarded the institutions as fair game, and the institutions erected higher and higher walls to try to keep them out.

Walls are an interesting preoccupation with missionaries. Ever since

Nehemiah, there has been an illusion that higher walls keep intruders out. Twaddle! What boy worth the name boy is deterred by high walls? I built walls 14 feet high to keep the Khokherke boys out of the technical center quadrangle—we had very expensive machine tools to guard—and while I was inspecting the roof for leaks, I would see boys dropping down the inside face to retrieve a soccer ball. They would scale the wall to be back outside, long before I could get anywhere near them.

Time came to try to demarcate our boundary along Church road. I did not like the barbed wire that was strung along the boundary on steel angle iron posts. A wall was called for. What kind of a wall? How high should it be? I realized that this wall needed to say something. What walls usually say is "Keep out!" I didn't want to say that. We were Christians living in a Muslim society. I didn't want to say, "Keep out!" I wanted to say, "Come on in and meet us; we don't bite!" Inside our wall would be gardens. Were these gardens to be reserved only for the occupants? By no means. We wanted to say, "Come on in, friend, and rest a while. Take the weight, for a few moments, off those weary feet. This grass is yours too, not just ours."

What was needed was a wall that marked a property boundary, but didn't provide a barrier.

We made a mold for a concrete element, shaped somewhat like a truncated cross with a hole in the center. We made hundreds of these similar pieces. We laid a brick foundation in cement mortar. On it, we balanced our pieces. Each one reached about two and a half feet up and along. When we had done one line along the length, we balanced a second piece on top of the other and mounted a coping to top it off. We had a wall that was just a series of holes strung together. Boys would sit in the holes; others would climb through them. Throughout the town posters assaulted every exposed, exterior flat space, especially at election time, but on this wall they could find no place to lodge. The wall was virtually maintenance free. This ridiculous, senseless, useless wall became the symbol of the Christian Technical Training Center which was known to some even as far as Lahore as the "place with the wall."

I digress, for I am telling about the Khokherke boys. Nazir Matthias, the head clerk, knew all the boys. He lived in Khokherke. He had grown up there. His father, aged over 80, had been an elder for more than half those years and was still an active elder of the local congregation. Nazir knew the sons, the fathers, and the father's fathers. He was a great source of information and good sense about the local community.

When I did my first interviews of new boys who wished to be admitted, Nazir was part of the interviewing team. After the boy had left the room, Nazir would just say, "He's a TM." I would mark TM on the top of the interview sheet. When all the interviews were done, I separated those marked TM and set them aside. No admission for them. Nazir had identified them as troublemakers. Apart from the staff, I had enough trouble from the students we already had without admitting more of them to cause trouble.

By the time the next admissions came round, I had time to reflect.

Again, Nazir assisted with the admission interviews. After all the boys had been seen, we sorted out the TMs. This time though, I told Nazir, all the TMs were going to be admitted, not refused admission. Nazir was thunderstruck. This was as good as blowing up the school! He knew these boys. Some of their fathers were criminals. Every boy was an introduction to discord and defiance of discipline. Did I have any idea of some of the crimes these boys themselves had committed? If I was designing to ruin the school, I couldn't have chosen a better or faster means to do so. It was letting a pack of wolves into a chicken run. It was . . . words failed him. He just looked at me in disbelief; he couldn't believe his ears.

I agreed it was a risk, but excluding them didn't seem to work. They had each gone to the trouble to fill in the application forms, have photographs taken, spruce themselves up, and come for interview. After all, why were we here? Surely it was to help boys like these, our own Christian boys, to somehow or other overcome the disadvantages they were born into. Wasn't it worthwhile, at least, giving them a chance? If they misbehaved, I would kick them out in a jiffy. We left it at that. We would see what happened.

Nazir left the room shaking his head with dismay.

Working His Purposes Out . . .
ABBAS MAURICE

Gujranwala
October 1971

Abbas Maurice was one of the Khokherke TMs who we admitted. He came from a family of three boys that had a disturbed parental background. All three boys, close together in age, were intelligent and capable. They were good at and interested in sports. They had pleasant personalities and looked you straight in the eye.

Samuel, who came to work in the Technical Services Unit, was a gem, reliable and quick-witted. He never gave a moment's trouble. Musa kept too close company with his Khokherke friends, preferred to mess around rather than apply himself, played with drugs, and when admitted into the electrician's course, dropped out halfway through.

Abbas, the oldest of the three, wanted to be a machinist. This was one of the best courses we had to offer. Initially it was a three-year course although later we reduced the length to two years. Some of our equipment, milling machines and grinders, dated back to the First World War. Wonderful old workhorses!

Abbas was proving a good student, full of interest and searching questions that stretched his instructors. His practical work was excellent. He had clear leadership qualities.

Then he blew it.

Several hostel boys reported that at about three P.M., after they had lunch, Abbas, and a couple of other boys from Khokherke who were not in the school, had come into their room and thrown them unceremoniously out of it. That done, the other two boys had positioned themselves as guards front and back, while Abbas had taken into the room a veiled girl or woman wearing a full-length burqa. They could only surmise what had happened. All four had now left the campus.

I was sorry to hear this. I was taking a special interest in Abbas. Through him, we might be able to reach the other Khokherke boys and bring about a positive set of relationships with the Christian institutions instead of the long-standing enmity.

I collared him after chapel the following morning and walked him off toward the playing fields to talk to him privately. He told no lies and made no excuses. Yes, he had been stupid. No, the girl was not a Khokherke girl, but a girl from the town. He had been caught out fair and square. He accepted that he was now going to be thrown out of the school. I pointed to a new heap of 500 bricks that had been dropped by a recent bullock cart near to the playing field.

"Abbas, don't bother to come in for classes. Move those bricks to the other side of the playing field and stack them there neatly. Let me know when you have done it."

"Yes, sir."

I left him to it and returned to the school office.

Toward the end of the morning, Abbas came in to see me. I looked at his hands. The fingers were puffed and torn by the bricks. Obviously, his hands were hurting him. He had had no opportunity to go home to get gloves. I walked out with him to inspect the bricks, now neatly stacked on the other side of the playing field. He looked at me expectantly.

"Now move them back to the place you got them from and stack them there, neatly."

Abbas swallowed hard. "Yes, sir," he acknowledged.

I left him to it and returned to the school office.

When the boys came back at two o'clock to the hostel, he was still at it. He had had no break since chapel finished at 7:30. All the boys knew why he was doing it. Some offered to help him, but he shooed them away. This was his punishment, and besides, he was nearly finished now.

He came to the house to find me. He was absolutely exhausted and his hands were screaming with pain. I went with him to check. The bricks were stacked neatly in their original position. I was proud of him, but I didn't let him see that. I dismissed him home and told him not to be late to school the following morning.

We used to preach through the Bible in chapel, starting in Genesis with a whole list of selected readings right through to the end of Revelation. A Christian boy on a two-year course attended chapel maybe 400 times. We aimed to give the boys a 20-minute sermon each day going steadily through the Bible. We had no chaplain; the staff preached. They were given their schedule showing their turn and the passage they were to preach. Most of them recognized the opportunity to nurture the younger generation in their faith and tried hard with their sermons. Compulsory chapel was the first part of each day for both Christian students and teachers.

Frequently, someone would hurry over from chapel to find me still in the office. "Mr. Old, it's your turn to take chapel. The passage is Romans 4, the whole chapter." By the time I reached the chapel, I would have to have a sermon prepared on that passage for instant delivery. Practice never made perfect, but it did hone some of the skills an impromptu speaker needs.

My favorite specific sin to attack was lying.

We lived in a culture where the lie was all too frequently taken for granted as having equal value with the truth. Expediency alone was the criteria by which you decided which to use. Judges in the courts had to make the basic assumption that all witnesses lie and perform their judicial duties within that rather limiting framework.

I asked the congregation in chapel one morning to make me a blind promise. "Put up your hands if you will do so." The boys all did so obediently, having absolutely no idea what they were promising. "I want the staff to put up their hands also." They did so, somewhat more slowly and raggedly. I outlined the promise they were making. "For one whole 24 hours, I promise not to tell a single lie. That is until 7:30 tomorrow morning. Furthermore, if I have told lies that have misled my listeners into believing something false, I will do my best to correct this by Saturday morning by the time school ends."

I was particularly interested in what Abbas Maurice might do. The previous Friday he had come to me because his grandmother in Lahore was ill. Could he please be excused attending school on Saturday morning in order to go to visit her? I have a weakness for sick grandmothers. "Certainly, Abbas."

On Monday morning I came to know from something that Samuel let slip that the boys had no grandmother in Lahore, but that Abbas had a wonderful day at the cricket Test Match between Pakistan and India.

I waited.

On Saturday morning, about 11 o'clock, there was a knock on my office door. Abbas came in and stood in front of the desk, shifting uncomfortably from one foot to the other and looking down at the floor.

"Yes, Abbas, what is it?"

"Sir, you are going to be very angry with me."

"You'll have to let me be the judge of that; what is the matter?"

"Sir, you remember you gave me permission to visit my grandmother in Lahore last Saturday."

"Yes, Abbas, how is she? I hope she's better now."

"Sir," he blurted out. "I told you a lie, sir. I don't have a grandmother who lives in Lahore. I had a ticket for the Test Match, and I was desperate to go so I told you a lie. I'm sorry, sir." Abbas looked as though he wished the floor would open and swallow him up.

I was in no mood to play games. Something wonderful had happened. "I already knew that, Abbas. What's really important is that you came and told me." I came round the desk to him and to his surprise gave him a hug. "Remember the lesson you've learned. Off you go."

Abbas graduated at the top of his class. I was able to find him a good job at a research establishment in Lahore. He developed tuberculosis and had to leave his job. While he was recuperating, I paid him a stipend to organize a sports and games program for the Khokherke boys. They used our playing field and basketball court for their practice and for their home fixtures. Before long, they had their own playing uniforms for basketball and soccer. Strangely, even by this time, the incidence of problems with the Khokherke boys, other than their smoking and using drugs on our soccer pitch, had dropped to almost nil.

Abbas recovered his health and was able to get work as a machinist in Iran at pay much higher than that available in his own country. On one of his breaks back home, he came to see me. He explained that he had made enough money now. He wanted to come back and help his own people. Would I give him a job as a machinist instructor in the machine shop?

I was delighted to do so. He was still working there when I handed over my job as principal and moved on to other activities.

God and Evil—the ultimate struggle . . .
TURMOIL AND WAR

Gujranwala
November 1971

B efore we left Taxila a year previously, we were receiving letters warning us to expect trouble as soon as we arrived in Gujranwala. The letters were written in pencil and in English on the pages of a copybook. The writer (or writers . . . we weren't sure whether there was only one) appeared to be sincere, and we guessed he himself worked in the Christian Technical Training Center. The staff had determined that they would get rid of us within a year, and there was to be a concerted effort to achieve this. They would work through the students to avoid receiving blame or punishment themselves.

We must particularly be aware of those who would pretend to be our friends. We should screen invitations to meals most carefully. There had been discussions about the use of poison. We should not accept gifts of food, fruit, or sweets. We would, the writer assured us, soon discover there was much dishonesty. We should trust nobody.

Fortunately, Brend and Marjet Kuyvenhoven were there. They were Dutch missionaries absolutely reliable and trustworthy, but it was soon apparent they had been sidelined by other staff and deliberately kept in the dark about much that was going on.

My immediate missionary predecessor had been ill and unable to exercise the controls he would have wished. During the summer closure, three of the senior Pakistani staff had been appointed as a triumvirate to manage things in the absence of a missionary manager.

First blood went to them. The three unanimously recommended, as soon as I arrived in early October of 1970, that I dismiss the storekeeper. I was believing nothing I was told and doubted the stories I was given about the storekeeper's dishonesty and incompetence. However, I did think that the stores were the untidiest, messiest stores I had ever had the misfortune to try to inspect, and I dismissed him on these grounds. It was a mistake, and I was unfair to Haider. The missionary principal of the seminary next door told me sadly that I had not started off too well; I had dismissed the only honest man on the CTTC staff.

My next move was better. I reorganized the administration of the Center dropping the position of headmaster that I was suspecting was the root of most of the problems. Instead I appointed Brend as chief instructor, a new position. Often, the cleaning up of a messy situation does not depend on the wisdom and acumen of a new administrator but just one or two fortunate decisions that are as much luck as foresight.

Brend's appointment was such an instance. He had come out from Holland in 1967 as an auto mechanics instructor when the Dutch Reformed Churches were re-deploying their resources after the independence of Indonesia. He had good contacts with a generous garage and workshop owner in Amsterdam who supplied a large quantity of training models and aids. Brend worked closely with his shop foreman, Kalim Alim, a jovial ex-Army mechanic who loved working with boys from his own community. The shop had its full quota of students and found practical work and income in repairing and servicing cars of local customers and missionary vehicles from all over the Punjab.

I was beginning to question whether this was a right strategy for training boys. The requirements of the customers seemed to override the needs of the boys to be educated properly, but this would require resolution later. No wisdom in rocking too many boats at once, the whole caboodle might capsize.

Brend proved a natural leader as chief instructor. He took his new job in his stride and covered for me when I returned occasionally to Taxila to consult over the completion of the operating block. He easily expanded his interests to include the other shops. There was a radio mechanic's shop, a drafting shop, an electrician's shop, a carpenter's shop, a machine shop, and a welding shop. None of them was really flourishing since the enrollment of the whole school varied between 60 and 80. Most course lengths were three years.

One that he didn't have to worry about was the photography shop and studio.

This we closed down when we became aware the facilities were being used to photograph, in pornographic poses, town women picked up at night-time in the school vehicle. Prints and negatives were then supplied to the local market and to other outlets in Lahore. We didn't need that kind of advertising.

Two other shops that had already been closed or had been slated for closure when the present students graduated were the tailor's shop and the cobbler's shop. These were where some of the least-educated village boys received training. They had been part of the boys' industrial home from its beginning at the turn of the century, but times were changing. Traditional methods of training shoemakers and tailors at the feet of a master tradesman were available and boys were not coming for these trades.

The staff were very successfully creating disturbances through the students, while pretending to cooperate in keeping the disturbances under control.

Although not all staff were involved, all were aware of what was going on. Most were enjoying the plotting, the playacting, and the subterfuge.

The riots, strikes, and processions continued. The Muslim boys brought to their rather naive Christian counterparts their considerable organizing abilities to supplement the instructions and counsel from their instructors. The country was full of turmoil. The Government was facing protests all over the country, with strikes and processions by students instigated to try to bring down the Government. Strikes and protests build excitement and make the adrenaline flow.

Several of the students instigated their own lawsuits, accusing me of breaking into their lockers and stealing their money and possessions.

It was a day in late November when the boys had absented themselves from classes and processed around the town. (All that is except Sultan, a very poor welding student from Sheikhupura who, despite threats of violence, would not join them and sat it out alone on the chapel steps.) Their banners by now were more outspoken. "Old Sah'b Murdebad!" ("Death to Mr. Old!") I accompanied them for the last hundred yards of their procession back into the school. Their chants grew less noisy and insistent after I joined them.

I called all the boys to listen to me from the chapel steps near the entrance to the quadrangle. The gates had not been opened that morning. The staff came out from the staff room to listen.

Since the boys didn't seem to want to come to classes, I was closing the school. The last meal provided by the cooks in the hostel would be today's lunch. There would be no further meals. They should go home, explain to their parents how they were using their time, and consider whether they wanted to continue studying here. If they wanted advances to pay for their bus fares home, they should go to the school office immediately after lunch.

One of the ringleaders from the hostel spoke up. "We won't go. We'll take over the kitchens and supplies and do the cooking ourselves. This is just a trick. You are sending us home without any intention of calling us back. You are just closing the school down. We need our education. We won't go home!"

"Boys," I responded. "This is not a trick. I know you need an education, but we can't run the school while you are behaving like this. I promise you that I will call you back just as soon as I think we can get started running the school sensibly again. You have my word that I will send you a letter, within ten days at the most, telling you when the school will reopen. We have exams for you to take before the Christmas holidays, and I want you to get back in good time. Take your books with you and study hard. Don't waste your time at home."

There was some further argument, but the boys were becoming less and less committed to confrontation. They had my word that I would call them back, and they could rely on that. Holidays are always welcome. Slowly, in small groups, they turned away toward the hostels. Their banners they took to save for a later occasion. The day boys headed for the school gates.

In an attempt to sort the staff out while the boys were away, I segregated them in the staff-room. One by one, I interviewed them before allowing them to progress through my office to their workshops within the quadrangle. I expected and required loyalty from each one of the staff. I was going to be here for years hence, and all disloyal staff would be gone long before I left. I told them what I expected from staff loyal to me and loyal to the institution. If they could not feel loyal to me, there was their draft letter of resignation waiting for a signature. I pushed a copy toward them. I was prepared to see everyone go and rebuild the staff from scratch. Staff who could not support me 100 percent should go, now!

"Where do you stand?"

Each member of staff, from Salim Mubarak down, swore his complete loyalty. More than one took the opportunity of a private talk to fill me in on things it would be good for me to know, including giving the names of the ringleaders of the staff plotting my ouster. A good proportion of the information I received was false, but I filed all that I heard in my head for later.

The staff was unusually quiet after their individual interviews. None of them knew what the others might have told me about their own particular activities and, without the boys to galvanize into instant crises, for a while I had the initiative.

Time was passing. I was conscious that I had promised the boys a letter recalling them, and that was a promise I would keep, but didn't want to keep. Nothing in the situation had changed or showed any sign of changing. I knew, as soon as the boys were back, the strikes and rows would start again over the slightest excuse. Any molehill would be a mountain within hours. I was writing the examination questions. Any one 'unfair' question could provoke disturbance and a walkout. Would we be able to keep the lid on until the Christmas holidays came round for another respite?

Both Marie and I were praying for some guidance and direction concerning the letter to call the boys back. It came from a most unexpected quarter that left me thankful and startled.

India and Pakistan went to war!

The struggle was for the independence of Bangladesh. Pakistan had two 'wings', the East Wing of Muslim Bengal and the West Wing where the lands drained into the Indus River. West Pakistan had refused to recognize the victory of Mujibur Rehman in the recent elections which would have seen him appointed as Prime Minister of Pakistan. In the ensuing disturbances, General

Yahya Khan had taken over. His foreign minister was Zulfiqar Ali Bhutto, who would replace him as President and then later become Prime Minister.

The internal protests in East Pakistan were being put down by General Niazi and troops from West Pakistan. India was sympathetic to Mujib's men and was feeding support to East Pakistan. Counter actions by Yahya involved stirring up the unease and the protests within Indian Kashmir.

It burst into open and undeclared war.

The seminary staff and students were playing a friendly match against our staff on our basketball court. Suddenly, a flight of three Pakistan Air Force planes burst overhead at about 300 feet at full speed heading due east followed by a tremendous ear shattering roar as their sound followed them. Below their wings was strapped a full complement of bombs. They were gone in a second. The basketball dropped from the nerveless hands of a casual visitor to the seminary. He had come from Thailand and had a day or so stopover in Karachi on his way back home to the States. The time was just enough to allow him a trip to Gujranwala to see his seminary classmate, Wilbur Christy. "HowdoIgetoutahere" he gasped desperately, frantically. We sent Salim Mubarak with him to get him to the frontier with Afghanistan. It was the wrong direction for Karachi, but any port in a storm.

We were just 35 miles from the Ravi border with India, and as in the '65 war, the Indians were attacking to the northeast of us on the sector between the Chenab and Ravi rivers. The two essential arteries of Pakistan's northern areas are the Grand Trunk Road and the railway that runs alongside it. They both pass through Gujranwala.

I went immediately to see the Brigadier commanding the Gujranwala garrison. A new cantonment was being constructed to the north of the city. We possessed a workshop, a vehicle repair workshop, and a machine shop. If it were to be needed by the armed services, it was available. Within hours, a unit of the army engineers had moved into our vacant hostels. Machine guns and anti-aircraft guns were mounted on the roof of the Kern's house and on the overhead water tank.

Each of the boys in the villages received promptly the letter he was expecting. Owing to the unexpected war with India, the Pakistan army was now utilizing the school workshops and the hostels. When the army returned the facilities to us, the boys would be recalled without delay. Meanwhile, they should continue their theoretical studies diligently at home.

I think it was the several loyal staff members who fostered the unfounded rumor that the Brigadier had offered to Mr. Old to arrest and execute by firing squad any CTTC staff members whom he construed were impeding the war effort.

God and Evil—the ultimate struggle . . .
THE TRADE UNION

Gujranwala
February 1973

B rend was managing the school while Marie and I were away in England with the boys looking for a possible family home. Shortly after we agreed to purchase Gibbins Brook Farm came a message from Brend to return immediately. Some of the staff had tried to take over the school by force.

Colin and Tim weren't going to let me escape back home by myself. Mom was capable of following after without their help. Why, they could easily be in her way! She would have no trouble settling up things in England and getting back to Lahore by herself. We would meet her at the airport. They were coming back with me!

The boys and I flew into Lahore airport. They were so happy to be back among the yells, smells, and bells of their own environment you would have thought they had been away for two years rather than two months. We caught a bus back to Guj from the railway station. The boys' dogs, two Samoyeds, went wild with excitement.

Normally, Brend was responsible for the training program. I dealt with the commercial operations that provided practical opportunities for the boys' skills. This was where most of the fraud occurred. When either of us was away, each covered for the other.

Last year I had a run-in with Khalid Alim, Brend's good friend, and the foreman in the Auto shop. Dissatisfied customers who had their cars repaired in the auto shop were taking up much of my time. There were far too many complaints. I began scrutinizing carefully the bills that customers were being charged. We charged for new parts at the market price we paid plus an additional percentage and then added our labor charges. Something was fishy, very fishy. Tim had worked in the auto shop the previous winter on his long holiday from Murree. He confirmed my suspicions.

I called Kalim into the office. He was taking money from the cashier for new parts, clutch plates, brake linings, what-you-will, and the customer was being charged for those new parts plus a percentage. However, the old worn parts were going back into the vehicle and a receipt for a new part was being purchased at one rupee a time from the auto parts store.

I showed him a whole pile of these false receipts. I had been down to the parts store myself and checked it out.

Kalim made no denials. They had to get their chaipani (tea money) from somewhere, didn't they? He wasn't robbing the institution; they were actually giving a percentage to the CTTC with every false purchase they recorded. As for the customers, the complaints they were making were non-sense. He only made false claims to replace parts when the parts were not badly worn. If they really were badly worn, they did replace them with genuine purchases. I doubted that.

I had not dismissed Kalim, although I should have done so, but had given him a strict warning. I also instituted a whole series of checks, includ-ing having new purchases brought to me for inspection and the old part being replaced kept under lock and key.

This would not, of course, stop the fraud; merely make it a little more difficult.

Brend told the story of what had happened while we were in England. One of the loyal staff, there were a number, had told him that Kalim Alim, Salamat Niaz, and Shamim Leghari, three staff members, were preparing to register a Trades Union, the CTTC Employees Union. Legally, this was not possible; there was needed a minimum labor employment of 50 persons. The country was however in the grip of student turmoil and labor unrest. Although Mr. Bhutto had become first president and now prime minister, his Peoples Party, the party in power, was having trouble controlling the genie that it had released.

Brend had acted promptly and decisively as soon as he heard. He closed down the auto-mechanics repair workshop and dismissed Kalim Alim and Salamat Niaz as redundant to the needs of CTTC.

They, and some others they recruited, countered by locking Brend in his office in the school, declaring that they were now the masters and that the school and its assets were under their direct control and jurisdiction.

Brend responded by escaping into the quadrangle, scaling a wall, and driving post haste to the friendly brigadier at the cantonment for immediate help. The school had recently been awarded an army citation for its assistance during the recent hostilities with India. The help he requested was promptly forthcoming. Brend regained control of the school, put on extra guards for both day and night, and cabled me to return immediately.

He had been served with nine different summonses to the Labor Courts in Gujranwala, alleging, as acting principal and defendant, he was guilty of unfair dismissal of employees and various other charges relating to the dismissals. He handed these over with some relief to me. By the following morning, I had a total of 14 summonses to answer as more charges were concocted and delivered and news of my return spread.

I shared my unhappy news with the English manager of a local strawboard mill. He laughed in derision. Only 14 cases! Did I know how many cases there were against him that he was fighting in courts from Karachi to Peshawar—240! His dilemmas brought little comfort though I agreed it proved that I was now accepted as a Punjabi by other Punjabis. Litigating against each other is a social pastime.

Brend had employed one of the finest advocates in Lahore as our legal counsel.

There was little time to waste. The Trades Union had not yet been registered. I presented myself at the Trades Union Registration Office in Lahore with registers and payrolls to prove we employed significantly fewer than 50 employees. The staff there just laughed. They did not care how many employees we had; they would be registering the union, and we could sort out whether they should have done so by due process of law in the courts.

So much for that effort!

It is now that I have to thank God for an intervention that I did not recognize at the time. I had no overt reason to change our legal representative, but I did so responding to a deep seated unease that I needed to do something about this right away.

Although I did not know, 17 years of well nigh continuous court cases lay ahead of me. I was to become unenviably the most experienced member of our mission as a defendant in court. The court cases were part of the struggle against evil. Almost all involved false trumped up cases where perjury by the plaintiffs was a given part of the process. The longest running criminal case of ten years began with a case of mistaken identity, where I was believed to be the representative of another mission also being victimized by court cases. When furloughs came around, the range of criminal cases against me governed when and whether I could leave the country. Civil cases were easier. A lawyer could represent me without my being present. Criminal cases required me to be present at every court hearing.

God had His eye on the future, and He works in mysterious ways.

We had an absolutely top-flight legal counsel, possibly the best in Lahore. He later became a federal minister, but I was uneasy whether his expertise lay in labor law or general law. He very generously agreed to my request that he surrender this particular brief and allow me to seek alternative representation.

I went to a retired judge of the High Court, a resident in Lahore and asked him who in his opinion was the finest labor lawyer in Lahore. He had no hesitation. Without doubt, the man I was looking for was Chaudri Altaf Hussain. He was now elderly, but he was the best. I thus came to know and rely upon, as a generous and skilled friend, a young Oxford graduate, the Chaudry's son.

Javed Altaf represented me in many court cases and rarely presented me with the bills his work on my behalf entitled him to charge. He saw our work as a sacrificial effort to help the poorest of his own people. This was a way he, too, could help them. He grinned as he told me that during attendance at his Catholic school in Lahore, before going to England for further study, he, a Muslim, had consistently had top marks in Bible!

Javed was clear that the cases against us would have to progress to the High Court level before they could be resolved. The Lahore High Court was proud of its reputation as a legal jurisdiction that was capable of acting independently of the power brokers and movers and shakers, even those as high as the Prime Minister and President. The legal system was based in English jurisprudence, reference to case law and precedent. It was long, laborious, and costly. Where Pakistan legal precedent failed or came short, Indian case law and English case law was quoted.

There were corrupt judges—one judge told me during the process of a case that nothing had been proved against me, but nevertheless, he would be finding me guilty—and there were corrupt lawyers. Even so, I felt the bulk of both judges and lawyers wanted to see true justice emerge.

I told Javed, we would be conducting our defense on three principles. We would tell only the truth, we would not pay any bribes, and we would trust that in some way God would bring blessing to Pakistan through this particular set of cases.

All three happened.

The case of the Trade Union took years to progress through the various levels of court. There were scores of visits to make from Gujranwala to Lahore and many returns home late at night. Perjury by the plaintiffs was expected and duly delivered as a commonplace hardly worth noting.

Javed reduced the issues in the High Court case 'Government of the Punjab vs. K. G. Old' to one primary issue. "Do the Industrial Relations Ordinances which regulate the relationships between employers and employees apply only to industries? If so, what are industries?"

Finally the High Court judge delivered a landmark ruling. In brilliantly concise legal prose, he defined industry as the interaction of capital and labor for profit. There was no appeal made against his ruling. Immediately, the pending cases against the University of the Punjab, The Pakistan Board of Control for Cricket, and a score of other non-profit organizations working for the public good, including the CTTC Gujranwala, were dropped for there were no grounds for the cases to continue.

There was a calming in the courts as the many industrial relations ordinances were restricted in scope and application to true industrial concerns. Cases in the other provinces also were calming. Several lawyers hearing my name mentioned sought me out in the court precincts to congratulate me and to thank me for fighting the government on this one right to the end.

I had done nothing, but Javed had fought brilliantly on our behalf, and the country as a whole benefited.

God and Evil—the ultimate struggle . . .
SALIM MUBARAK

Gujranwala
August 1973

S alim Mubarak was the most powerful member of the CTTC staff threatened by any new broom that might come to try to clean things up. He had grown up alongside missionary children and spoke English fluently. He was able and intelligent. He thought he understood missionaries well and despised them in his heart. He had to learn to swallow his pride, concur with and approve their actions even when they were so obviously mistaken. He had learned what pleased them and how to please them. Many a time he had swallowed his pride and had taken the blame for mistakes his missionary seniors should have foreseen and avoided. He was more efficient than they were and often was quicker in appreciation of problems and their prevention. From his childhood, he had worked assiduously at rising to the top of the ladder open to him. He had been anxious to learn, asked questions constantly, and stored away in his mind the answers he received.

He was a good machinist—a troubleshooter on a whole range of problems from broken down vehicles to faulty milling machines. He was the right hand man of the missionary principal, called upon automatically to deal with the emergencies that were always cropping up. He knew how to smile and how to mix, when to defer to the missionary's superior wisdom, and when to speak out offering his own views.

Many missionaries counted him a good friend and a fine example for the young Christian students to emulate.

He could preach well and led the Gospel Teams out to the villages. His sermons in the chapel were well developed, to the point and hard-hitting. He was involved actively in all aspects of the school's life. The school was his life. He was the headmaster of the school, the senior Pakistani appointment.

When I came, he was one of the three national staff making the interim decisions for the school. Like Iqbal, the accountant, he had developed his own perquisites of the job, and these benefits and other activities he was involved in were now threatened. However, he either controlled most of what went on within the whole network of corruption or was aware of it and allowed it to continue to happen for his own reasons. He would need allies in fighting off this new challenge I represented and in securing himself for the future.

Overtly, Salim was 100 percent with me, smiling broadly and cooperating earnestly and wholeheartedly as I carefully picked my way through the ramifications of an educational institution. I had never worked in an institution before, and I had come in direct as principal. I was accustomed to the straightforward challenges of a building site and not the feuding, nit-picking, advantage seeking of one long-service teaching staff member over another. The whole ethos of the school workplace was alien to me; I was just grateful I had never had to be a teacher.

I began to ask questions about the boys' security funds. Each boy had to deposit 70 rupees to cover the possible costs of breakages of tools, loss of textbooks, and student damages. Credit balances were returned to the individual boys when they graduated. Iqbal's ledgers had no record of these funds. No, that was right, those funds went straight to the headmaster. He kept the records for each boy, received the security money when the boy arrived, and repaid the boy his credit balance when he graduated. A very cozy, little ready-cash arrangement with all sorts of possibilities.

By the time I was ready to check the headmaster's records, all the boys' security funds were back correct to the anna in a tin box in the headmaster's desk, 7,000 rupees. The tin box was emptied, the money went into the bank, and a new page was opened in the ledgers. The boys' individual accounts were credited and security funds abolished.

Salim was responsible for the photographic studio and publicity. It did not take long to recognize this was no asset to the training program and the closure would enable Salim to concentrate more effectively on his role as head of the machine shop.

By now I was pretty sure of the structure of the opposition at CTTC and who was masterminding it. A female relative of Salim was using similar tactics to cause trouble for Marie Allison at Pasrur.

I began checking where the various imported tools for the machine shop were. We had recently received a good supply of small machine and metal working tools from Germany. Why weren't they being kept in the main stores and being duly ledgered there? Well, they would be eventually used in the machine shop, and the machine shop had its own tool store where tools were issued to the boys against numbered brass tokens. There was a tool store-keeper. I was assured the system worked well.

The boys were on Easter holiday. I let Salim know that on Monday I would start checking the physical presence of the recent tool imports, *all* the recent tool imports, together with the entries in the ledgers. I was prepared to take a week doing it and had scheduled my time accordingly. Where were the invoices? In his desk. He would search them out and let me have them by Monday.

When I arrived at school on Monday, I was faced with dealing with a burglary. From the Church Road side, a burglar or burglars had smashed a window into the machine shop and then further smashed a window into and entered Salim's office within the machine shop. The desk had been ransacked. Papers were strewn all over the floor. What was missing? Micrometers and depth gauges for sure and other expensive precision tools kept locked in the desk for security. Some papers also could not be found. Why had the burglars not just broken into the tool store? Salim explained that they probably thought the security money of the boys was still in the desk, and they were after money.

I told Salim to go immediately to the police station, report the burglary, and make sure it was entered in the police register as a first information report. This was not going to remain a mystery for internal solution. The police had their own methods. They would start by interrogating the watchman, if not the first informant, hard. Salim's face turned gray and ashen. He was not anxious to go. I repeated my instructions to him. He turned slowly, took the proffered bicycle, and headed for the police station.

Before the police questioned the watchman, I questioned him first, carefully and privately. He had some very sensitive relationships, but he would rather tell me confidentially than have it extracted by the police and have what he said become public to be later used against him. He told me enough to show the whole burglary was a staged drama. He had no part in it but had stumbled upon the 'fixers' while they were at work. He told me who they were.

I declined to accept the loss of the invoices and other documents, purportedly among the materials stolen, as limiting my checking of the tools and obtained from the suppliers further copies. Considerable tools were missing.

Now we begin to glimpse a divine concurrence, a congruence, an intervention. This is God's battle we are fighting, and He is steadily taking care of the unraveling of events. It is akin to a great conductor leading an orchestra. Although his musicians may be out of sight of each other and the sounds they produce may emanate from very different sections, He can bring them into a split-second harmony. A previously unheard player now adds his own few notes to the music.

A German machine shop instructor who had previously worked at the CTTC was working at the Pak-German Technical Training Center in Lahore. Searching Brandreth Road for a set of precision-made blocks of stainless steel known as slip gauges, he located a set in Farrooqi's Hardware store. They were a German set and expensive. He would have to check whether the price was affordable.

Franz comes up from Lahore to see me. Where are the slip gauges that he had been using in the machine shop? They are not to be found, anywhere. Yes, the reason they are not to be found is because they are available for sale at

Farrooqi's Hardware store in Brandreth Road. Yes, the actual set, not a similar set. There are identifiable marks on the gauges, some he has made himself. Thank you, Franz.

I gain the assistance of the police inspector at the Naulakha police station in Lahore. He likes this cloak and dagger stuff. He will cooperate with a posse of policemen and himself in attendance. They hide behind a stack of rubber tires across the corner and pretend to be interested in a car parked across the street. Franz and I go into Farrooqi's. Do they have any precision slip gauges? No, I am not interested in Chinese slip gauges. I am only interested in the best, from Germany. Yes, I am fortunate; they do have just one set. Farrooqi brings them out from below the counter. I examine them carefully. I take each gauge out to examine it for scratches. They are all strewn across the counter. Franz is calling to the police by a prearranged signal.

They take ages to come, but are eventually there, filling the shop, a whole posse of them. The police inspector is all for arresting Farrooqi himself on the spot for theft and burglary and dealing in stolen goods. Much brouhaha and excitement! I am adding to the confusion by loudly accusing Farrooqi of stealing my tools. I can prove that they are mine. Farrooqi is all innocent and spreads his hands open wide; he has bought the slip gauges from a Gujranwala man who regularly brings in tools for him to buy. He has known him for years. No, he doesn't know his name. Yes, of course, he can recognize him; he would know him at once. He is slim, about 40, light moustache.

I produce a photograph of all the CTTC staff taken at a graduation. Is he there? Yes, no doubt at all. That is the man! He will swear to it in a court of law. Yes, he will swear an affidavit today. It is Salim Mubarak.

I place a charge of theft against Salim Mubarak in the Gujranwala Courts and dismiss him.

The case drags on for years; there are well accepted ways to defer hearings on court cases. The slip gauges, held as evidence, acquire marks and damage while in police custody and thus become useless. Salim Mubarak accuses another member of the initial managing trio of involvement and reluctantly, although believing him to be innocent, I suspend him for a while on full pay. Eventually, his suspension is lifted, but the court case itself never reaches a conclusion. Salim Mubarak gets another job elsewhere. With his departure from Gujranwala we see the beginning of the end of the staff and student problems that have plagued us since I came.

God and Evil—the ultimate struggle . . .
THE DAILY QAUMI AWAZ, LAHORE

January 30, 1973

An extract from the Daily Qaumi Awaz (*The People's Voice*) of January 30.

CHRISTIAN TECHNICAL TRAINING CENTER HAS BECOME A SPY CENTER. EX-SERVICE MEN ARE WORKING DAY AND NIGHT IN SPY ACTIVITIES. PRINCIPAL OF THE CENTER HAS GONE ABROAD TO GET INSTRUCTIONS FROM HIS FOREIGN MASTERS.

By a staff reporter.

The Christian Technical Training Center has become a center of spy activities of the foreign agents. In this center there are more activities related to spying than there are to technical education. It is learned that the agents of an international group have spread out their net of spy activities in the country. The spy ring working in the center is obtaining military secrets and passing them on to their foreign masters thereby causing the country a great deal of damage on an international level.

On investigation it has been found that in this center ex-Servicemen are working and their leader is also an ex-Service Britisher. The vice-principal of the Center, too, is an ex-Service man of the Dutch army. These people have employed under them ex-service men on important posts and through them spy activities are carried on.

The head of this Center frequently goes abroad and it is learned that in these days he is out of the country. It is thought that after obtaining instructions from his foreign masters he is due to return in a few days time.

Ostensibly these people have taken on the cloak of missionaries and technical education work whereas they have no experience of running an institution of the type of the Christian Technical Training Center. From the information which we have collected in respect of the head of department and vice principal and other workers in the Center it has been learned that the Pakistani workers do not mention anything about the activities which the foreigners are carrying out against the country as this group either dispenses with the services of anyone complaining or they are threatened with dire consequences. Consequently many of the employees have already been punished by throwing them out of jobs.

The head of the CTTC is an old ex-service man, Mr. Old, who, before the coming into being of Pakistan was a captain or a major in the Military Engineering Service. On the establishment of Pakistan he took up an appointment as building engineer for Gunman and Co. in Pakistan Ordnance Factory, Wah. In 1953 Mr. Old married an American missionary nurse who was residing in Sialkot and through his wife he came into the mission service. The mission appointed him as the building supervisor in the missionary hospital at Taxila. By establishing himself in a bungalow in the mission hospital just near the army headquarters in Rawalpindi he obtained many secrets.

After this, when in 1965 there was a war between India and Pakistan he was appointed the building engineer in both Murray College in Sialkot and the Mission Hospital in Sialkot from where, by placing himself near the border, he took part in activities against the country.

Thereafter in 1970 he was sent to Gujranwala Christian Technical Training Center as Principal and this area is also very important from the army point of view.

Consequently he stepped up his activities in this area and during this period he always visited Pasrur and Sialkot on one pretext or another and stayed with a girl friend of his wife and continued his spy activities.

These days he has again gone out of the country for specific instructions and will be returning in a few days time.

WE DEMAND THE GOVERNMENT INVESTIGATES THE ACTIVITIES OF THIS SPY CENTER !!

They have spread their spy ring network through their bearers and cooks who have access to the bearers and cooks of army officers for getting information.

It is surprising that the officers of the C.I.D. of the Pakistan Army have not so far given attention to this group working against the country and who have had a sort of leave to pursue their activities for the past many years. They are working day and night to harm our beloved country.

God and Evil—the ultimate struggle . . .
WHITE ANTS AND DAYBREAK

Gujranwala
August 1973

The Pakistan Government necessarily had to pay attention to reports coming in from the public about spies operating within Pakistan. It was inevitable that we would receive regular visits from the Criminal Investigation officers at provincial and federal level.

For years, I had to give monthly reports of all my movements outside the town and the reasons for my journeys. This was no bother; the authorities had a right to know what foreigners were up to within their borders.

Many of the investigating officers became familiar acquaintances. It did not take them long to figure out we were doing what we said we were doing.

They would do their preliminary investigations locally and then come to see me. The head clerk came to recognize them, and he knew what to do. He would ply them with sweet tea to put them in a good mood and then answer all their questions without hesitation as truthfully as he could. There was never anything to hide.

After one flurry of reports against me, there was a very zealous, new, young officer from the Federal office in Islamabad. Several afternoons, after school was over, he was questioning me for prolonged spells, referring to papers he carefully kept hidden from me. Finally, he closed up his file. He had only one question left.

"Mr. Old, how do you get rid of white ants?"

It so happened that I knew. Termites are a considerable menace and problem to any cellulose-based materials such as paper and wood. The two-foot thick mud walls in our house were host to colonies of white ants, and sometimes the only solution was to dig and excavate until the queen was located. However, one of the major oil companies was marketing two very effective chemicals that could either be injected or mixed with earth to form a mud barrier virtually impenetrable to white ants. I knew where these could be obtained, had used them successfully in various locations, and so I became the unpaid technical consultant to a small company of termite exterminators operated on the side by my C.I.D. interrogator.

Nothing came of all these investigations into spying for the simple reason there was nothing in any of the accusations.

It was probably in August 1973 that Marie, our missionary women neighbors at the United Bible Training Center, and I suddenly noticed the same thing, daybreak!

For almost three years, we had been living in an oppressive atmosphere of intrigue and hatred, of student strikes and staff corruption, of court cases and of confrontations, and of plain spiritual darkness, almost palpable.

Before we had come to Gujranwala, I had experienced this feeling, this atmosphere of foreboding darkness in one place only. Marie had served on a hospital train in Italy during the war and was showing me around some of her remembered places. We had visited Casa Materna, a children's home in Naples, and now this day we were visiting Pompeii. I never went beyond the entrance to the Roman village buried by an eruption of Vesuvius. I could not. There was a frightening atmosphere of darkness that was overwhelming and halted me in my tracks. I could not go on. It was like a wall ahead of me.

Gujranwala, ever since our arrival, had been like that. There was an overarching sense of present evil around the Technical School. Little occult symbols hung from some of the trees. I had come to realize that this was why Marie and I had been put in this place. It was not to accomplish good things, but to quite simply face down and try to deal with entrenched evil. It would not matter whether we survived the struggle, but it would matter that we were found faithful. We had not been able to sort things out with one great cleaning of the stables, but one by one, we had seen ongoing evil brought to light, and then we had dealt with the issues and individuals that were exposed.

All of a sudden, one morning we awoke, and it was daybreak!

It was amazing. The darkness had gone, vanished as though the denizens of hell had just gathered all their remnants together and had fled away before the rising dawn could catch them. It was as though after weeks of continuous monsoon clouds drenching the land, you awoke one morning to find almost unremembered clear blue skies. No particular incident appeared to have triggered this change, but Marie and I remarked upon it simultaneously and so did others. The darkness once gone never came back.

Oh, yes, the troubles continued; the accusations and the lawsuits continued. They became just a part of the normal life; other problems faced us, but the darkness was gone. Somehow, we had come through the dark wood and emerged out onto the other side, and we were, thank God, unscathed. Not only that, but the way forward was now clear to claim the blessings of God for this place, whatever they might be.

Working His Purposes Out . . .
NATIONALIZED!

Gujranwala
September 1972—June 1974

Even before Pakistan came into existence as a nation God saw that the Punjabi church which had seen such a great inpouring of His power a half a century earlier, would be beleaguered to the point of despair in 1972. That is the year when the ruling powers of the land would, in a stroke of the pen, take action to destroy the means by which it was nurtured and educated. The state is an Islamic state. Its founding principles guarantee the rights of minorities to worship, but not their right to be educated according to their faith and understanding.

We will see now His interventions on their behalf.

At the end of September 1972, the Government issued an order whereby, overnight, all previously independent schools and colleges in Pakistan were nationalized. The argument privately used to explain this was that it was the Government's attempt to bring to heel the fundamentalist Islamic institutions where opposition to the Government of Mr. Bhutto was fostered.

Few Christians believed this. It was "dominant Islam" using its power. It was absolute calamity. It was the Government's way to breach the founding guarantees concerning minorities. The lifeblood of Christians had been taken away. Christians maintained that only in their own institutions would and could Christians be treated fairly. What they understandably meant was "favorably."

I hurriedly arranged a Punjab wide seminar of Christian educationists and other leaders to meet at the Christian Technical Training Center in Gujranwala. It was well attended. Principals of Christian Colleges, headmasters, headmistresses, teachers, and community leaders presented excellent papers. Missionaries present tried to point to new opportunities, but of the national leaders, only Frank Khairullah of Murray College and Zeb Zaman of Kinnaird High School were willing to explore the challenges and opportunities of a radically different situation that had come overnight. For others, there were no relieving rays of light in total darkness. This was the coup de grace. All the efforts to build up the Christian community over more than a century had been brought to nothing. The Prime Minister's Minister for Religious Affairs was a Muslim priest who for some time had been warning that if the Christian drive towards education was not halted they would soon think themselves "as good as we are." Moderate Muslims dismissed the Minister's ranting as nonsense, but to Christians trapped in their powerlessness, he was speaking prophetically of the pogrom to come.

There had been an interesting exception. Schools that taught in the English medium rather than in Urdu or Punjabi were exempted from the nationalization order. This meant that many Catholic schools catering to upper-class children were excepted. This was seen as the Government taking care of its own back door since many children of Government officials attended such schools.

The Catholic policy was to run schools in English medium with high fees that created resources, enabling schools for poor Catholic children to be financed. Protestants ran few such schools, and among them, the wipe-out was almost total. The Sialkot Mission had operated over 60 village and rural schools—all gone. They had operated boarding schools for boys and for girls coming in from the villages. They were gone. They had operated schools of high caliber and good administration in the towns. All gone. Gordon College in Rawalpindi and Forman College in Lahore were gone, together with sister institutions Murray College in Sialkot and Kinnaird College, the women's college in Lahore.

I read the nationalization order carefully and decided to ignore its provisions.

Forms requiring immediate details of all moveable equipment, including ceiling and pedestal fans, (which were disappearing from the nationalized institutions rapidly), I put into the waste paper basket. I reassured the staff that they were still my employees and not government employees and thus still subject to my discipline. The staff, or some of them, halfway expected or hoped to see Mr. Old marched off one morning never to reappear. Missionary friends who had previously been involved in the institution wished us well, but warned it was a lost battle. You can't buck the Government.

However, the months passed by; the forms continued to come demanding more and more information and as usual there were no replies made.

My argument against compliance was a simple one, undoubtedly reinforced by that Cornish streak of stubbornness that said, "What can they do to me, anyway?" As a non-Pakistani, I undoubtedly had a greater freedom of maneuver than would have had a Pakistani defying his own Government and risking his own job and security. My argument was that the nationalization order was flawed. It had not nationalized all privately operated educational institutions. It had nationalized all privately operated schools and colleges.

And WE, alone among them all, were neither a school nor a college. We had *been* a school. We had been the Christian Technical School—BUT, and I had records to prove it, before the nationalization order had even been thought about, we had presciently changed our name to the Christian Technical Training Center. That had been in 1970. The boys were even wearing imported badges showing they attended not a school, not a college, but something other-named.

Semantics? Perhaps. But law is argued on the meanings of words, and I was prepared to take the Government to court should they try to impose illegal rule over the CTTC. The courts would act independently and arrive at judgment based upon law.

The potential significance of this tiny technical training center to the Christian community was becoming increasingly obvious.

I continued to receive imperatives from Lahore and from the Board of Technical Education, always delivered courteously.

We carried on. Then the showdown! I was called to a meeting with the various Technical Education officials at the Provincial Assembly Chambers to be chaired by the Deputy Speaker. Something or someone was going to have to give!

The Assembly Chambers in Lahore has the central site in the busy metropolis, where the major junction at the Mall occurs. Set well back from the junction, the building has a great dome. Between it and the Mall is an open area that once held the statue of Queen Victoria. The lofty central needle of the memorial to the Islamic conference and an open Q'ran has now replaced this.

The Deputy Speaker wasted little time. "Mr. Old, I understand you are not complying with the order to nationalize your school. Please tell me, why not?"

I explained. The order issued by the Government only nationalized schools and colleges. It did not affect me. I was neither a school nor a college. The Speaker laughed, as did the officials with him. "Mr. Old, you are playing with words. Do you not realize that it will take less than a half an hour in this very Assembly to pass legislation that will include your technical training center? That becomes no problem; you are merely splitting hairs. What else?"

I continued.

"Our center is not the normal kind of training center. We are not interested in academic results of themselves. You are. You will insist that the boys we educate already have a minimum level of education before they can be given admission. We instead tailor our programs to fit the needs of the individual boy. We have no minimum level of education. If necessary, we teach the boy how to read and write.

"You will also tell us how long the courses should be that we offer. We are focused on getting the boy up to a level where he can earn a living as a skilled tradesman in the marketplace. If he can achieve the standards we require more quickly than another, then he can graduate more quickly.

"Then you will tell us what it is we should be teaching. Syllabuses in an educational system such as you operate become frozen and eventually lose touch with the present day. We are constantly revising and altering our syllabuses to accommodate the changes happening around us.

"Then you will set the examinations that the boys need to pass to graduate. The examination systems become corrupt and emphasize eventually skills of reading and writing questions and answers. That does not suit the barely literate Punjabi carpenter who nevertheless can make a fine table or chair or the auto-mechanic whose skills lie in his fingertips that we all like to find for our cars.

"Furthermore you have made all the teachers of the schools you have nationalized civil servants. My authority to employ, dismiss, discipline, promote and to demand and insist upon excellence which enables our institution to flourish, would be gone.

"Yes, you can wipe us out of existence, but what have you gained?

"You need us, in just the way we are, doing unorthodox things, teaching in unproven ways, taking risks that bureaucrats can't, won't take, making mistakes that you, from your security, can laugh at and learn from—probing the lower limits at which we can give young men skills that will benefit themselves and their country and all the time not costing the Government a single rupee. We pursue the same ultimate goals you do, the welfare of our people."

I paused and looked around. Several were politicians, several were educationists, all within the system. They had given me a fair hearing, but my cause was not theirs.

"Will you please wait outside a few moments, Mr. Old? We will discuss what you have said."

When I was invited back and was seated, the Deputy Speaker said, "Mr. Old, we accept all your conditions. Now will you sign your agreement to nationalization? We will allow you to work uninterrupted, and you will not be interfered with, but you cannot avoid nationalization. The Director of Technical Education will be in contact with you. Thank you for coming. Good day."

I knew the promises of politicians change with the wind. I made one last effort. From back home in Gujranwala, I wrote to the technical education officer I was dealing with who had been present at the Assembly Chambers.

I listed the commitments that I understood had been made at the Assembly Chambers and concluded, "If you will confirm to me in writing that the commitments made at the Assembly Chambers are binding upon us all, then I will concur and comply with the nationalization order."

I received no reply by letter, but a request by phone to come in and see him.

"Mr. Old, do you realize you are asking me to commit suicide? You know how things work well enough. You have been here a long time. You know I can't sign such an undertaking. I would be finished. Totally finished. You are a Christian, Mr. Old. Do you have faith? Yes? Then start walking by it!"

I smiled and sighed. He was right. He didn't dare sign confirmation of any agreement. It had to be operated by mutual trust. Did we dare? Interesting that a Muslim, and a man I respected, should remind *me* about walking by faith. What he had expressed was an ultimatum and there were no choices.

I excused myself. "I have to leave; 'I have promises to keep.'"

He amended the quotation for me with a smile, "and miles to go before you sleep."

Somehow, across our divides, with the help of Robert Frost, our souls had touched. How would things work out now?

THE SPHERE

Not enough simply to be aware.
Awareness is not linear nor planar
But spherical
And we the center of our sphere
Receiving calls from everywhere.
Eternity speaks through whispers
As well as in the thunder.
Infinity draws near and sings surprises
In the sheer simplicity of trivia.

Working His Purposes Out . . .
WRITE A BOOK!

Gujranwala
June 1974

S oon after the graduation ceremonies at the school for missionary children in June of 1974, Marie left for England with Colin. Both carried as hand-luggage some precious carpets that had the ability to transform a house into a home. Tim was already in England staying with his grandmother and involved in the servicing of church and cathedral organs in the south of England.

I followed one month later. We moved down to Gibbins Brook Farm, where my brother, Tony, had been working flat-out to get the old house ready for our occupation. Marie had been looking forward with both anticipation and some nervousness at getting into shape the first home that was ever really and truly hers. What a challenge that promised to be! I was not going to be able to help much, for it was going to be an interrupted furlough. I would return twice to Pakistan before my final return in June of 1975. Marie would remain behind in England for what she would later say were the most difficult years of her life.

In early September, I returned to Gujranwala in time to help write the exams, have graduation, and begin new admissions—more boys than ever were applying and being admitted. Brend was running the school with his usual élan and enjoying having his head. There was no difficulty in getting back to Marie in time for Christmas. We planned to go to the States in April for mission interpretation in the Synod of Washington-Alaska, our home Synod. I promised Brend and Marjet that I would be back before the end of June so that they could plan their own furlough from July.

Towards the end of March came the telegram: "SCHOOL NATIONALIZED RETURN IMMEDIATELY BREND". Just five words. Within three days, I was on the plane. I could do nothing, of course, but I needed to be there with them, the boys, the staff, Brend and his family. It couldn't be for very long. I had a long-standing speaking engagement at a Seekers' college-age conference at Wanapum on the Columbia River in the States on April 8. I could only be there in Guj one week.

I reflected that we had two and a half years of freedom more than all the other schools and colleges so we had been able to help a lot more kids. In the end though, it had proved right, "You can't buck the Government."

However, God had other plans!

Brend met me at the airport in Lahore. It was Sunday. I would have to leave the following Sunday. He told me that he had been informed by the Director of Technical Education that the school was nationalized under the provisions of the Nationalization ordinance. Brend thought that there might just be a hope, if I could see the Minister of Education and persuade him, they might review their order. This was just straw into the wind.

"No, Brend," I said. "This has gone beyond that. There is no way a Christian missionary is going to persuade a Pakistani Minister to act in that way when, after all, we have been the only ones standing out against their previous order. Think of the pressure they have already had from the alumni of the colleges they nationalized, and it's made no difference. No, the only hope we have is our certainty that God has an especial purpose for this place, and we both know it. He's going to have to do something quite remarkable this time if we are to escape."

In Chapel the next morning at seven, I spoke to the boys. They were glad to see me back.

I put to them a question.

"Boys, who does this school belong to?"

They didn't know how to reply since I hadn't given them a lead how to respond.

I helped them. "Does it belong to me?"

Yes, that's right. It belongs to Baba Old; he's the Principal so it must belong to him. "Han, ji."

"No, you are wrong; it doesn't belong to me. Does it belong to the staff?" I pointed to the staff sitting in the front rows.

Yes, that's right. They teach us so it must belong to them; that's the answer Baba is after. "Han, ji."

"No, you are wrong. It doesn't belong to them either. Does it belong to you?" I swept my hand towards them all.

Oh, so that's what Baba is after. Yes, of course it belongs to us. After all, if we weren't here there would be no school, would there? "Han ji."

"Wrong again; it doesn't belong to any of us! It belongs to your children and their children and their children and their children. And if we do not prevail with God, who is the only One who can save this school, not one of them will have the opportunity you are having to be attending their own school and their own chapel for worship before school each morning.

"I am going to ask you to spend the day with me in prayer and fasting. Just gather in your groups, in your dormitories, and in your classes. There will be no teaching today. I do not want you to do this reluctantly. The cooks will prepare the meal at lunch and this evening, and they will serve anyone who comes for a meal without any question or criticism. But I am asking you to go to prayer today with me and to fast today, not for yourselves, but for your children and for our people, for there is no other place left to us now except this place, and we have almost lost it."

I dismissed the chapel. The boys were silent and serious as they left. Not one meal was served from the prepared meals in the kitchen all day. All over the campus little groups, staff, and students were gathered in prayer and subdued conversation.

At about 2:30 A.M. the following morning, I suddenly awoke. Where was I? In Sellindge? No, back in my own bedroom in Guj. I struggled into wakefulness.

A voice spoke to me. A man's voice. Urgent.

"Ken, you must write a book, and this is what you must put in it." The voice gave me a list of chapter headings. I switched on the bedside light. There was, of course, no one else to be seen. I grabbed my spectacles, slipped out of bed, went over to my desk, and wrote down in pencil the chapter headings I was given. I went back to bed and fell immediately asleep.

I awoke at the usual time, a little before five. I went to the desk, rubbing the sleep out of my eyes and looked at the scrap of paper. It wasn't a dream. The chapter headings were all written there. All related to what we were doing at the Christian Technical Training Center, the boys we were doing it with, and how we were doing it. How we could help the poor and disadvantaged move into opportunity for prosperity by their own efforts.

Brend was somewhat surprised that at a time when some decisive activity was obviously called for and time was so limited that I was going to write a book, but he took it in his stride. I must have it written and completed and a copy in my hands by Friday morning when I would take it into Lahore. This would be the last working day of the week and my last chance. He did not question the event leading up to the decision. By eight o'clock, after chapel, the typist and I were at work in a makeshift office in the house. Occasionally, I would go over to the school to gather information and outline and give data for graphs that needed to be drawn. All the help I could use was there at my disposal.

I titled the book *Community Development through Craft Skills*. It indicated only eight percent of Punjabi Christians were literate, compared with double that number for Muslims. On average, the monthly pay of fifty percent of the parents of students was less than £10 ($15). Step-by-step, the 15 goals of the development plan of the school were analyzed, goals focused on assisting the poor. I derived and shared lessons that had been learned. In all the change and turmoil of the early seventies, which experienced very considerable student unrest, there had been no discipline problems, even from the Muslim students. In fact, some students had transferred in from other schools and colleges in order to benefit from the discipline at CTTC.

David, the typist, hammered away as the hand-written drafts were given to him. He was way ahead of me, waiting. By Thursday noon, the writing was done. David had worked up a cover sheet. By evening, the mimeographed copies had been stapled and compiled. It was a poor apology for the glossy professional productions that can be achieved these days, but it was done. Now to deliver it. One day left.

Working His Purposes Out . . .
GO AND SEE THE SECRETARY!

Lahore
March 1975

I drove the 45 miles into the center of Lahore alone. Behind me, I knew people were praying, but the odds that I should succeed in even meeting anyone who would give me a hearing were very long. I also had a shopping list in Brandreth Road, the electrical and iron-mongery supplies street, for Brend. As usual, there were several horrible bus and truck accidents along the Grand Trunk Road to sober even the most light hearted, had I been feeling that way.

I had been to the office of the Minister of Education previously and had been amazed at how almost all of the minister's time had been taken up with dealing with supplicants of one kind or another, for appointment, for transfer, or for promotion. How on earth did the poor man ever find time for any work?

I drove straight down the Mall to the Minister's office. It was not in the Secretariat, the complex at the Tee junction of the Upper and Lower Mall, which housed the principal administrative offices of the Punjab Government.

The Punjab was the largest of the four States—Baluchistan, Sindh, and the Frontier Province were the others—that made up Pakistan. When we had first come to Pakistan, the population was about 39 million; as I write, it is about 150 million. Yet in 1975, the population was probably about 84 million. Sixty percent of the population of the whole country was in the Punjab, and half that population was 16 or younger. That gives an idea of the educational load facing the Punjab government.

Right away, as I approached the minister's office, I knew we had failed in our efforts to save the school. It had been at best a remote chance. Even that was now gone. There was no activity; there were no messengers sitting outside the door. An inquiry confirmed the end of our hopes. The Minister was in Islamabad meeting with the Prime Minister and would be away several days. So much for that! The book had been an exercise in futility.

No point in crying over spilt milk. I shopped for switches, carpenters' tools, hinges and locks in Brandreth Road, ate a bowl of lentils from a food-stall in the road, and then went back up to the Mall to complete shopping there before heading back to Gujranwala.

As I was walking towards the travel agent to confirm my flight home to England, a voice spoke to me. It was not a human voice but it was a voice that I had learned to recognize. It bypassed my ears and went into my mind. Such a voice I heard but rarely, yet I knew it did not originate in my own mind. "Go and see the Secretary of Education!"

The Secretary of Education? Who gets in to see the Secretary of Education without an appointment? I kept on walking.

Again the voice insisted, "Go and see the Secretary of Education!" Look, this is silly. It's three o'clock; the Secretariat closes at two. Even if I could get in through the main gate, there will be no one there in his office. I kept on walking towards the travel agent, away from the Secretariat.

This time, the third time, it was an order. "GO AND SEE THE SECRETARY OF EDUCATION!!!" I turned in my tracks. This was going to be a stupid waste of time that I did not have to spare!

I parked the car up a side street and walked down to the main gates. These were always guarded by a squad of police. I knew they would not let me in without an appointment or permission from inside. I knew no one within the Secretariat who would instruct that I be allowed to enter. As I crossed the Lower Mall, my heart raced with amazement. Where were the guards? Over the next 15 years, I went to the Secretariat many times. Always a full squad of gate police, checking cars, checking pedestrians, was present. Never did I encounter an absence of guards, YET on this one critical occasion, there was not one single gate guard in evidence. The whole of the Secretariat was incredibly unguarded. What had happened, I had no idea.

I did not hesitate in my stride. I walked in as though I knew where I was going and as though I had every right to be there. I turned to the right into the education complex. I saw, to my surprise, sitting on a bench along the corridor, an office messenger. He was sitting outside the office of the Secretary of Education. This was amazing. All the staff had gone home. The Secretariat was closed. There was no activity; the place was lifeless. Yet here, sitting outside the Secretary's office, was a messenger!

"Where is the Secretary?" I asked.

He nodded his head towards the door.

This was no time for questions. "Please will you give him this card?"

He waited for the bell inside to ring its summons. When he returned, he nodded for me to enter and resumed his patient seat.

I knew immediately as I entered the room that I might have gone further than I thought, but I had still lost the battle. Behind a huge desk was a kindly looking middle-aged man. To either side of him on the desk were two great piles of bureaucratic files, each tied with a pink cotton tie. The situation was obvious. This poor man had had a horrible morning. Like the Minister on my earlier visit, supplicants of one kind or the other had overwhelmed him. Hardly a single piece of the work that he had intended to accomplish had he achieved. When two o'clock had come, he had instructed his office peon to remain and had been making some progress in moving files from his right hand pile to the left hand side of his desk.

And now the enemy, the public, in the form of me, had even discovered him in his own private time and was invading that too.

He looked up as I came in and motioned me to sit down. He completed the file he was studying, tied the tapes, and placed it on the left hand pile. He looked at the visiting card to ascertain my name and said wearily, with the weight of exhaustion in his tone, "And what do you want, Mr. Old?"

"Sir, I don't *want* anything. I want to give you something, and I want to tell you something, and then I will go. Here is a small book. If you can find time, read it, for it suggests a different more effective way of teaching people. And the thing I want to tell you is this, you are a failure!"

He eased himself back in his chair. I had his full attention.

"What do you mean, I'm a failure?"

Working His Purposes Out . . .

THE FAILURE

Lahore
March 1975

"**W**hat do you mean, I'm a failure?"

I launched straight in.

"Sir, you have, probably apart from the Prime Minister, the single most important job in the whole country. The children of the country are our future. The Punjab has the bulk of those children, and you are charged to see to their education. They are wonderful material. Where in the world is there better raw material to build a nation than here with our own children?

"All over the Punjab they are waiting, wanting to be educated. Their minds are full of dreams. They can't articulate their hopes, and if they do they are not heard. They want, want desperately, to understand the world in which they live and why it is like it is. They want to know whether their lives mean anything, and whether, by their own efforts, they can have any goal beyond the one of mere survival.

"Our villages are full of the potential of a great nation. They are like tiny buds waiting for warmth and nurture that will enable them to flower and bloom and create beauty and happiness, but they do not have the power to create that nurture and warmth themselves. That has to come from a previous generation. They have imaginations that need to be fired to the stars and across the seas and into the inmost parts of nature and of knowledge. They need to be charged with fantasy and a sense of the impossible to be striven for; they are waiting to be excited about the process of learning and of growing.

"Do you know what we are doing? We are taking those tiny buds, hundreds, thousands, nay hundreds of thousands of them, and we are grinding them underfoot into nothing in the dust of our own soil. And YOU are the man in charge of the process, and you are destroying their dreams, and they have a right to expect better!"

The words had been tumbling over themselves, and I reined them in and halted them and was silent.

We looked at each other for a long moment.

"You are wrong, Mr. Old. You are wrong. I am not a complete failure; I am a complete success."

He leaned forward, earnestly, not angrily.

"You see, our goal is failure—and we hit the target 100 percent of the time! I have been Secretary of Education for six months. I have not visited one single educational institution during that six months because I know you are right. Our population is bursting, we need hundreds more schools and many more colleges, and yet what are we to do? Are we to multiply the examples of failure that are all around us? Is that the best we can do? Yet that apparently is as far as our minds can take us. Tell me about your school, Mr. Old."

I did so.

I told him I knew little about education; I was a civil engineer not an educationist. I had, therefore, little to forget and a burden for the poor on my heart, and it started from there.

How did we best help them and equip them to achieve for themselves?

We were now giving preference to the boys with limited means or limited schooling, preferring villagers to urban dwellers, failures rather than successful students, boys from the lowest levels of society. Our criterion for admission was need, not ability. We were lowering admission age levels by two years. We were developing extensive new facilities, scholarship programs, and dormitories. We were reducing course lengths to the minimum compatible with the skills needed to be learned.

We were teaching more and more in Punjabi as well as Urdu and reducing the English content of the courses. Because of the paucity of texts in those languages, we were developing our own. We were conducting examinations quarterly with high minimum pass marks to quickly identify and help the boys having trouble. We were insisting on the highest quality of teaching, selecting staff from the best of our own graduates and running concurrent staff training programs.

We were emphasizing the acquisition of manual skills rather than theoretical knowledge; we were eliminating all material from syllabi not directly involved with employable skills or human and spiritual growth and development. We could not afford the luxury of broad, general education.

Our goal was one hundred graduates a year, but already we were exceeding that goal. We were watching the job market closely to quickly match training to new job opportunities. We had graduations and admissions twice a year, and no long summer holidays. Boys studied within a strongly disciplined environment.

We were, as we had expected, observing exceptionally high motivation, and there were few discipline problems.

The Secretary looked at his watch as I finished. He had an appointment with the Minister of Finance to discuss the budget, but he wished to continue the conversation. Would I meet him for coffee? He described the location of his residence. He would see me there at eight o'clock this evening.

When I met him there, he had obviously skimmed the book I had brought. It was on his coffee table. He took me out to dinner at a restaurant and then back to his house. We talked until after midnight.

I had designed and built, as an offshoot of the housing project, a village primary school of concrete and brick in the shape of a cross where none of the four classrooms had more than two walls. It could be shipped out to any village on our local trucks and be erected within three days. There was a sample at the school. He was very interested.

As I left, he confirmed he would be coming up to the center tomorrow, Saturday, to see things for himself.

I woke Brend up when I returned to the compound; he would see to getting things ready for the visit and then I went to bed.

The school was spotless. Brend had pulled out all the stops on getting the school clean and tidy. The workshops already were tidy; we had just had a board meeting and a graduation. Everything was always spotless when that happened. I walked around the campus with Brend to check; not a thing was out of place. Then we waited . . . and waited . . . and waited . . . waited all day. We let the boys go, and those who were going home were allowed to leave. Night fell, and with it, the realization came anew that I was going to England tomorrow. Despite the encouragements of yesterday, we were still nationalized, and would there be anything to come back to?

It took more than a week for Brend's first letter to arrive. Marie had been as disappointed as I had when I returned having no encouragement for her. She had been reluctant to go to Gujranwala from Taxila but had quickly reacted to the opportunities to use her gifts that were all around her. She, too, would miss Gujranwala if a consequence of nationalization would, as seemed possible, be my replacement as principal.

Brend's letter was brief. The Secretary had been driving up to Guj in his own car on his day off, Saturday. No official car. His car had broken down, and it had taken him much of the day to get himself and his car back to Lahore. Instead, he had come early on Monday morning. Brend had shown him around the school and even the dormitories; he had been fascinated with the village school design. He had lunch with Brend and Marjet.

On Tuesday, the Director of Technical Education for the Punjab had come from Lahore, had delivered a message from the Secretary, and he, too, was shown around the school.

The message was brief. Marie and I looked at each other with amazement.

"Tell Mr. Old that on no account will we nationalize his school and will he please assist us in the development of our own plans for the improvement of education in the Punjab."

What a wonderful God!

One of the precious fruits of what has happened is the participation and sense of ownership in this remarkable "about face" by the Government that the staff and students take to themselves. Their children will bless them for this; for have they not prevailed with God? Their prayer and fasting have saved this school, saved it for those who will follow after. There is renewed vigor in their own personal walks with Him who answers the prayers of His people!

God and Evil—the ultimate struggle . . .
BREND

November 2, 1975

M arie was in England with the boys, longing with all her heart that she could be back home in Pakistan with me. In mid-September though, she was encouraged by a visit from Brend and Marjet Kuyvenhoven. They had planned only a two-month furlough because they knew I would be alone. I had written behind their backs to their Mission Board in Holland, urging them to insist that they take a three-month break. I could manage.

When they returned, they rebuked me for that extra month, but it was with love, and they had been blessed by their extra time at home.

The two letters I wrote those first days of November 1975 I wrote with a breaking heart.

November 3rd   Gujranwala
Dear Friends,
Some of you who will read this were with us just a week ago at one of the happiest times in the 75 year-old history of the Christian Technical Training Center. We were dedicating new buildings and new equipment and at the same time graduating 45 new craftsmen.
It was a truly happy day, with much spiritual blessing.
Six days later, on Sunday morning early, just two days ago, tragedy struck. About 1:45 A.M., thieves broke into the home of Brend and Marjet Kuyvenhoven. Brend had been here almost nine years, and largely as a result of his efforts, the new training center had come into being.
The thieves entered through a ventilator above a verandah and into the living room. After ransacking this and a room where two of the three young children were sleeping, they entered the main bedroom. They were in the room for some little while, taking a jewelry box to the living room and removing its most valuable contents before again going to the bedroom.
What next followed is uncertain. One thief removed Brend's watch and the alarm clock from the bedside table near him. Brend awakened. The man moved to the wardrobe and with an armful of clothing had probably reached the door when Brend, slipping quietly out of bed, grappled with him. In another corner of the room was a second man with an automatic pistol. At least five shots were fired.
Marjet awoke to the sound of a fusillade of shots and men shouting

but within seconds the men had escaped through the back door and over the neighboring wall. She saw no one.

Brend was able to call out to Marjet before he became unconscious. He had been mortally injured in his leg, back and abdomen.

Marjet closed the doors against the cold night air, protected Brend with a covering and ran for help next door where a Dutch guest was staying. Brend was carried as quickly as possible on a string bed to the nearby civil hospital but soon after arrival there he expired.

The funeral that day was a triumph of Christian hope.

As the news spread Brend and Marjet's friends, the 'little' people, laborers, trainees from the villages, women folk from the crowded dwellings nearby soon far outnumbered his own colleagues and his missionary friends. Muslims and Christians alike wondered in tears how this could have happened to one who had no enemies.

The chapel was too small. The service was held in the gymnasium. Wonderfully strengthened, Marjet testified to the continuing love and renewing grace of Jesus.

None could recall a funeral procession like it.

The choir of trainees from the Christian Technical Training Center singing 'Walking in the light with Jesus' led a procession of more than 2,000 who followed Brend. Women, who usually stay behind, remained with the others. The air was laden with the dust from many feet. Buses and tongas pulled to one side and stopped. Men who are so separated by church struggles they cannot talk to each other were companions behind him. Muslims and Christians shared in carrying him. In the crowded little cemetery at Khokherke, Brend was laid to rest as Roman Catholic sisters sang

> *"Rejoice in the Lord always,*
> *and again I say Rejoice . . .*
> *Rejoice, Rejoice . . ."*

Ben Bavinck, of Brend and Marjet's own church, who was here that day will accompany Marjet and the children back to Holland in a few days. The children, Simon 7, Heleen 5 and Reinier 3 are behaving wonderfully. The family had returned from Holland just one month ago.

Last week we were praising, as a staff group, for the clear signs of a turning to God among the staff and trainees. This morning, as we reassembled after the special holiday awarded to the boys on the dedication day, we met again in the gymnasium. More than a hundred trainees and staff signed pledges of commitment to Jesus Christ and a new walk with Him.

Do be constant in your prayer for Marjet in the days to come. Do pray for us all here. We can't replace Brend and we shall grow differently because he is not here. Pray we all grow towards Him individually and together.

Brend's favourite verses from the Bible were 1 Thessalonians 5:18 and 2 Corinthians 5:17

> *Therefore, if any man be in Christ, he is a new creature:*
> *old things are passed away; behold, all things are become new.'*
> Ken Old

Several days later I was able to add a little more to those brief details.

An American woman said to me "Never have I felt more like a Christian than when I walked in the thick dust of Brend's last journey with so many others. I seemed to glimpse the Calvary Road."

Streams of grief stricken Christians have been coming, often over long distances, to give us the strength of shared grief. "He was ours, he loved us and we loved him because he loved us." All strife between various factions of the Christian community has merged into an uncommon pain that all are sharing.

Workmen I tried to pay today for digging and preparing Brend's grave all through last Sunday, both Christian and Muslim together, refused. They are poor but not that poor! Brend was theirs!

And who is this Brend whose passing has reduced a whole community to an appalled sense of loss?

This morning in chapel the technical trainees, his boys, nearly 200 of them, mostly from the villages, were given opportunity to make a token of their remembrance in a gift for Marjet, Brend's wife. They were limited to the equivalent of one Dutch florin. But the lists are full, every boy, and many oversubscribed. They needed some way to show what they felt. Brend, you see, was theirs.

On Tuesday when the Center reopened in the dusty Punjab plains of Pakistan after a day's holiday, many trainees learned for the first time of Sunday's tragedy.

Brend had immense energy. For nine years not only had the training center in which he worked been steadily growing. He also had been growing in many ways and carrying others with him as he grew.

In the early years since he came from Holland, he was building up a department of auto-mechanics. When in 1970 he became vice-principal and chief instructor, his gifts of organization flowered. He was assiduous in detail and tireless in pursuing excellence. He was persuaded that Punjabi boys, given hope and opportunity, were as good as any anywhere and he was out to 'liberate the captives and set them free.'

And how they responded! As admission requirements were lowered from ten to eight years of schooling we discovered how highly motivated these youngsters were. Graduating standards and achievements rose rather than diminished. The graduates this fall averaged 69% in their examinations, higher than ever before.

What they learned however was not only manual skills but something much more important. They learned what it is like to live for a while in a 'loving' community, in a 'nourishing' community, and they became men who are able to stand for the right because they have seen it and known it. Brend became a glowing example for them. He played volleyball with them. He prayed with them. He listened to their problems and shared them. They were important to him, not as a group but as individuals, as younger brothers.

Through the years Brend himself was changing. His anger at the inequality of society became increasingly mellowed by a gentleness of increasingly shared experiences.

A little over a year ago Brend and Marjet experienced the reality of 'If any man be in Christ he is a new creature.' Almost it was as if he were seeing like a child on tiptoe into a room of breathtaking treasures. The sense of wonder he brought back never left him. Every experience, every struggle, every challenge and every opportunity for him now had to be related to, and be seen in the light of, a discovered splendour. From thence forward for him the burning bush still burned and the glory of the Lord filled his house. He walked and lived in a sense of the Presence of the Holy Spirit.

It was as though there was a purging away and a preparing for what was to come.

We who worked with Brend suddenly realised how far and in such short time he had sped ahead of us. His smile would suddenly flash on a situation that perplexed us and he would bring us into a different perspective that brought a light he had captured to play upon us all.

A few days before his death we discussed Brend's tasks ahead. He was to be the lynch pin around which the school would develop and his priorities he had clear—to enhance the quality of the boys' lives in the hostels and to improve the quality of teaching. He did not see the boys as students from 7 am to 2 P.M. but as golden opportunities sent by God to be polished in every facet of their lives.

These were the building blocks of the church and they were to be fashioned fit for the Lord's service. Little gave him more joy than sending busloads of boys off to 'Camp of Blessing' for a week's teaching in the Murree mountains—the boys and staff who came back just days ago with a strange deepened joy and commitment ran to tell him of it first of all.

In the week before Brend's death we were caught up in a wonderful sense of expectancy. In chapel on Monday morning Mushtaq, a young electri-

cal instructor, told of his blessing at Camp Mubarak and of committing his life to follow Jesus. Our hearts were strangely stirred and we felt a strange Holy Presence among us. We met twice more that day for prayer. The following day chapel spilled over for an extra hour and almost fifty of the trainees and staff committed themselves to Christ and remained most of the morning for teaching.

The whole week was a week of blessing.

Then, on Sunday, November 2nd, tragedy struck and Brend is gone. He was only thirty-four.

Brend's relationship with his staff colleagues was of unbounded confidence in them and trust that called forth a like response.

We shall miss him. There can be no replacement for one like him. We shall grow differently because he is not here. He belonged to all of us and we are proud he called us 'friend'.

> *These strangers, who cross our paths*
> *All too infrequently,*
> *Have been enabled*
> *By the splendour and might of Him*
> *Working within themselves*
> *To know the One who calls them*
> *To the mysterious way.*
> *Reality has broken through*
> *And they reflect His likeness.*
> *His promises are the door*
> *And through it they escape*
> *The tainting and corrupting*
> *Of a world that is sick.*
> *Instead, thrusting ahead,*
> *They are come to share*
> *The very being of God.*

(Excerpt: Roses for a Stranger—2 Peter 1:3–4)

The years have passed.

Heleen, my favorite five-year-old, is a nurse. She has married a doctor, and they have a son and a daughter. Simon is also married, to Marjolein, and they too have a son and a daughter. He has been back on a couple of occasions as a volunteer at the technical training center. He has had a spell in Guatemala and in Tanzania. Reinier is studying theology in Amsterdam. Marjet never remarried, continues to have a radiant Christian witness, and long ago forgave those who took her husband from her.

God and Evil—the ultimate struggle. . . .
REFLECTIONS

December 1975

We have reached, with Brend's death and just before it, the creation of the Society for Community Development, a turning point. Our path now will be different because Brend is not here to help guide us. The next 15 years will see large blessings but only because of these years that have just passed. We shall broaden our activities into other areas of human concern and the flow of the river of activity will widen from a rocky torrent into an estuary.

What are some of the lessons these past five hard years have taught me?

I was to observe ten steps in the struggle I have narrated. Only much later in hindsight was I to recognize them as features of Christ's own life and ministry. What did young John say of Him?

> *For this purpose the Son of God was manifested,*
> *that he might destroy the works of the devil.*
> ***I John 3:8b***

The steps in the struggle were:

1. The primary evil is entrenched within the status quo.
2. *You* are vulnerable.
3. *You* are expendable.
4. *Your* friends will fall away.
5. *You* can't use the devil's weapons.
6. The way to meet evil is head-on.
7. Hold on, stand fast. It is for this you are here.
8. It gets still darker, but the darkest point of the night will be followed by dawn.
9. Let God work.
10. The victory is His. Enjoy the blessing.

At the fall 1975 meeting of the Christian Technical Training Center Board, it moved to broaden its ability to respond to the opportunities around it. It re-formed itself and reconstituted itself as the Society for Community Development. Its goal was now "to assist the Christian community in its growth and development by witnessing to the nature of true Christian service in such a way that this community shall be encouraged to relate its life and work to the Will of God.'"

The decks had been cleaned and cleared. The way forward was now open to the unknown seas ahead.

The Way He Works—The timing is always perfect . . .
ASIF RABBANI

Taxila, 1969

John Haines is a young American working with us. I have sent him off into the boondocks far from civilization, up into the mountains to help get water into the village of Jhokund.

John Haines' diary, Sunday, June 22, 1969

Back at Taxila (from Jhokund). Asif, a 27-year-old man who converted to Christianity four years ago is here to see Ken with a problem. He was unable to find a Christian girl to marry so he found a Muslim who was a relative. After the wedding he was accused by her parents and his father of pretending to have returned to Islam when all he did was to say nothing. He has been disowned and beaten by his father, ostracized by his old community. The Pakistan church doesn't treat converts well because it thinks they are after the Mission's money. His questions are, as his wife is now living with her parents, how does he get her back and guarantee her a financial security. His ability to get work and retain it is reduced by the fact that he is a Christian. If his wife goes to live with him her parents will disown her and they, the young couple, will be deprived of their wedding gifts and dowry.

––––––––––––––––

Gujranwala, 1974
I had given Asif an introductory letter that was intended to assist him to get work.

I have a short letter on my desk:

Dear Uncle,
I gave the letter to Mr. Wolf yesterday but he slipped me with lame excuses. Do pray for the problem for it is third month going on. I am fearing it would not be a cause created by Satan to spoil my testimony for Jesus Christ.
Yours in His Love, Asif

It was from the Qadiani sect of Islam that Asif had come. Convicted of sin and his need for Christ by an itinerant Muslim convert preacher, he was rejected by his father and ejected from his home near the Indian border. His wife, a cousin, returned to her family and is divorced from him. His search for work has been unsuccessful but his deep commitment shines through in his gentle spirit and intensity of faith.

Lahore, 1976

Asif and I have met in Lahore. He is staying for a while in the servant quarters at St. Andrews Church in Lahore. He is planning to go to Karachi to sell Bibles. He tells me he has stopped smoking. I am surprised because he has been addicted to tobacco. Tears come to his eyes as he explains, "One night, Uncle, I had a dream:

I saw Jesus. It was not Jesus, the carpenter of Nazareth. It was Jesus glorified. He was unutterably holy, shining with the light of the sun. He was pure beyond words. He held out his arms to me and I knew I was unworthy to approach Him but I knew He loved me. That was all. The dream faded and then I awoke.

"From that moment I have not smoked a cigarette, I know He desires me to be pure in my body also as well as in my thought and belief."

Lahore, 1980

I am shopping in Brandreth Road in Lahore. This is always a full day's work, and often I do not leave the street until evening, having eaten chicken curry or lentils from a street stall or a restaurant near the electricians' shops. Brandreth Road is a wonderful street. It sells tools, electrical equipment, locks, hardware, hinges, screws, nails, pumps, rolls of plastic, window screen, and cable. It sells almost everything that would be consumed by a school that is training technicians and craftsmen or that will be used in the buildings that house them.

I am well known amongst the shopkeepers. After many years acquaintance, they will trust me with anything. There is a fascinating interplay of shrewdness and trust among the traders; they seem to act as agents for each other using little scribbled notes that somehow sort themselves out.

By the end of a shopping day, I am almost afloat with soft drinks and tea that I have been plied with in shop after shop. In one shop, I forgot my briefcase loaded with many bundles of ten rupee notes that I intended to spend. Several hours later, I returned to look for it. It was where I had left it; the shopkeeper had been guarding it for me. He would not have thought of looking in it or taking anything from it although it was loaded with money. He knew it was mine and that I'd be sure to be back for it. Marie would shrug. "You didn't leave your money AGAIN!" Although this almost became a habit with her forgetful husband, I never lost any money this way.

It is about 9:30 in the morning. I am in the small hardware store beside the Alley of Locks. Suddenly, out of the blue, I am hit by a thought. *Go and find Asif Rabbani*! It is a peremptory thought, almost an order. I know this is not a 'voice' in the sense of hearing something externally uttered. Job uses the phrase "the arrows of the Almighty." This feels like one of those. I ignore the thought and carry on with my order for tower bolts. Again, more insistent and more commanding. "Go and find Asif Rabbani." Asif Rabbani is in Karachi, 800 miles away. This is ridiculous! "GO AND FIND Asif Rabbani." This is stupid, utterly stupid. Asif Rabbani is 800 miles away, and I have a full day's shopping ahead of me that will allow no interruptions if I am to complete my list.

I excuse myself from the shopkeeper with a promise to be back a little later and complete the order. I walk back to the car. I haven't thought about Asif in months. We've been out of touch since he went to Karachi. Where on earth should I start? This is ridiculous! I'd better go to St. Andrew's Church and start my enquiries there. I turn up Empress Road and pull into the church compound. A gardener hoeing a flower plot looks up as I drive in. I'll start with him, and then I'll go and see the pastor, if he is there.

"Do you remember, mali ji, some time ago, some years ago, a young man stayed here in the servants' quarters before he went off to Karachi? His name was Asif Rabbani."

"Yes, sir, I remember. He's over there!" He points towards the servants' quarters at the back of the church. I am staggered that he is here now. The gardener takes me over to the first servant's quarter and points. The double door is closed, not latched outside, signaling someone is inside. I walk over to it and knock and wait.

Let me go back a short while in time and tell you Asif's story.

Several days previously, he had come back from Karachi, penniless. The pastor, an Australian missionary, had allowed him to stay in the servant's quarter as he had previously. In the quarter was a string bed without a mattress and a crudely cobbled together rickety table. Asif had no money. He did not want to beg, but for several days, he had no food.

That morning, reluctant and desperate, he had knocked at the pastor's door and asked if the pastor could let him have some money to buy food. Sid is a man of prayer and great spiritual qualities. "Yes, of course, Asif. You need food. Let me first go and seek the Lord's leading. Sit here; I'll be back in a moment."

Sid was longer than a moment, but when he came back, it was with a puzzled look on his face. "Asif, I can't pretend to understand what it means, but I have no leading to give you anything. I'm genuinely sorry, but that's where it is."

Asif went slowly back to his room. What was happening? Didn't God care? He did not doubt the pastor. He was not a man to use the Lord as an excuse. He sat slowly on his bed. What to do now? He thought of the friends he knew who might help. There weren't many. Uncle Ken and Aunt Marie would help him; he knew that. If he had the bus fare, he would go the 45 miles to Gujranwala to see them but perhaps they might not be there. Perhaps they were on furlough. Perhaps they were in Taxila.

He searched in the small bag that contained all his earthly possessions. Here was an envelope, here a sheet of paper. Pulling the table close, he addressed a letter "Dear Uncle Ken and Auntie Marie, . . ." and as he wrote his heart began to break and tears began to fall. Wiping the tears back, begging them to come to see him soon, they would find him at St. Andrew's Church; he signed his name.

He put the letter in the envelope, addressed and sealed it, and then as the extent of his poverty burst upon him, his heart just broke. He didn't even have ten paise, less than a penny, for a stamp!

What was God doing! He'd lost his family, he'd lost his wife, and he'd lost everything and everyone he held dear. He had gone hungry and thirsty. What did God want from him? His very life and breath? He didn't even have a stamp to post a letter. He was kneeling beside his bed, his body wracked with sobbing when a knock came at the door. He wiped away his tears with his sleeve and opened the door.

A moment of stupefied silence. Then a look of great joy came across his face, and he flung his arms around me, sobbing and saying over and over, "What a wonderful God, what a wonderful God! I asked Him for a stamp, and He sent me a reply-paid telegram; what a wonderful God!"

The Way He Works—The timing is always perfect . . .
PAUL WHITEHOUSE'S GIFT

December 1981

Marie and I went on furlough in September 1980. This time we went to the States. It was Marie's first furlough back home since 1968 and only her third since Mac's death in 1953. Normally, the area assigned us for speaking engagements was the Washington and Alaska area, but part of this time, the first three months of 1981, we spent in the Michigan/Ohio area of our church.

Several times I was able to return to Pakistan to help Bob Thomlinson, the English bursar, and his colleagues who were running the technical center in my absence.

Our return in September 1981 was met with orders for my arrest on a false charge laid against me in the courts of Lahore. The bailiff suggested that for a consideration he could report that he had been unable to locate me. I declined the offer, but immediately went underground and apparently disappeared from the face of the earth until bail before arrest had been arranged and I could re-emerge.

I asked Bob how he had managed financially during my last period away. Bob is an accountant. Red ink is anathema to any true accountant. Bob had been teetering on the edge of a lake of red ink for far too long. He was very glad to have me back and to be able to resign the responsibility for ensuring the income needed and go back to balancing the books.

From my earliest days at the school, I had been able to relax with the assurance that the Lord's prayer teaches us to ask for today's daily bread but not tomorrow's. I seemed to remember from somewhere in Scripture that Jesus said, '*the morrow shall take thought for the things of itself. Sufficient unto the day is the evil thereof . . .* '

Even so, it had often been a close run thing. The end of each month was always tight. Our rapid growth had entailed increased staff and many additional expenses beyond simple salaries. The funding of the development plan had included an endowment fund for scholarships, but we had planned for a growth from about 60 to 250. We were now over 400 boys.

Approaching the end of November, I felt it necessary to remind God, just in case He wasn't aware of it, that we tried to pay our December salaries in the middle of the month. The staff wives needed to buy cloth to get new clothes made by the tailor before Christmas. They also needed to get their own gifts and supplies. Some families would be traveling away for Christmas.

"Please, God," I asked, "remember that we need to have enough money to pay wages by the middle of the month. We just can't wait until the 31st this particular month. Please make sure we have enough money to pay salaries on December 15. You have always made sure we have had enough money at the end of each month, but this time we only have two weeks."

I just could not see where the salaries were going to come from, so my prayers were a little more frequent and urgent than usual. There were no bills receivable or remittances due that we could expedite.

I was working alone in the staff room early in December when Bob Thomlinson came in. He was holding an open blue envelope in his hand and looking somewhat dazed. I inquired what the trouble was.

"Oh, there's no trouble," he responded. "I'd better start at the beginning. During the summer, while you were away, I think it was about early July, we had a visit from the local manager of Pak Oxygen. (Pakistan Oxygen supplied the industrial gases we used in our welding school.) He had a visitor from Britain, an efficiency expert, who had come up from his head office in Lahore. He didn't quite know what to do with him so he brought him up here. He asked if I would show him round since we were customers of his. Well, I showed him the welding shop, but I also showed him around the school. He was here for less than an hour. He seemed to appreciate what he saw—said it was the most impressive Christian work he'd seen in Pakistan—and then left."

Bob paused, his story apparently only halfway finished, and removed a letter from the envelope he was carrying. "This letter has just come."

Dear Mr. Thomlinson,

You probably won't remember me. I made a very brief visit to CTTC in June. The Lord has shown me that I should give £5000 for the work of the Society for Community Development. I have made arrangements to transfer the funds to your account. Every blessing in Christ. Yours sincerely,

Paul Whitehouse

Bob looked at me in surprise.

I was crying.

What a fool I was! How many times would God have to show me that He was absolutely reliable, until I'd eventually get it into my thick head? He said, *Before you have asked I have answered it.* It was a stronger promise than any promise to pay of the Bank of England. During 25 years of experience since the early orphanage days, I had never once been let down; I should have learned.

In this letter there was the promise of money, not just for December salaries, but also enough for January and February as well.

Psalm 81:10b says,

> *. . . open your mouth wide, and I will fill it.*

God also says,

> *Prove me now . . .*
> *if I will not open you the windows of heaven,*
> *and pour you out a blessing,*
> *that there shall not be room enough to receive it.*
> ***Malachi 3:10b***

Bob passed me the letter. I looked at the postmark on the envelope. It had been posted in England, before I, in my stupidity and blindness, had started reminding God that He had better get moving—as if I couldn't have just trusted Him.

Have you ever wondered about the *mechanics* of Providence—the apparent coincidences, the concurrences of events, places, and people? Madame Guyon writes, "All things conspire to one great end to those who love the Lord."

That is another way of saying what we find in Romans 8:28 from the apostle Paul. *We know all things work together for good to them that love God, to them who are the called according to His purpose.* I suppose we could rephrase that as "We know all things work together for good to them that love God, who make sure they are in the center of His will and purpose."

It seems to me there just HAVE to be angels. If they weren't there initially, God would have had to invent them to implement His purposes.

How did it happen that this unknown man was prompted to send this large sum of money to us in such a way and at such a time that it concurred completely in timing with our need? The amount itself far exceeded that immediate need?

Yesterday, more than 16 years after he wrote that letter, Paul Whitehouse came to visit me in connection with his ongoing interest in Gujranwala. This has led him to make a number of visits to Pakistan. He explained how that letter happened.

"After the conclusion of a consultative assignment after my redundancy and after my visit to Pakistan in 1981, I had £22000 in the bank. What would I do with it? I could practically pay off my mortgage, but the idea of taking a sabbatical appealed to me. I would be financially independent for a couple of years and could correspond with various Christians and be the hub of a network of Christian activity. On reflection, I see how arrogant that was.

The vision was centered on my independent ideas and myself rather than the Holy Spirit's prompting. The Lord was about to deal with my pride in a decisive way.

"There began to form a faint, but growing impression in my mind that I should give some money to the work in Gujranwala. At this time, I wasn't working, so I had no income. I quickly concluded that this didn't make any sense, so I tried to ignore it. I consider myself adept at ignoring the Spirit's gentle pressure, but even so, this just would not go away.

"When finally I opened my heart and asked God how much I should give, I got the clear impression that the sum involved was £5000. Periods of cold fright were then punctuated by cold sweats! £5000! I lost my peace and found that this nonsensical notion was now dominating more and more of my thought life and waking hours. Surely, it couldn't be right to give away your redundancy money, the seed corn, the only financial security you have while you are not working?

"I struggled and struggled with God.

"Knowing my weakness, the Lord graciously strengthened me in an unusual way.

"I had a dream in which I saw a large briefcase rise into the air, turn upside down, and open. Out of the case fell lots and lots of small pieces of paper, scattering everywhere. The dream made a deep impression on me. I knew immediately its significance. The papers were bank notes, pound notes, and I was called to give away the money I had accumulated, not some but **all** of it. This was of the Lord. I could resist no longer.

"I wrote a letter to Bob Thomlinson, and after I had remitted the funds to SCD, it became easier to give the remainder to other Christian causes until it was all gone."

I wonder how many other prayers Paul Whitehouse's faithfulness answered?

The Way He Works—The timing is always perfect . . .
THE ENGLISH LANGUAGE INSTITUTE

February 1983

This is a story of the almost instantaneous funding of a dream. Its speed even left me gasping.

It was an apparent lull at the school. There were no crises. It was afternoon. I was busy in my office. Marie was over at the house. Nathaniel Nawab, who would succeed me as principal later in the year, had gone home for lunch. The boys had all dismissed at two o'clock. Only the office staff was still at work.

I looked across at the new campus buildings, the workshops, and classrooms. Only one eyesore now remained, the north side of the inner quadrangle. The building that initially had been the hub of the Christian Technical School, housing the offices, the photo lab, and the drafting shop had outlived its usefulness.

The high, flat roof leaked. The walls of brick laid in mud mortar and pointed with a cement lime mortar were cracked. The concrete floors were cracked. I would really need to see that the whole building was replaced before Nathaniel took over. I was a civil engineer; building was my trade. Nathaniel was an electrician. He shouldn't have to inherit that particular problem; there would be many other problems for him to tackle when he became principal.

Now my mind was active, exploring, and dreaming. What should it be replaced with, what kind of a building? Well, it should have two floors instead of one; that was certain. Most of the other buildings only had a ground floor, but we could no longer be extravagant with space. Maybe, just maybe, we could build the roof of the new building on top of the roof of the existing single story building before it was dismantled. That would save the cost of expensive shuttering and formwork. We would build in reinforced concrete framing with brick cladding.

We would also pre-cast the steps of the staircase and build the staircase within the building early on for easy access for the building workmen to the upper levels.

I built the building inside of my head. We would not pull down the inside wall which provided security to the training quadrangle until after the new building had its outside wall complete. That way we would not impair our internal security. Although there would be cross walls breaking up the line of sight, hopefully we could get the south columns in a straight line and build them within the existing building. We would have extended cantilevers for shade along both long sides.

I got up from my desk, having mentally completed the building except for the division of space, and walked across the quadrangle. I paced along the length of the existing building. The columns would need to be at roughly 22-foot spacing, five spans. The roofing could be inverted pre-cast troughs, each 11 feet long. They would be covered with sheet plastic, three inches of earth to absorb heat and a surface cladding of bricks.

By the time I got back to my office, I knew what the building would be used for. On the ground floor offices for the Society for Community Development, the academic registrar, classrooms, a filing room, and perhaps a computer room. Upstairs—an English Language Institute. We, as an organization, had a peculiar strength. Many young volunteers from the United States and Britain, occasionally also from Australia and New Zealand and Canada, were anxious to come and work with us. Let this really be a mutually beneficial project where these young people could gain experience of the loveliness of our Pakistani culture, while sharing with us the one valuable thing they possessed that they could give immediately on their arrival, their own language.

Gujranwala had a million people. It had companies engaged in international commerce. Much of the communication was in English. Colleges, and even schools, used texts in English. The town needed a school for the English language, and this should be it. None others were better fitted to provide it than we were. That would not be the only benefit. As our own Christian children started progressing through the educational processes that we were providing, they would get the benefit of English language teaching tailored for them. Perhaps they could even be taught through the medium of one of the modern, simple English texts of the Bible.

I sat back once more in my office, looking at the old building, but seeing instead the new building. In my mind's eye, students of both sexes looked out from the upper windows over the quadrangle to which they would have no direct access. This would be a way to broaden our help out to girls as well as boys.

My reverie was interrupted. The Head Clerk knocked and showed in a lady visitor.

She was a stranger, a westerner, a Canadian. She had happened to be passing and had seen our sign, the Christian Technical Training Center. Did I have time to tell her a little about what was going on here? Nazir brought in tea. As we talked, I gathered she had come from Islamabad on what had proved to be an abortive errand. She had come unannounced to visit a school for the deaf that had requested some aid funds. She was on her way back to Islamabad when she had noticed us and called in. We walked through the empty workshops, and I explained what we were trying to do by tailoring our vocational programs to the needs of the poor.

Her questions indicated that this particular visitor was astute and well educated about Pakistan. I invited her to come over to the house to meet Marie, but she wanted to be on the road toward Islamabad. It would be after dark when she arrived. As she prepared to depart, she asked, "Do you happen to have any projects, Mr. Old?"

"Oh, yes," I replied enthusiastically. "Do you see that building over there? I want to replace it with a double-story English Language Institute where young native English speakers can experience our hospitality and give the one thing they are able to give immediately, their own language."

She let me ramble on. It was clear the building was already built in my mind, although its freshness, little more than an hour, would have surprised her.

"How much will it cost?"

That took me by surprise. I hadn't really got around to thinking about that. It would probably be about 400,000 rupees but that sounded a very random figure. It needed to be more precise than that. "415,000 rupees," I declared without hesitation.

She was similarly without hesitation. "Well then, get your request for funds into the Canadian Embassy before the end of this month, please. We make our decisions then."

By the end of the month, the outline drawings had been done, and they accompanied estimates submitted to the Canadian Embassy with a request for funding. The request was granted. The building was built within the estimate, was one of our finest buildings, and was everything I had dreamed of.

The Canadian Ambassador came down for the ceremony of dedication. The foundation stone read simply:

We build
That,
Following After,
You Might Grow
To The Glory Of God
December 3, 1983 Matt 5:16

Matthew 5:16 reads: *Let your light so shine before men, that they may see your good works, and glorify your Father which is in heaven.*

The English Language Institute and its twin institution, the part-time Barr Training Institute, inaugurated a new range of part-time educational opportunities for our Gujranwala young people.

Working His Purposes Out . . .

THE ONE HUNDRED RUPEE BUILDING SCHOOL

Summer 1978

I nursed a dream. Our Christian boys out in the villages were struggling to attain educational levels of tenth class to equip them for admission to the Christian Technical Training Center. For most of them, it would prove impossible. It was true that carpenters only needed eighth class pass, and we were experimenting with a shortened electrician's course that would require only eighth and permit them to do house wiring and domestic installations. Villages were getting electricity, and there were jobs there for our boys.

My dream, though, was to establish on the vacant field, north of the road to the chapel, a large parallel institution to the Christian Technical Training Center. This would teach the building trades where perhaps only five years of prior schooling would be necessary for many of the courses.

I had never even been inside an institution teaching the building trades, and I wasn't aware whether Pakistan possessed one. The idea that we could open the whole area of skills trade training to our boys in the villages at the end of primary schooling and at the same time help meet the country's needs for skilled construction workers excited me. We could continue development of the pre-cast concrete buildings we had developed for flood housing. We could also do basic research and development of construction techniques suitable for a developing country where the needs were more practical application than scientific study.

Such a development would also create the need for additional hostels to house the boys. Maybe if we couldn't manage new dormitory buildings, we could get away with putting an extra floor on the three new, single-story hostels. An additional study hall and dining hall would also be needed.

These were details that could be sorted out in the planning stage, and I set Justin Joel, the draftsman, to work developing the plans for what we would need on the new campus.

The kind of institution I was dreaming of, ten teaching blocks and four residential buildings, would mean a price tag of between $750,000 and $1M. Since I didn't have a single spare rupee, I put that in the back of my mind. That would be God's business, later. We had just about completed the construction of the new buildings for the Christian Technical Training Center, and now it was opportunity to begin to think of the next step forward.

How does a dream become reality? More often than not, it never does!

There are, though, certain basic principles. The first is that you make sure you are in the center of God's Will over the dream. This means you ask Him to confirm to you that the dream you have has originated with Him—that it is His design for the present situation and for you.

The rest is plain sailing. Start moving.

Perhaps that oversimplifies; often the ride is very bumpy.

However, when this confirmation happens, you can act and go on acting as though you have all that you need. You do not wait for the resources you will require to be safely in hand before you start changing your dream into reality. If you try to do it that way, you will never start! You just launch out and press on. All you want each day is your daily bread, not a larder full of goodies that will carry you through to Christmas.

In retrospect, I can see that the Building Trades Center was indeed God's plan, but not in the way I expected, planned or anticipated. Those buildings are now used for a school of more than 800 boys and girls, all of them Christian children. The Building Trades Center has moved away to work out its life on the other side of the Technical Training Center.

Once more, it was a case that God knew the end from the beginning, whereas I was the tortoise in the middle struggling along with tunnel vision.

Alistair Watson from England is visiting the women's United Bible Training Center. He comes across the road to visit us. As we walk down toward the school, he takes out his wallet and gives me a 100 rupee note. "Use this on your boys," he says.

"No," I decline (after taking the note). "I'm not going to use this on my boys, but on boys I do not yet have. I am going to build a school with this." I explain my dream and point out the buildings that in my mind's eye I already see. "The drafting shop will be there and there and then will come the two surveyor's blocks." I show him round my dream buildings while he looks quizzically at grass burnt brown by the sun. "There are the plumbers and gasfitters, and up there the painters and the decorators. The carpenters are on the upper two floors right over there above the trowel trades."

Alistair sees that his 100 rupees is going to have to go a very long way, but that same afternoon as soon as he has left, I take it as far as it is going to go, to the United Bank in Khokherke. With it I open a new account called *The Building Trades Center*.

The dream is beginning to move.

A few days later, the whole body of technical students and staff gather in the corner of what used to be Woody Bagwell's fruit garden, and we have a service of dedication of the Building Trades Center. We always read on these occasions Psalm 127 and then sing it in Punjabi. It begins

> *Except the Lord build the house,*
> *they labour in vain that build it:*

That afternoon the hostel boys, in their work assignment after their lunch meal, begin shifting dirt and broken bricks and hard-core to make the road onto the site. They use wheelbarrows that we have manufactured ourselves. We may only have 100 rupees, but we will do what we can with what we have, boy labor, and broken bricks. That way, 100 rupees can go a very long way!

Working His Purposes Out . . .
Swift Memorial Primary School

September 1985

The Building School (the one hundred rupee school as I called it in my own mind), intended to provide opportunities for rural, undereducated boys, was under way, and sure enough, God was providing the resources to build it.

We now had available for the students, complete or approaching completion by our own labor force, the first three blocks, each two stories high in reinforced and pre-cast concrete—a total classroom and workshop area of about 13,000 square feet (together with covered walkways and toilets and staircases).

It was, however, a case where I had one thing in mind and God had another far better use in view. Things now begin to move in His direction.

"William," I asked of our pastor, "don't you think we should be doing something for our own poor children?"

At this time, William had a congregation who had faithfully followed him to worship in our school chapel, while the Swift Memorial Church building downtown was virtually empty, run by the remnant Session and a replacement puppet pastor. William's session (board of church government) at this time consisted of one elder, myself. I was also the church treasurer. For the first time in a long, long while, the church accounts were being reported to the congregation regularly and accurately, and we had a positive and increasing bank balance even after William's salary and rent was paid.

The time had come to move forward.

I had a dream.

Just suppose that from preschool on up through kindergarten and then through the five years of primary school, our children were not just taught to remember. Suppose, like the children I had seen at home in schools in England and in the United States, they were stimulated by bright colors, by inspired creative teachers, by group activities, by good texts, by schooling being fun, and by encouraging them to think as well as to remember. Could we not begin to turn around our people and have them think in terms of creativity as well as imitation?

There was no better way to achieve that than to start young and train them in the way that they should go. We needed a test-bed for what we were going to be doing in our rural locations, and the raw material was on our doorstep and challenging us to move.

I explained.

We had many village schools that were ministering to our own rural, poor children. We had to go out long distances to help them, but we were doing so and our people were being helped. Did not the children on our own doorstep also want help? Was there not a need to invest our energies in the youngest and most needy segment of our own community while we still had opportunity? It might be too late if we waited too long.

Things were getting tougher all the time for our minority community, but if we kept to our own children, no one was likely to interfere with the Christian teaching we were giving them.

Private schools run by Christians, especially since nationalization, were proliferating to offer alternatives to government primary schooling with its requirements of Islamic religious teaching even for the Christian students. Christian families were looking elsewhere, often desperately, for their children. Many of the private Christian schools offered good education and good religious teaching for children, but inevitably, they were operated as businesses with a profit motive. They had to make money to survive. They did what they could to help poor children with scholarships, but prestige meant attractive school uniforms and Muslim children that could pay the high fees they needed to charge.

Why should we not operate a school ONLY for Christian children with minimal fees? We could start with children up to third grade. The older children would already be in school somewhere. I would provide free the classrooms in empty unused dormitory rooms together with electricity and fans. Wilbur, the pastor's son, had a science degree, and Florence Smith, an experienced teacher with a great spirit of service to her community, could kick it off. We would charge only what was necessary to cover expenses. If it sometimes didn't cover all the costs, we could ask the congregation to help from its own funds. It would be sure to help if asked.

We would have a school management committee. I outlined people who might serve. William brightened when I agreed to be chairman of the Swift Memorial Church Primary School. We were on the way.

We were caught by surprise. We announced in church one Sunday morning that we would be having admission interviews the following three days. It wasn't long before we realized we had an elephant by the tail. The children and their parents queued up for admission and kept on coming. The numbers steadily mounted. Wilbur and Florence had a simple school uniform in mind, white shirt over white shalwars and a navy blue sweater. That would keep costs down for the parents. The carpenter trainees in the building school were busy making little stools for the children to sit upon, blackboards, and easels for use outside. First one, then two, then three dormitory rooms were needed, but the numbers were over a hundred and steadily rising. We weren't going to turn any children away for lack of space because from these children would come our future leadership.

We also faced an unexpected question. Would we please admit the children of one of the senior members of the Commissioner's staff? The Commissioner, the divisional governor, was a personal friend, and his assistant had just come into the area and had to find a school for his children. He had no objection to his children participating in the strong Christian program we had developed for our children. They had good Islamic teaching at home and to learn how other people thought would do them no harm. We, on our part, wanted to help. Could we afford to unbutton the focused use of our limited resources into the needs of our own people to help a Muslim child temporarily transferred into our community? Contrary to the decision in our rural schools, we decided that we should maintain the strict rule of Christian children only.

The overflow was inevitable. The need to have the dormitory rooms returned for the use of the hostel boys steadily increasing in number matched the availability of alternative space elsewhere. The school moved over to the building school and numbers leveled off at about 350 Christian children.

Volunteers from England helped teach them English, and the 17 computers gifted to us by the British Government for our computer school eventually, when replaced by upgraded equipment, moved on to our primary school children. Work was being provided to teachers in the community, and Florence was a superb headmistress.

Now the question was a different one. Where does our graduating fifth class go?

Working His Purposes Out . . .

THE CHRISTIAN HIGH SCHOOL

Spring 1986

Around Gujranwala, a ring road is being completed that will enable much through traffic to bypass the city. The ring road will cut the various roads out of the city, and each junction will be a hub where buses will interchange passengers. Just beyond the Sialkot Road junction is agricultural land. To the right is Vanianwala village, but to the left are open fields.

Our rural population is flooding into the squalor of overcrowded slums in the cities in search of work. Relatives squeeze in on relatives, and still more arrive a short while later trying to move into something better than the brick kilns on the fringes of the towns where they first found work.

IF it were possible to acquire 100 acres of this flat land, it would be possible to create a dormitory town for the workers needed in the hundreds of little factories that Gujranwala possesses. Their transportation into and around the city would already be available and assured.

I have been working for years, on and off, on outline plans for a new town which I am calling Kanaya New Town. I am visualizing the creation of an extended, partially prefabricated settlement of homes somewhat akin to the colony, Brend Colony, of staff housing that we have already erected. We would set up a pre-casting yard on the site to supply building elements. This would provide work for some of our rural laborers displaced by the coming of tractors. Our Christians are largely landless, but if they had regular jobs in the city, they could pay an installment toward purchasing their own homes. This would give them a stake in their own land. There could be a thousand homes and all related facilities. There would, of course, be problems over squatters who move in and then do not pay their installments, but after all, what would life be like without problems to face?

My thoughts run on to the education of their children. They would need a middle school and a high school. If there were only Christians in the school, it should be possible to run a coeducational school with separated boarding arrangements for girls and boys from distant areas. In a recent paper on the education of the rural Christian community, I have advocated the establishment of several boarding schools strategically located around the Punjab to replace those nationalized. One of the recommended locations is the Gujranwala area.

Why are we waiting?

I go over to see Nathaniel Nawab, who has replaced me as principal of the Technical Training Center, with a proposal.

I can find space in the hostels and make arrangements for the accommodation and care of boys two years younger than any boys we have now. Does he have a spare classroom in which we could start a middle school?

Does he have a teacher he can spare to teach sixth class, non-technical subjects according to the Government curriculum? If we open sixth class now, the children in that class will move up to seventh in a year's time and into eighth a year later. Other younger boys would be following after at yearly intervals in age. I will try to find scholarships to help pay their educational fees. Each year we could add a further class until we are on into high school in three years, and if God prospered, into post-matriculation education two years later. The boys in the new school can be given practical training in metalwork, woodwork, and basic electricity.

This will be a new venture for Nathaniel and for the Christian Technical Training Center, but I am talking about his own people and reaching out to help meet their needs. He wants to help. He is thinking practicalities. There is a classroom just inside the machine shop door beside the examination hall that could be used. Anwar is a young teacher recently employed who could teach the boys their academic subjects. It *is* possible.

We agree. The Technical High School is launched. Little expense is involved and little fanfare. The initial class is one student and one teacher, but by May, we have 28 boys in the first class of sixth grade.

Each year thereafter, we are needing an additional classroom. Nathaniel is acting as principal of the school but growth is steady, and we are now increasingly encroaching on his time and upon available space. It is time for another step forward, the appointment of a full-time principal for the new high school and a move to other quarters. The senior staff selection committee makes an excellent choice in Evert Lall's wife, Pamela. She is fluent in English, a graduate, an experienced teacher, and highly competent.

The Building Trades Center, which now has three of its planned ten blocks, finds its carpenters squeezed back into one of them as the nascent high school also move in. The primary school already has the ground floor of the second block and is well on its way toward its eventual enrollment of 350. The procession of sixth, seventh, and eighth classes of the middle school from the technical training center to their new home at Easter, 1988, is joyful and noisy with the boys smart in their blue and white uniforms. The first graduating class of the Swift Memorial Primary School, including some girls, will join them after the summer! The doors for girls are just beginning to creak open.

I know very little about education, but I take this wonderful opportunity of the removal to a new location to think through what we are trying to do and to set down as an educational outsider some principles that are to guide the development of the high school just coming into being.

It shall be a coeducational high school, and only Christians will be admitted.

(The Christian community is becoming increasingly under pressure as Islamic fundamentalism gains ground politically and middle road political parties compromise on principle with fundamentalist factions for the sake of internal stability. No longer can the policies we have followed in the Technical Training Center of equal opportunity to all comers hold sway. Harder times are ahead, and we must focus on the equipping and training of our own people. A further important factor is that with the risky course of coeducation being tried, it would be very difficult to control or manage problems that might arise between Muslim boys and Christian girls. There is a good chance that within the Christian community such problems could be managed.)

There will be no long summer holidays by right for the teaching staff. We will pay them well, but they will work the hours and days of the rest of working society without being a privileged sub-community. All children failing to obtain high grades in each subject at the end of spring term will have required remedial teaching for much of the summer holidays to bring them up to standard.

There will either be no homework or at worst a very minimum. Kids need to play and not be burdened outside school hours with additional schoolwork. This burdens the teacher with marking assignments and parents with the task of ensuring the child is compliant. Most homework is totally unnecessary. It should be possible to teach the kids what they need to learn in the classroom, and school life should be ordered to ensure it by focusing on fundamentals and encouraging extra curricular, voluntary learning activities that broaden the individual child's mind.

The essential educational tools for development worldwide now are the fluent use of the English language and competency with mathematics. These two subjects will be our strongest focus, together with the practical acquisition of some manual skills. Because of our contacts with the West, we can expect volunteer teachers with English as their native tongue to come and help give our children an edge over others.

All teachers must be involved in continuing education to improve their qualifications, and we, the employers, will pay the examination fees of all successful students and give them the opportunities to take those examinations.

The consequences surprise. Our Christian children are the disadvantaged ones in society. We have always been at the bottom of the scale. The children's homes are not the homes of the affluent; newspapers cost money and they do not have books other than the Bible in Urdu. However, television is bringing English language programs into many of the poorer homes, and the children are learning at home by listening.

Pamela reports one year that ALL her students in tenth class achieved the matriculation standard, the best results of any school in the city, even better than the long-established prestige schools.

Something good is beginning to happen to our people.

Now for a hostel for girls to complement the hostels for boys!

Working His Purposes Out . . .

SHALOM CHRISTIAN CENTER

Jhelum
1980

This is really Rennie's story, but I suppose I began it.

It began before 1975, while Brend was still alive. We were recognizing, at that time, a holy strangeness in our situation in Gujranwala.

After the struggle of the first three or four years had dispersed and cleared, it was as though a holy light began to shine over the place where we were working. It was as if, in some mystical way, we were at work in some cooperative venture with God, as though a degree of attunement had been reached where the whole resources and power of God were being brought to bear on present problems in our own peculiar location. We weren't dealing in generalities or principles. We were dealing in specifics and in details, and somehow God's Hand was in those too.

It wasn't only that the financial resources for a development plan, which we had considered daring and visionary, had been abundantly and promptly provided; it was that we were recognizing that our vision had been far too small. Had we really had the vision to dare and believe, as we should have had, so much more would have been forthcoming and so much more could have been tried for and achieved. It was as though almost before we had time to express a need the answer was forthcoming. There was a buoyancy of expectancy in the air. Nothing was impossible. We were restrained only by our own lack of imagination.

It was a wonderful time to be alive. We were stretched, there weren't enough hours, we were tired, and we were challenged—but oh! God was somehow in the air.

Brend and Marjet and I had even more opportunity to talk about our Punjabi church after Marie went to England with Colin. The church was a discouraged church and a struggling impoverished church. Its roots were rural. So many of our people were illiterate. Our people were born into their faith, two or three generations down the line now, from those first conversions with their invigorating claims upon the newly baptized. Even so, there was no doubt that our people would pay whatever sacrifice might be demanded of them for the cost of following Christ. Their understanding of God was rooted in what had happened centuries ago to Jesus in Palestine rather than in their own present and personal experiences of God.

We had reorganized ourselves into a Society for Community Development; how could we help our community grow in individual, personal experiences of God? That surely is a key component of any development. How can it be encouraged to happen?

We thought that there was no better opportunity than now. God was at work right where we were. Let us encourage, invite, and meet the costs of groups from our rural church to come and stay in our hostels. The newly completed hostels are not yet filled with boys; watch and share what is happening. Let us put resources and effort into the spiritual arena of our church's life. Let us challenge them to pray with us, to share our goals, and wait to see those prayers answered. Let us share our experiences and encourage them to share their own. We could learn from each other. The villages of the rural church could begin to sing a new and even richer song.

Rennie and Melloney Gold had just arrived. Rennie was English, and Melloney was Welsh; they had visited Marie in England, and she thought they would do well. They were appointed by the Church Missionary Society of England and were nominally under the jurisdiction of the Bishop of Lahore. They were assigned to work with the Society for Community Development. This arrangement worked well, and others also came from England to serve in this way.

The Golds had only been with us in Gujranwala a short while when Brend was killed. So many dreams came to an end that day. My replacement, Shafiq Jalal ud Din, the principal designate, had been killed in an accident earlier that year. Now all additional activities had to be shelved as we who remained drew on the strengths we had to accommodate these losses.

Time passed. Marie, in the fall of 1977, was able to return and add her considerable energies and wisdom as growth continued, and with that, a new search for a Pakistani replacement for me as principal. There was no renewal of the lapsed idea for a spiritual retreat activity for the rural church in Gujranwala. The new hostels were full, and space was at a premium.

A glimpse of new opportunity was, however, presenting itself elsewhere in Jhelum city, nearly 70 miles to the north. The disused Mission hospital and the district missionary house (a large, double-story bungalow across the road from the hospital) were going to be put up for sale as no longer needed for the work. After Evva Hartig's retirement, a missionary family had been located in the hospital to run a youth center for the West Pakistan Christian Council, but it had only been for one missionary term, and the center was now closed.

I requested that instead of selling the hospital property it be turned over to the Society for Community Development for a small lease fee. We would guarantee to spend annually a certain substantial amount on maintenance and improvements. We would establish a retreat center for the use of the whole Punjabi church on a year-round basis. There was no such center available in the Punjab. There were a couple of camp centers in the mountains, but they were distant and not available year-round. Although there were no funds to meet the commitments I was making, I was sure that as they were needed they would become available. This center could more than fulfill the dreams that Brend and I had shared and be a source of blessing to the Punjabi Protestant church.

For recreational activities from the Center, there was the wide Jhelum River just to the east and the old Moghal Fort of Rohtas not far away in the other direction.

Somewhat to my surprise, the authorities controlling the property concurred with the proposal.

On May 2nd, my birthday, Shalom Christian Center was born in 1980. Our first director was Aslam Ziai. This fine young man was one of the graduating students at the Seminary next door where I was teaching a class on 'Conflicts in Scripture.' West Side Church in Richland, Washington, hosted Aslam and his wife Sudaish for a summer spell to give them the experience of U.S. church camps.

When Aslam left Shalom to join the seminary as vice principal, Rennie and Melloney were ready to move up to Jhelum. They spent 15 years there developing and operating a center that became widely used and accepted by the entire Protestant church.

Working His Purposes Out . . .
GREEN WHEELS

October 1984

Rennie was somewhat like me, more than a little crazy. Craziness, or a certain degree of it, can occasionally be an asset in the unusual environments in which missionaries find themselves. The tendency to act irrationally, however, is not always God-led and great patience is called for in dealing with such people. I used to consider that my purpose in life was to create chaos, for only when chaos was overwhelming were the reluctant participants in the turmoil ready to act radically to gain any shelter in a storm. To me, creating chaos seemed to come naturally. Equally natural was Marie's ability to restore calm and order after chaos had erupted. We made a good team.

Rennie's craziness was of a more moderate and less disruptive form. It was always governed by the fact that I held the purse strings, and there was virtually never any money available for Shalom apart from building repair work.

For instance, who would go to British Airways in England and try to book as a piece of personal baggage on a flight to Pakistan . . . a 14-foot-long fiberglass mold for a kayak? It might have been under the maximum weight allowance for a package, but . . .

Rennie had decided that he would develop outdoor kayaking on the mile-wide Jhelum River, just outside his back door, as an activity for the participants at the Shalom camps. I, of course, doubted his wisdom . . . seeing in my mind's eye rows of shrouded bodies laid on the riverbank. I didn't even know whether there had ever been a kayak in Pakistan.

On Rennie's second leave in England, he busied himself acquiring the means to create kayaks. British Airways just blinked, swallowed hard, and with true resilience felt that rather than putting it under the seat, it would be better in the cargo hold. There would be no extra charge.

In June of 1982, a month after arrival back in Jhelum, Rennie had his first kayak, and a year later, he had three more.

This led on to another problem. The most suitable part of the riverbank for activities was a mile away. Rennie really needed a vehicle. It was a long and often hot walk for many campers, and there was, in addition, much to be fetched and carried to maintain the activities of Shalom at full stretch.

Vehicles and the availability or non-availability of them are a constant preoccupation with missionaries. The poor people usually are just that—underfunded. Their salaries frequently are inadequate to permit the ownership of a personal vehicle, and even when that acquisition becomes possible, the vehicle will end up being used more for the work than for leisure. Those who work in institutions such as schools, colleges, or hospitals may have the use of an institution vehicle. Those who work on their own are less fortunate. Rennie had scraped up enough for a tiny personal vehicle for himself and Melloney, but he needed something very much larger for the work.

I was sympathetic, but unable to help. Any funds for Shalom were directed into saving the buildings from collapse. Rennie was on his own on this one. Was he praying about it? Yes. What was he praying for?

Rennie recalled later, "Ken asked if we had prayed, because we were still unsure what kind of vehicle we needed.

"'God loves to hear specific prayer,' Ken said. 'For instance, if you were to pray for a white Ford Transit van with green wheels or for that matter, a blue van with pink wheels, it's not at all beyond God's power to provide, even down to the colored wheels.'

"This was how Ken could typically avoid the issue he was faced with, and at the same time, come up with something spiritual."

Driving back the 67 miles to Jhelum Rennie and his two foreign volunteers were again discussing the need for a vehicle. They were hamstrung without one and had drawn a blank with me. They agreed that God seemed to respond more positively to specific prayers than to general ones. Probably, this was due to the fact that God's responses to specific prayers were more readily recognizable.

Rennie pulled over to the side of the road near Gujrat and stopped. The three bowed their heads and Rennie prayed. "Heavenly Father, we are told that you want our prayers to be specific. We want to ask you for a Ford Transit van with green wheels. We really need it for the work you have given us to do. And we need it soon please. And we are not joking. Amen."

Rennie was now looking at every Ford Transit he happened to see. Ford Transits were the most popular middle-size vehicle in Pakistan, used for taxis, minibuses and as personal vehicles of choice. He was seeing hundreds of them; they were everywhere. He just had not realized how many there were. Not one of them had green wheels! Rennie began to doubt that a Ford Transit with green wheels actually existed. His specific prayer had put them into a dead end with no way back!

Rennie had, by this time, involved his camp participants. They recognized he was crazy, majoring on the color of the wheels when what he really needed was any vehicle that worked, but he was popular, and they played along with serious faces while probably smiling inside. Rennie was now explaining that the green wheels were the evidence that would be needed to convince his inquirers that it really came from God.

Another problem was arising with this hypothetical vehicle that only existed in prayer conversation. Even if they did get it, it would be too small! Rennie often had a full busload of boys from Gujranwala dropped onto his doorstep and left for a week.

That was 40 boys or more. In addition, there were the kayaks. By now, he had four of these. What he really needed was an Army truck, a 3-ton, or a bus.

Just at this point, a third person with the gift of partial craziness enters the picture. Blame God! He turns up at Jhelum. This is Alan Whit. Alan is, I think, initially from North London. He is a small, wiry man, middle-aged.

For many years, he had been a bus mechanic at one of the London Transport bus garages. He seemed to have a gift for getting himself in jail. He would fill his knapsack with tracts and Testaments, and sooner or later, he would find himself in jail in Russia or Romania or India or Pakistan or Afghanistan. He seemed to thrive on these jail experiences, using them as opportunities for sharing his faith with other unfortunates inside. How he did this I do not know, for he did not seem to be gifted as a linguist. Nor could I fathom what strings he used to pull in order to get himself released.

Out of the blue, he called on Rennie at Jhelum, and Rennie shared his need for a vehicle. What advice did Alan have about buying an Army 3-ton truck?

"You don't need a truck," Alan retorted. "What you need is a bus! And it just so happens that I have a spare bus right now! It would serve your purpose very well."

All Rennie was seeking was some advice from someone who was knowledgeable about larger vehicles. He was getting more than he expected. Alan dug around and produced a picture of the bus. It was a Green Line bus, still wearing its original livery of green and a destination sign for Oxford. Its wheels were green! Alan told him he had just not been praying big enough.

If my recollection serves correctly, Alan had been wandering around in the countryside in Scotland or possibly it was in northern England. He had been surprised to discover, parked in a field, a London bus. Well, he was a bus man himself, and he was intrigued how the machine had found its way to this out of the way place. It might even be a bus he had worked on. He climbed over the gate and into the bus, looked at the tires, and looked at the engine. The bus was 30 years old, a single decker, but there was very little wrong that couldn't be put right with a little tender, loving care. He loved buses. A conversation with the farmer led to the owner being convinced that if he gave it to this curious little stranger God would find a use for it somewhere in the mission fields of the world. Alan became its owner and spent months working the machine over ready for the Lord's work wherever He would dispose it.

Rennie told Alan that we just had no money to pay for it. Alan's response was that if the bus could do our job he would be quite willing to drive it out to Pakistan and then give it to us free. Rennie was undecided, and that was where it rested. Alan returned to England, and Rennie came on down, without much hope of encouragement, to see me in Gujranwala.

I was distinctly less than enthusiastic. We did not need a bus! I gave an example. MIK, the Christian Publishing House in Lahore, had bought a printing press. It was the last thing they had wanted or needed. They had ended up serving the printing press, running around trying to get orders to keep the machine going. Eventually, wisely, they had sold it, and were once again able to pursue their original goals. The tail had been wagging the dog. Rennie would end up serving the bus. No one else could be trusted to drive it. Think of the accident liability. What about the cost of fuel at 12 miles to the gallon! Who fixes the breakdowns? And more immediately, what about licenses? Who pays the bills and taxes and customs duty and . . . ?

Rennie takes up the story again.

"I was quite indignant. We had prayed specifically as he had encouraged us to do. Then when God gives us a London bus with green wheels, Ken comes up with all sorts of insignificant and imaginary problems. Until this time, I had always gone to Ken whenever I had a problem, and now I felt God was trying to take me from underneath him. I asked God in prayer what the situation really was about the bus with green wheels. Was it something He was doing, or was I having some sort of mental breakdown? In order to find out if it really was God's will, I decided to put a test to Him. I would see if I could get an Import License for the bus."

This was a good and difficult test. I told Rennie it was a waste of time and he should use his energy elsewhere. It would be extremely difficult, if not impossible, to procure an Import License without paying bribes and/or telling lies.

Now the chase began. Only those who have negotiated the pitfalls of bureaucracy in third world countries armed with truth and innocence and an aversion to bribery and corruption can fully appreciate Rennie's dogged journey.

He started in Lahore. "What, you want to import a BUS? You cannot. It is not personal baggage." Rennie quietly told the full story, from the very beginning. He wrote out an application, three pages long.

The personal assistant read the story. He, a Muslim, commented, "I don't know what to say about the green wheels, but you will certainly get it after much struggle. Inshallah. If it is the will of God."

That hit Rennie like a ton of bricks. He would stick with it right up to the very end.

Rennie was refused in Lahore.

The next step up was the Chief Controller of Imports and Exports in Islamabad.

Rennie was refused there. There was yet one last step.

The Secretary of Commerce.

Eventually, Rennie was before the secretary himself in the Federal Government Secretariat. The secretary heard him out. He probably had rarely heard such a petition, presented so naively and yet patently so honestly.

The Secretary paused a moment or so before replying. "I would like to help you because I believe that God does answer prayer. You will get your import permit."

On October 22, 1984, Alan arrived with the bus in a dense cloud of black smoke. Shalom had transport.

But Rennie had overlooked one thing. He had thought that there would be no import duty to pay on a 30-year-old bus. He was wrong. Duty at 30% of the original price would be 60,000 rupees.

Rennie was now faced with the prospect of driving the bus back to England when he went on furlough in six months UNLESS this could be sorted out. Yet he was convinced that this was God's answer to his initial prayer, and it was too soon to admit defeat. He knew full well it was no use coming down to Gujranwala to see if I could produce 60,000 rupees.

Rennie started again.

He started with the Third Secretary of the Central Board of Revenue in Lahore to see if he could get an exemption from Custom duty. That was the first of many refusals, but through refusals and appeals, he eventually, after the passage of months, was nearing the top of the ladder again. All the officials concurred. It was impossible to entertain his submission, because it would create a precedent. Every mosque and Islamic Center in Pakistan would clamor for free import of Pajeros.

At last Rennie reaches the secretary, a different secretary, the summit of the ladder of authority. Again kindly treatment and the Secretary hears him through. "Come back in five days."

The Secretary greets him on his return by saying, "Congratulations, Mr. Gold. We are giving you exemption of import duty on the bus. We are also waiving the additional 5% surcharge. We are doing this simply because of your trust and faith in God."

Who says bureaucracies don't have a heart—and a soul?

Working His Purposes Out . . .
KABIRWALA SCHOOL

It has been a sad day. Babu Khattu Mall and I have been to see an elderly pastor, long past retirement, who lives in a village near Kalaswala at a minor crossroads a few miles from the Ravi river.

We had called on him a month or so previously. He lives in great poverty in a small dark and gloomy pastor's house, by himself. We had come to see if we could help him as a person, for we knew he was in straitened circumstances. The burden on his heart, however, far outweighing his own needs, was how to defend the property of the church building a few doors up the street from shopkeepers and others who would move in and take the property as soon as he was gone. He dared not retire for he loved that church; he had served it for more than 40 years. There was not enough vigor or power in the congregation to defend it successfully against the local men who wanted their hands on it. Couldn't the 'Mission' help?

We had encouraged him, inspected the condition of his church (it was cared for and freshly whitewashed), prayed with him, left him a small gift of rupees, and had then gone on our way, promising to return.

Today we have kept that promise, but it is too late to be of benefit. The pastor's house is closed and empty. The old Padri Sah'b, they tell us, had died a week ago; he had been found dead in his house. They have no idea what will happen now; they are just waiting for someone's axe to fall.

I have had to sit in the car for a while, choking back my tears. What is happening to our people? Why should an old man in his eighties have to die alone and in poverty at his post, because we who are coming along after him are unable to carry the responsibilities that are rightly ours, not his? Why have not we, the Punjabi church, allowed him to die in dignity, if not in comfort? Why could we not rise to the challenge of the continuation of his tiny rural congregation and its building? Was his death, and thus his life, merely an exercise in futility?

The next village, Kabirwala, is beyond the crossroads along the back road to Shakargarh. Just beyond the roadside mosque where Khattu Mall used to debate with his friend, the maulvi, we turn right along an earth track. The area, once severely affected by saltpeter on the surface, has been successfully drained and returned to cultivation.

In this particular part of the rural Punjab, we are checking the condition of church buildings in need of maintenance and repair. We have the means to help with some of them. This particular church is obviously well used, well cleaned, and well kept. The woodwork has recently been painted green and the walls whitewashed.

Babu Khattu Mall takes the keys offered by one of the Christian children crowding round us, and we go inside. The familiar trails of the white ants on the creosoted four-by-two's are their own warning. All the timbers, except the main wooden beams, are sagging under the weight of the dirt on the roof and the effects of the termites. Recent rains have left mud marks and streaks on the walls. Obviously, rain is entering into the earthen walls from the top, and during the rains, it is spurting out in streams lower down the wall.

Inspection done, I turn to look at the cluster of excited children around us. Punjabi children are very beautiful. They have a light brown complexion, always sparkling brown eyes, attractive features, and little self-consciousness. The girls particularly have a natural dignity and walk with easy upright grace that is more a 'glide' than a bouncy walk. There are no overweight children. These children are ragged, dirty, unkempt, barefoot, and happy.

They stop chattering among themselves as I talk to them.

"How many of you children go to school?" It is afternoon, so the school children would be home by now. "Come on now, how many of you go to school? Put up your hands." Shyly one little girl puts up her hand. The children laugh, not at her, just out of excitement. She points to the distant village across the other side of the road where she attends school. It is a long way for a little girl to walk alone to school, although she would soon join with other children from the nearer neighboring village. No, none of the other children (out of about 20) go to school.

The parents, both men and women, are gathered watching us near their homes beside the garbage dump. It has been years since a missionary came to their village. We walk over to them followed by the chattering, dancing, and skipping children. Babu Khattu Mall tells them how we might be able to help them with their church.

Then I break in, still hurting from the memory of our earlier visit elsewhere that day.

"Why don't you send your children to school? Do you know what you are doing? Each of you is so saddled by debt that you will never escape from it while you live. Not one of you is able to handle any kind of crisis because you have no resources. When you get sick, you can't buy medicines, and you can't afford a doctor. You can't afford your weddings, and you can hardly afford to bury your dead. Your daughters die because you have to save the medicines and medicine money for your sons. You even have to borrow for your bus-fares. You are at the mercy of the people who employ your men-folk. Not one of you possesses any land or anything worth having except your children.

"God has given you a wonderful treasure, your children, and you are wasting it and them like spilling a pot of gold coins on the ground as you walk along. You are condemning them to the same life you yourselves will never escape from. What kind of parents are you? You owe your children more than you are giving them. At least you could give them hope, hope they can escape from the situation you yourselves are in, and you are not even giving them that."

The children have fallen as silent as their parents under this outburst, but I am angry. I'm angry that the futility and hopelessness of their own lives are being passed on down to their children, and they aren't even going down fighting.

"If the nearest school is too far away, why don't you start your own school? You at least owe that to these young ones. Look at them! Do you know what they will be when they are just a few years older? If you don't know, look at yourselves! Is that what you want your children to be like too?"

They shake their heads. No, they don't want that. "Sah'b ji," one woman ventures, speaking for them all, "we are very poor."

"Poor!" I snort. "You are not *that* poor! You just need to do something; you are not helpless! Why don't you run your own school, educate your children on your own doorstep? They may as well do that as play in the garbage."

An idea strikes me.

"Suppose I give you 400 rupees every month to help pay your teacher. Could you run your own school then?

"I'll help you with running the school, and you will have to follow my rules if you are to continue to get my help, but do you think you could do it?"

Their eyes answer for them for they sparkle with surprised animation. They nod violently, affirmatively, excitedly, as though someone has just offered each of them an acre of land.

"Han ji, jihan!" Four hundred rupees was, in those days, the equivalent of about 13 English pounds or 20 American dollars. It is the best bargain I have ever been involved in.

That is the monthly cost to give the village Christians of Kabirwala hope and to change their world.

I don't have 20 dollars a month to spare, but I know it will come from somewhere. It always has in the past, and it will come again. I'm not nervous about that. Money is never really the problem.

I begin to set out the rules as they flow out of my head. I know nothing about primary schools and precious little about education, but I know about accountability and responsibility and plenty about cheating and manipulation and false receipts and the dangers of unsupervised handouts. If I can take care of the things I know about, the education process will take care of itself.

"There will have to be 25 children on your register."

"I will make surprise inspections, never telling you when I am coming. When you think you can relax because I have just been, there will I be, back again. Whenever I come, I will expect to find not less than 20 children attending school that day. I am very strict, so if you want to keep your school, you will have to run things very firmly and well. You will have to make sure your children are in school every day.

"It will be your school, and you will run it with a Village School committee of at least four people. At least half of your committee MUST be women. You must tell me who your school committee will be before I leave today. I will have nothing to do with your school buildings. You have to sort that out yourselves. You can always sit under the tree.

"I will pay the teacher direct the 400 rupees I will make available. I will not give that to the school committee. If you need to pay the teacher more money, then you will be responsible for that. If I don't come out to pay the teacher at the end of the month, then the teacher will have to come in to me at Gujranwala to get paid, and I will pay the bus-fares too.

"I will provide a blackboard, an easel, a teacher's table, a chair, and some school books for the teacher to teach from. When I come out, I shall test the children to see what they have learned. If the teacher needs supplies, you will have to provide them.

"The school is for your own children, and you must teach them Bible as well as all the other subjects required by the Government, except Islamiyat.

"When your children graduate from fifth class, then we will see what scholarships are available to take them to boarding school. You can be sure we will try to help them.

"Your teacher must have at least eight years of schooling and preferably have been away to boarding school at CTI or Hajipura or Narowal or Pasrur, with ten years schooling up to tenth class. Do you have anyone like that in this village?"

The cluster of parents is animated and excited. Do they ever! There are nieces and nephews from other villages—Robbina and Farhat at Hajipura, Nargis will be out of Pasrur this summer, and Jamil is just finishing tenth at CTI. The lone, little schoolgirl's big sister Adwina is at Narowal and finishing this summer. She actually lives in Kabirwala, so she is a natural candidate for teacher!

Question: If they can get 50 children in their school, will they get 400 rupees each for two teachers?

Answer: Yes, in for a penny, in for a pound! If they get even 40, I will pay for two teachers.

They are nodding their heads with each of the conditions as I set them before them. There is not one they cannot meet. "When can we start?"

Question: "How soon will you be ready to start?"

Answer: "Two weeks."

I check with Babu Khattu Mall. He nods in agreement. I promise to be back two weeks from today to meet the village school committee and either one or two teachers and for Babu Khattu Mall to inaugurate the school in Kabirwala under the peepul tree.

Working His Purposes Out . . .
VILLAGE SCHOOLS

1984—1990

We are seeing a rapid growth in the number of our rural primary schools. When Evert Lall, who will soon succeed me as Secretary of the Society for Community Development, joins us, his first assignment is the rural schools. His gifts flourish as he rediscovers his own distant roots in the villages beyond Sialkot. Something good that started with Kabirwala is happening in the villages and keeps on spreading.

Years later, a Korean girl has now come and will soon be directing the Christian Primary Schools program.

That first school, starting in such an unpremeditated way, would spawn within a few years a rural education system approaching 50 such schools. They were all operating on those initial spur-of-the-moment principles, with between two and three thousand village children getting daily schooling they otherwise were unlikely to have received.

A few of the schools met in the church buildings, but most met in an open space under a tree or in the sunshine or in the shade of a wall. There were soon schools in all directions of the compass from Gujranwala.

An unexpected question now arose. Could, and should, we admit Muslim students? Parents of Muslim students were asking whether their children could attend our primary schools. The possible reasons were several. Maybe there wasn't any other primary school in the village. Maybe our school was the nearest school. Maybe the government primary school had a teacher more absent than present. Maybe our primary school teacher was considered a better teacher. Children from both communities played together; maybe the children wanted to go to the same school as their friends.

Our natural instinct was to say *yes*, but what trouble could this lead us into? Christians are only about 2% of the population of Pakistan. The Government had made Islamiyat, the teaching of Islamic religion, compulsory in all schools with Muslim students. The Government had also in 1972 nationalized more than 50 rural primary schools previously operated by the Sialkot Mission or its successor bodies. Our people were already feeling oppressed and threatened. Our own village schools had a strong emphasis on equipping our children in their faith by Bible teaching, class worship, memorizing and singing the Psalms and generally supporting the hard-pressed, rural pastors in their ministries. Would admitting Muslim students throw all this into jeopardy? Would we just be recreating another primary schools system to be taken over by the Government in the next Islamic surge forward, to the detriment of both the quality of the schools and our Christian children?

In the end, the needs of the children swung the balance. Muslim children needed schooling as much as our Christian children. To say *no* could mean a kid might not get any schooling at all, and it would not be consistent with our desire to help the poor. It wasn't only our people who were poor. We should '*suffer the little children*' and let God take care of the consequences.

At one of the monthly paydays for teachers, which also included a training time and a social time when the teachers became acquainted with each other, I explained.

The teachers must interview *both* of the parents of any Muslim child wanting admission to our primary school and explain to them, very frankly, that we are Christian schools with Christian teachers educating Christian children. This included educating them in the Christian faith. The parents would already be well aware of this, but it should be made very plain to them by the teacher. We would not reduce any of the Christian content of the schooling. The parents must each agree that they had no objection to this. No Muslim child who was admitted would be required to remain present during such lessons. The child could be given leave to be absent or alternative work. There would be no attempt, there must be no attempt, overtly or subvertly, to take advantage of a child's need for schooling in order to ram an alien faith down his throat or into his mind. We, as Christians, didn't like it being done to our children through Islamiyat, and we would respect others with similar convictions.

It was not long before, in addition to 2,000 Christian students, there were several hundred Muslim students enrolled, and the number and proportion of Muslim students has continued to grow slowly, steadily without any inter-religious difficulties or problems from the Government.

Another question that very soon arose was the use of the church building. The village schools were managed by their own school committees. I had insisted there be at least an equal number of women on these committees, and this set-up worked well, although I wasn't aware of precedents. I had a long felt sense that women everywhere are the better, more sensible members of the community, and this was a method of enfranchising their good common sense.

One of the early questions that arose was whether the church building could be used as a school building during the intense heat or summer and winter rains. There was no general consensus.

Some congregations wholeheartedly gave over their church buildings during weekdays to the village schools educating their children. The buildings provided a place where the teacher's chair, table, blackboard, the matting the children sat upon, and the various school books could be stored, even if the lessons were held out of doors. Sometimes the school had little, low, individual stools for the children; they also needed storing.

In the very next village, you might find such use of the church building, God's own house, regarded as anathema. By no means! Let the children get wet in the rain. Time had shown that eventually children dry off. Store the school furniture? By no means! Would they have stored blackboards in Solomon's Temple? Of course not! Then why did you even ask?

The village school committees worked these matters out with the local pastor within the environment of the village community with common sense and tolerance, and I only observed the results with curiosity. Each village school was different and was managed differently.

At each end of the month, on the last Friday, the teachers are coming in to Gujranwala from the primary schools up to 150 miles away for their pay. They catch tongas, the horse drawn taxis, to the nearest bus stop and then a series of buses to get them to Guj as early as possible. The numbers coming are increasing. There are more female than male teachers. We are achieving another goal, creating rewarding work for educated, young Christian adults in a rural environment. About 50 teachers (some schools have two teachers) are being enabled to remain in their villages after schooling rather than joining the flight to the urban centers searching for work. They are contributing to their own communities by their working presence among them.

We always have a training program for them when they come to Gujranwala. Sometimes it is a course in teaching techniques, sometimes sharing problems in a group discussion and listening to answers others have found, and sometimes one of the United Bible Training Center staff comes over to help with Bible Training methods. I also interview the teachers individually about their own school, and so we are getting to know each other well.

We are anxious to foster a sense of fellowship amongst the teachers. There is tea when they arrive, a shared meal at lunch and tea before departure. Over months and then years, these teachers who are isolated in their primary schools develop close friendships with each other and look forward to meeting.

In the summer, they come either to Gujranwala or even go on an expenses paid trip up into the mountains to Murree for a month's residential training so they are in the process of becoming qualified primary school teachers. If we can get their training certified by the Government, then we will open up a career avenue for them into the Government schooling system, and they will be very good teachers with much to contribute. Meanwhile, our Christmas party at Gujranwala for them becomes the social event of the year with fun, skits, games, decorations, and gifts all thrown in to make the celebration memorable.

The bulk of our children are normal primary school age, from about four years old until about 11. By this time, they are ready to move on to middle school which will take them on another three years to eighth class. High school is a further two years to tenth class at an age of about 16. Before nationalization in 1972, the Sialkot Mission had a half dozen boarding schools to which these children could have gone. Now the whole network of primary schools and rural boarding schools has gone, and there is nothing in its place, although Gujranwala is beginning very slowly and tentatively with tiny steps to try to fill the gap. From 1972 onwards, the children, both primary and middle school aged, have been lost in the limbo.

I am noticing on my visits to the schools quite unselfconscious teenagers of both sexes sitting amongst the little ones. Most of the over-age pupils are boys. The teachers explain. The word has spread that I have promised to try to provide scholarships for further education in boarding schools for our village school children who complete fifth class. I am not sure how well I can help girls, for their boarding schools have gone, but I know I should be able to help the boys.

It has not taken long for the penny to drop. If an uneducated boy can just complete his fifth class, then there is a way opening up, maybe two or three years hence to be sure, to go to Gujranwala for training in a skill. Ken Old had better get busy! There is a deluge gathering in the villages to rain down upon Gujranwala!

In a continuing marvel of God's economy, we never seem to run out of money to pay the teachers their wages and their travel expenses and to meet the overheads of school visitation and training.

Somehow, during the journey from Kabirwala to the present day, more than $250,000 has been given by people beyond the shores of Pakistan to help take more than 12,000 village children through primary school.

God alone knows where it has all come from. It is the way He works.

Over the years, the Rotary Clubs of Japan became interested in helping. Individuals and congregations in the United States underwrote a village school and are still doing so.

Working His Purposes Out . . .
PIETER

Among the volunteer groups that came to work with us in Gujranwala was a Youth With A Mission team with members from several countries. They came in 1983. Among them was a young, Dutch primary school teacher, Pieter.

During the late eighties, the number of our primary schools was gradually growing, but oh, they were just so primitive! Learning by rote. Memorywork with no release of the imagination helping children fly on wings of fantasy. Occasionally, in spite of little precedent, a child's dreams broke through. We were interviewing a boy from a distant village for admission to the sixth class of the high school. He wanted to be an astronaut when he was through with school. Wonderful! He hasn't made it yet, but I hope he's still trying.

We needed to do more than just replicate the products of the scores of thousands of primary schools scattered throughout our rural economy. How could our children ever jump the gap unless we could give them the kind of stimulating educational processes early-age children receive in the primary schools of England and America? How could they learn to think, really think, instead of relying on their memories to carry them through? How could they fathom problems through to the end by their own nurtured initiatives instead of remembered solutions derived by others? If we were really to help our children and their teachers, we needed a different way of teaching and learning. It was probably necessary to import that. Could it be done?

Pieter, who had returned home to Holland, was willing to come back out to help us. His Dutch church would help support him. He applied for a visa for three years. After long delay, it was refused. The refusal was understandable. Naturally, Pakistan, an Islamic state, did not want Christian missionaries. He appealed the refusal. No answer. Months passed by. Reminders from both Pieter and us were fruitless. Pieter, with his own personal needs, sent a frustrated letter to us. He would not wait, but would come on a tourist visa and see if he could arrange things from inside the country. That was no good. I telegraphed him to stay where he was; I would have one more try from my side.

I went up to Islamabad, to the Central Government Secretariat.

I had always been impressed by the high quality of the top bureaucrats of the Pakistan Civil Service. The lower and middle levels were inefficient and frequently corrupt. If you persisted and pushed on high enough, however, you would usually find that the really key positions requiring integrity and initiative and broad views rested in the safe hands of good men. The country-wide administration was similar. It was virtually unchanged in structure from British Raj days with Commissioners, Deputy Commissioners, and Senior Superintendents of Police controlling divisions and districts. Rarely were these other than excellent men.

I am in the office of the deputy secretary. Pieter's file is on his desk. I want a visa for a Dutch primary school teacher for three years. Three years, not one or two years, three years. He smiles. These foreigners! "Mr. Old, this country has hundreds of thousands of primary school teachers. Why do we want another one of them? Are you trying to put one of our teachers out of a job?"

I smile back at his quip, but I am deadly serious. "That's just the trouble, sir. I would like to see them all out of a job! You know what they are doing to our children. They are turning them into ever better memory machines. It's not their fault. They get no help from the Government, for the Government itself works in the same way. How will our children ever grow up to be able to compete on level terms with Western children? How will our people ever learn to invent things instead of just copy things? They have no chance of doing so. I am not asking for a visa for an educational expert in primary education; I would have no trouble if I wanted that kind of visa.

"I don't want an expert. I want our rural primary school system, we have more than 40 rural primary schools within a radius of 100 miles from Gujranwala, to have the benefit of an ordinary primary school teacher from Holland who will bring the way he does things at home to us here. He will teach our teachers how to help children think. He will only be able to help a few children and train a few teachers while he is here, but he is ready and willing to come and help us. He'll find his own salary; it will cost us nothing. That's all I want; some way to help our children learn to think. If there is any better way to achieve that, then please tell me how."

The Deputy Secretary eases himself back in his chair. "Mr. Old, we have to be careful that you missionary organizations are not trying to feed in Christian evangelists under the disguise of people who are coming to help us. We don't need that kind of help. Moreover, if you had asked me for a visa for an educational expert, you would not get any visa. We have experts telling us what to do coming out of our ears. They are based in Islamabad and Lahore and Karachi, and they know all the answers. There are just too many of them, and they are crowding the swimming pools at the hotels. I am interested in what you are proposing. It could indeed be useful. Tell me more about your village schools system. Who is financing it? How are the schools organized? Where do you get your teachers?"

We part friends, and I leave with a promise of a three-year visa for

Pieter. He should wait two or three days and reapply at the Pakistan Embassy in The Hague.

Pieter came and gave valuable service to the Christian primary schools for three years. He was working alongside Evert when we left on retirement in 1990.

Working His Purposes Out . . .
THE AFGHAN RICE HUSK LOG STORE

F our times I have designed buildings for one purpose and then God has used them for another far better purpose.

These examples have convinced me of three obvious truths:

1. God knows where He is going and what He wants. Just stop arguing, keep quiet and tag along.
2. He is wiser than we are.
3. It is sometimes better we don't know what He knows or what He wants.

The first was Joe Alter's memorial school to his wife Margaret in Lyallpur. This became a Bible correspondence school.

The second was the Building Trades Centre in Gujranwala. This became a high school.

The third was a hostel for unmarried staff at Gujranwala. It now houses thirty girl students until an even larger hostel for two hundred girls can be constructed.

The fourth was a temporary portable building to store fuel for Afghan refugees.

This is the story of the fourth building that we never ever built as a rice husk log store.

Will Ericson is beginning to get his rice husk log factory on the outskirts of Gujranwala turning out logs. The project is funded by the United Nations High Commission for Refugees. It is heaving sighs of relief that, at long last, the logs are going to be flowing toward the fuel hungry refugee areas of the North West Frontier province.

Will faces another problem not related to Gujranwala. Where are the rice logs going to be stored in the refugee camps? The first loads can be distributed directly to the men, women, and children clamoring around the newly arrived trucks, but the goal is to build up stocks and establish distribution centers.

Will talks to me about getting contractors to build mud-wall stores which will later need to be roofed with traditional wooden four-by-two's and burnt clay tiles. The construction will need to be supervised from the word go.

I fall to thinking. Over a decade ago, we had been supplying portable prefabricated concrete buildings for flood relief housing, carried on the small local trucks and designed to fit those trucks.

Could the same be done again, using not concrete this time, but steel framing and corrugated sheet roofing?

This time I sketch out a steel frame ten inches deep and just six inches smaller all round than the bed of the Bedford Rocket truck that is the Punjabi standard. The angle iron, to keep costs to a minimum, will be 1 1/2 inch by 1/8 inch thick. For columns, I will use 2 1/2 inch diameter water pipes sitting on the standard, concrete foundation pads of the past. For bracing, I will use slender, mild steel bar. Eight of the modules can bolt together to form a roof for a basic building, 26-foot-square. These squares will themselves bolt together to make any required size.

By this time, becoming enthused with the possibilities of this kind of construction, I am forgetting Will's needs and seeing grain stores, refugee housing, workshops, factory buildings, village schools, filling stations, general housing, assembly areas, covered walkways, bus shelters and even churches.

We make a first 26' roof square and support it at its four corners. We then apply a load of filled cement bags right in the center to see what will happen. I have estimated, in addition to its own weight, a maximum dead load of 1,000 pounds.

It is carrying more than 2,500 pounds when we give up; it has deflected just over two inches in the center, and we have used only 15 pounds of steel for every 10 square feet of area covered. We are in business!

Will tells me he has made arrangements for his first rice log store to be constructed of local materials in Mianwali. We never did make any portable rice log stores, but . . .

———————————

Evert Lall in Gujranwala writes to me:

"So far we have put on 71 church roofs and if we count others like the Pasrur school that will add another ten roofs."

Some of the Khokherke rapscallions that we described in an earlier story have found a mission in life. They rattle around the Punjab on top of FitWeld roofing modules that have been loaded and roped into trucks or tractor-trailers. After a dusty and hazardous journey they are welcomed with sweet milky tea by the waiting Christians at some remote village.

There is always a worship service within the bare and wobbly walls of some church shell, and then they set to work with a will.

Some of the stories follow. They tell not only of simple buildings, but also of a community struggling to survive and grow in an adverse environment, a community for which God has great purposes.

Working His Purposes Out . . .
THE CROSS IS TOO SMALL!

November 1987

It is the turn of Chehal Kalan to get a roof on its church. The village, on the outskirts of Qila Didar Singh, is 17 miles west from the workshop at the Christian Technical Training Center in Gujranwala, Pakistan.

The two tongawalas (horse taxi operators) in the congregation have arrived to collect it.

Ladha and Bashir have hired a two-wheeled trolley pulled by a Massey Ferguson tractor. It is costing them ten dollars to take the roof to the village. Oho! It won't all fit in. They and the young men helping them load stand back and then squat on their haunches to contemplate the situation. Another trolley will cost another 175 rupees. Wow! Silence for a while and then an idea . . . try the roofing pieces not flat but standing on their edge. There are five long ones and five shorter ones to get in somehow.

Five long ones and four shorter ones are squeezed in sideways. Good enough. Slide in the gable end and ridge flashings, and then the last module is loaded on top of everything else outside the gate for the gate is too low. Let's hope the load will go under the drooping power cables along the way without touching. The roofing sheets are already on. Everything that needs to go has found a place. The nylon rope that also has to go lashes everything tight. Ladha and Bashir balance precariously behind the tractor. The roof is on its bumpy way to Chehal Kalan.

Corrugated sheets from Lahore are expensive. We find, in our local bazaar, an ancient corrugating machine that will turn pristine rolls of flat, pre-enameled steel sheet from Canada into corrugated roofing sheets cut to the lengths we might need. Needless to say, sheets are rarely identical and tend to vary in length an inch or two, but we can adjust the amount that is tucked underneath so that the eaves will look straight.

It takes between three and six days to roof a village church.

The Christians in Chehal Kalan form only a small part of the total community. In the good old days of McArthur and Milne, their district missionaries, they numbered 65 families. Then they all belonged to the 'Amreecan Mission,' their name for the Punjab Synod of the United Presbyterian Church of North America. Things are different now. About 40 families remain; many of the others have become Roman Catholic.

In 1947, the year of Partition, the Sikh and Hindu Jat landlords for whom they worked fled to India. Muslim refugees came flooding in. Land was reallocated to them. The place of the Christian peasants did not change. There was nothing in Partition for them except that their lives were now to be worked out in a state vibrant with Islam.

Their religious mentors were no longer there to help them, for the day of the district missionary had come to a close. Wilbur Christy was the last of them to come to Chehal Kalan and pitch his tent on the edge of the village near the pond and hold Bible schools.

For the Chehal Kalan community, days are now harder. One of their number sells his house to a Muslim resident of the village. It is adjacent to the little mud church. The unity of the community is broken. When the summer monsoon collapses the church building, the new neighbor wants that land for his courtyard.

Six or seven years of litigation ensue as the poor and powerless community fight for their right to their own church land. In spite of the wealth and influence of Mohammedi, their right is upheld. Then quickly, hurry, hurry, get digging, get the foundations and walls in at least part way up before Mohammedi tries to repossess the land. No time to check levels and angles or the shape of the church . . . hurry, hurry, enclose as much of the land as possible.

When they reach door lintel height, work comes to a halt. All their money is spent; every brick they can afford to purchase (and they buy them one by one) is in place, bedded in mud mortar for there is nothing to spare for cement.

Their adversities have bonded them together even more closely. They refuse to be swayed by bitter divisions within the newly independent United Presbyterian Church of Pakistan that has succeeded the Sialkot Mission in most of its work. The Carl McIntyre faction finds no response there, nor the faction led by Pastor Mumtaz. They continue to give their tithes of rice and wheat to Yunus Muttoo.

It is Yunus who in 1986 hears that the 'Amreecan Mission' is again helping rural churches through an assistance fund. Not only are they now sharing in the cost of repairs, but also they are supplying whole church roofs. This is frequently beyond the resource of the local congregation.

The Presbyterian Church, U.S.A., is indeed helping. Proceeds from local land sales are being used. Almost 300 applications for urgent help are soon on my table. In most cases of new or rebuilt or extended churches, congregations are given a deadline to complete the walls to eaves level. When this is achieved, then the puzzle is to devise a roof light enough not to collapse the very weak walls on which it will rest.

Chehal Kalan starts work again. Ghulam Masih goes around with his subscription book. Every rupee will buy two bricks, and rupee by rupee the money comes in. The walls begin to move upwards. Now the target is to get the walls up to the eaves before the summer monsoon. This year, though, the summer monsoon fails amid fears of drought, and the great pond diminishes to a quarter of its size.

On a Tuesday evening in November, the roof arrives. On top, Ladha and Bashir ride in like conquering heroes.

Wednesday morning the erection crew arrives.

Gujranwala is the industrial center of one of the administrative divisions into which the fertile province of the Punjab is divided. It is a congested city of more than 1 million people, and its one traffic light long ago gave up the unfair struggle. To the east side of the city is the Christian compound. An adjunct of the Building Trades Center, FitWeld makes the roofs, and young Christian men from the local community vie with each other to be on the team to erect them.

Before starting work, there is a short service. The floor inside the four walls is strewn with straw. The women and children are there and those menfolk that are not in the fields working. Some of the young men remain on duty to help each day the crew is here.

Now the work goes with a will. The church is a small one, only 30 feet by 16, and soon the roof frame has been completed, all manhandled into place and bolted together. The bricks on the highest course of brickwork fall away underfoot, and the wall bows when a lever is applied to reposition the frame.

Evert Lall, a retired Air Force officer committed to serving his community, is leading the group. With him are four of the boys and two young Presbyterian volunteers from Washington State. I am along too, for there is a looming difficulty.

Right angles are rarely a problem in a village. Wherever the wall goes, the roof is apt to follow. However, the roof to be positioned has right angles and the walls below do not, by quite a long chalk. There is three feet difference in the diagonals of the walls.

And, to the consternation of all, one corner of the roof inevitably sticks out almost two feet into Mohammedi's courtyard.

Something needs to be sorted out.

Whispered conversations and a shaking of heads—it's just too much to hope that Mohammedi won't notice it. There is still time to put on a few roofing sheets, but I defer it. Instead of the villagers, I offer to go and talk with Mohammedi. Mohammedi is in the fields. At dusk, he has not returned. He has gone to another village.

After the evening meal of spinach, vegetable curry, and unleavened bread, he has still not returned. Yunus and I go off to see Chaudry Sah'b, one of the leaders of the village and a relative of Mohammedi. He is in bed, the warmest place there is. *Greetings, Peace, welcome to my poor house. May God's blessings be upon you.* Then the explanations. We are neighbors, and we have to live together, but. . . . We are sorry, but what can we do now? We must not allow divisions to come between us. Would Mohammedi be willing to allow the roof to jut into his courtyard? *Yes, it is very difficult. Yes, he will not be able to build against that wall.*

Suddenly, an apparent corpse from the other bed sits up, uncovers the shroud, and discloses a young man who joins in the discussion. The apologies and contrition continue. *It will all depend on Mohammedi.* The chaudry will talk to him when he returns. Farewell, may God's blessings be upon your house, Peace.

I am asleep in my sleeping bag in the common sleeping room in Bashir's house when I am awakened. The room is carpeted with beds. Bashir's house is one of the two houses in the community that can afford to have electricity installed. Mohammedi is there. He has just come back, and the chaudry has sent him. We talk earnestly. Yes, it is a problem; he cannot now build against that wall, but we are neighbors, and we have to live together, think no more about it!

Ghulam Masih, close to his eighties, cannot now labor, but he can keep watch over the tools and equipment and make sure nothing is missing. He takes from his wallet a well-worn piece of folded paper and passes it to me after kissing it. It is a letter of many years ago from Wilbur Christy, informing whomever it may concern that Ghulam Masih, son of Dana, is authorized to defend the church property of Chehal Kalan and any other church properties in the district.

Each day, when the predawn call to prayer awakens the faithful, Ghulam gathers together the young children of his own community and teaches them Bible stories and memory verses. In the evening, after their meal is done, he again gathers the children for teaching.

The roof is complete. One last task remains. I stand with the elders as Gulazar fixes the cross at one end. They somehow find a cheap little corrugated sheet roof beautiful.

Bashir looks for some time and then sadly says, "You know, **the cross is too small**."

And I imagine, a long time ago in Heaven, a conference between God and His angels. Michael, the fiery one, breaks in as God reviews all the ways He has tried to bring these earth people back to Him. "Sir, You should take the earth in your hands like a ball, and shake it until their teeth drop out."

And God in answer says, "No, Michael, I have a better way. I am going to send my Son to die upon a cross."

And Michael stammers "A cross? A cross, but Sir, with respect, it'll never work. They need earthquakes and fire and lakes of brimstone. For what they need and the mess they're in, a cross is just too small."

And God smiles, because He knows. He knows that the one thing that cannot be defeated is Defeat itself. The courage of the defeated is unassailable.

Ghulam Masih (whose name means Servant of Christ) and others like him, who are dotted over this land, are reasons why the cross may be small, but it is always big enough.

Working His Purposes Out . . .

A ROOF FOR CHRISTMAS

December 12, 1987

Poet Rupert Brooke talks about "a first bird's drowsy calls." There is nothing drowsy about my night adversary, the Satiali Kalan cockerel. Even before the early call to prayer that intrepid bird is on its way. I find myself, from the depths of my sleeping bag, wondering whether roosters have the same call the world over, and whether this one hurt his throat when young or has distorted it by over exertion. His call is distinctive and searing. Distant normal cockerels eventually respond; this excites still further this unique bird. I assume it is so dumb it cannot tell the full moon from the sun. It keeps on until early light shows the mist on the cotton and sugarcane fields, and the chattering of the girls outside warns that it is time to move.

Evert and I share with Peter, our young American volunteer, a small mud-wall room with a low roof that is crowded with furniture, mainly beds. In the corner, a carpet loom with a carpet in its first few inches of length awaits attention.

Across the alleyway, in an even smaller room, is a larger loom, and in bed, a woman with her baby. The room is open at one end and has no door. Behind the loom, in a tiny space not two feet wide, the three girls chatter. It is not yet 6:30, and they have been at work some time. The middle girl calls the colors by their nicknames. "Three of white, two of cinnamon, four of yellow." Her two companions deftly respond with her, knotting, cutting, knotting, cutting, combing, almost too quickly for the eye to follow. The small bare light bulb, on during certain hours only, gives them light. Yesterday there were four of them.

"Can you manage with only three?" I ask.

"Oh, yes, we can manage with three or two or even one."

"How old are you?"

"I'm 15, and these two are 11." The girls giggle, never a pause in the knotting and cutting, knotting and cutting. In some of the larger carpets, there are a million knots; each one individually tied. At the end of a month, with all four working together, they can earn a total of about $120 U.S., so there's no time to waste.

In the Christian corner of this Punjabi village there are around 30 looms, only two owned by the weavers themselves. A Muslim entrepreneur who provides the loom and the yarn and collects the carpets for washing, trimming, finishing, and marketing owns the rest. The loom in our bedroom is the weaver's own, and in spare time from the fields, he is weaving his own carpet to provide extra income for Christmas.

Last night I met Yasmin (Jasmine), a girl trying to escape this kind of future.

All six of our building group are hosted among various homes in the village for accommodation and meals. We have finished our evening meal of rice, vegetable curry, flat bread, and tea, and I have already left the house when I am asked to return.

The table is cleared and the oil lamp throws a dim light. Mother, father, two daughters, grandfather, and brother come into the tiny room and sit down. They speak in Punjabi, but I understand enough. Yasmin speaks first, a pretty girl with her features largely masked by the cloth over her head. "Take me with you." She is about 16.

Her mother joins in. "Take her with you." I play for time and try to find out why. It is soon clear. Her older sister is illiterate and has no interest in schooling. Amin giggles self-consciously. Yasmin is now halfway through her ninth year of schooling, and what is going to happen to her? She may well be the first literate one in her family.

"Take me with you," again the plea.

I encourage her to complete her tenth year of schooling, to try hard for a high matriculation, and then she should find us in Gujranwala, and we'll try to get her into nursing school. She likes that idea—1989 is not too far away.

It is still early morning, and Peter and I are back from the fields. Abid, the pastor's seven-year-old son, hobbles over to the hand-pump to provide us with water to wash and shave with. He has a valgus foot from polio in his infancy. Doctors have advised nothing can or should be done. However, Dr. Margaret White, in a chance meeting on Sunday, confirmed something can certainly be done, so a letter is written and an envelope found and addressed to register Abid for admission into the Mission hospital at Sahiwal.

I had thought I'd be leaving visitors behind with Marie when we left from Gujranwala 70 miles away in a Ford van loaded with equipment. This time the church roof, a larger one 52 feet by 22 feet, was in Satiali Kalan. The village is socially interesting because there is only one mosque rather than several, and the Muslims, when they migrated from India during the 1947 Partition, brought with them their Christian peasants and servants. A church in Baltimore has helped to meet the balance of the cost of this roof not met by a grant from the Presbyterian Church, U.S.A. We allow one day to erect the prefabricated roof trusses made in our workshop and five days for the sheeting and finishing.

Visitors, however, don't just come to Guj; they also come to Satiali to see us. I am called away from the work to meet the various notables of the village and the Catholic candidates for election to the local councils. A delegation from Nizampura presses its claims for help with its church. Then come Padri Ghulam Masih from Mandiala, the elders from Mailiburji, and Padri Samuel Khokhar from Kot Amin. They all want a church roof. Please, can we have it by Christmas? Well, it's now December 11, and there is Trigri roof to do next, so Kot Amin may get its roof, but Mailiburji, perhaps January, certainly before Easter.

Elder Gulzar's face drops. They are all ready. Just come and see . . . they are nearby.

I will never learn. Punjabi distances are flexible to the point of absurdity. Miles of fine, thick, billowing dust—first to Nizampura, where they are up to ground floor level then Mailiburji.

Sure enough . . . since my last visit, they have pulled down their old mud church and erected a 31' 5" by 20' church—the walls, that is. Surprisingly, the diagonals are almost equal. The bricks don't seem to run in very neat courses. The walls are a brick thick in mud mortar. One of the problems is to get the roof up without the walls buckling. We usually lose a goodly number of bricks underfoot as we work on the walls 12 feet or so high. Another problem is to prevent the roof from blowing away in a high wind. How do you anchor a light roof into thin walls laid with mud mortar?

All things are possible to them that believe, and please, can we have our roof before Christmas?

Working His Purposes Out . . .
A Cross for Manianwali

January 7th, 1988

Manianwali is the first of our 1988 church roofs. As a Punjabi village, Manianwali, as far as we know, is unique. It is a village where only Christians live. They also own the land around the village. This has given them an independence of spirit rarely seen among the serfs and peasants who work for other landlords.

In 1947, about nine Sikh families and their Christian menial workers who tilled the fields for them lived in Manianwali. Strangely enough, the Sikhs never built a gurdwara there. Nor is there the usual brick built house in the middle of the village on the highest ground that denotes the landlord's house. Through the summer of that year, all in the Punjab waited anxiously to hear where Sir Cyril Radcliffe would draw the future frontier between India and Pakistan. When the news broke, it was about 15 miles to the east of the village. Within a day or so the Sikh families had fled from the orgy of killing that was to follow.

The 14 Christian families took counsel together. They were going to possess this land or die in the attempt to hold it. Neighboring Muslim families from the next village tried to move in and were repulsed. Court case after court case followed, and the little community stood firm until, against all expectation but their own, they were eventually confirmed in their ownership as sitting tenants and the land was theirs.

Elder Samuel was appointed the headman by the Government to be responsible that taxes were paid, and a Government watchman, one of Samuel's relatives, was appointed to assist him. There is no need. There is no stealing in this village, and no need of a watchman.

Thirteen years ago, Pastor Gulzar came to live in the village, first in a room of another family and then in a room the community built for him. Two years ago, they added another room. There may have been a little, mud-wall church that fell down in the monsoons, but if so, there is no trace of it now. The village has no electricity, although the lights of Dhatewal and Talwandi Bhindra are not far off, and the early call of the muezzin to the faithful carries clearly across the level fields. The fields are now full of rice stubble, sugar cane, or the young sprouting of the winter wheat. The two previous wheat harvests were bad ones, but the last rice harvest was good so things are better.

About a year or so ago, the first foreigners to visit the village in more than a decade came for just an hour or so while the whole community was rejoicing at a wedding feast. The interruption was welcome, for they had come from the 'Amreecan Mission' to which the whole community belonged. In the 'old days' the 'Amreecan Mission' was the Sialkot Mission of the United Presbyterian Church of North America. Since 1958, most of its work has devolved upon the United Presbyterian Church of Pakistan or its various boards and committees. There is much dissension in this church, but communities identify themselves by the benchmark from the past, the 'Amreecan Mission.'

The elders broke away from the feast to show Old Sah'b and Mr. Nick the selected place near the pastor's house, right adjacent to the open well where there was barely space to build even a small church. Measurements were taken, estimates were made, and heads nodded in agreement. Yes, it could be done, and if the 'Amreecan Mission' would provide the roof then the walls would soon be up.

A young Pakistani bishop of the Church of Pakistan had asked Marie and me if we could help with a church in his own village, and he would help too. His village is only a few miles from Manianwali, and after a visit there on a day soon after Christmas, we drove across the fields from Talwandi to Manianwali. I had brought a tape with me. The two diagonals of a rectangular building are not, in villages, necessarily equal. So it proved again. The Manianwali ones were almost three feet different. Not only that, but the church was no longer near the well but on the edge of the village near the lambardar's (headman's) house. Land had been gifted by his brother to the community for its church. This was a much better location. Although in mud mortar, the walls were a brick and a half thick. Everything was now ready.

So, too, but only just, was the roof we were preparing at Gujranwala.

On January 2, Elder Sardar came in all smiles and salaams to collect his roof. Finishing touches were made as Sardar went down to the bazaar to hire a truck. When he returned, the trucker refused to unbolt the hoops that held the top of his truck body together and drove away. By now it is afternoon, and the village is 60 miles away and much of it bad road.

Samuel is sent off to the bazaar to get another truck, and he returns with the same one. An extra 50 rupees has made the difference.

Just after the truck has left, we find a 22-foot tie bar has been left behind. So it goes.

Our erection party is polyglot. I say only four of the local Khokherke boys will be needed, but six climb in, and I choose not to count. There are three other young men—a Samoan and two Americans from Youth With A Mission. The poor old Ford Transit is hard to start, and its battery is so weak that we take our battery charger with us—but, of course, not a power point is in the village.

We arrive right on time at 10:30, in spite of delays in trying to make the spare wheel usable. We don't succeed, and in this instance, fortune favors the foolhardy.

First of all, we have worship. Sitting on the floor, the gathered people thank God for giving them a roof and both sing and read that familiar Psalm 127 that we all know by heart . . . *Except the Lord build the house, they labour in vain that build it . . .*

Now things go with a will. Within a couple of hours or so, all the roof modules are in place to hold the roofing sheets. The upper courses of brick-work have spaces knocked in them to take the concrete blocks that will hold the roof down in a storm. By half past five when work stops because it is dark, the roofing sheets are already on their way.

We eat and sleep at Elder Sardar's house. The family has vacated their two rooms and 11 beds have somehow been squeezed in with no room to walk between them.

By seven I am asleep and do not hear the commotion as they look for the thousand rupees a woman has hidden in the bedding she loaned. Only half of it is found.

Noises outside at 4:30 indicate breakfast is being prepared as two men squat on their haunches feeding the little, outside cooking fire with twigs. I take a quiet walk around the village which is otherwise asleep. From Dhatewal and Talwandi flicker electric lights, and the maulvis are calling prayers. I pass a pile of bricks where the second church is intended to be. The villages, above the flood level of the fields, stand proud like ships at sea. Our village is quiet. There is no machinery, not even a tractor. Oxen turn the crushing wheels that extract the juice from the sugar cane. First flickers of light promise the new day. Breakfast is already ready. Wake up!

The walls are three and a half inches out of level. The YWAM boys level the trusses with wedges and bricks as we continue sheeting. Mid-morning the Land Rover, more decrepit than the Transit, arrives with Evert's wife, Pamela, and four of our foreign girl volunteers. They are out to inspect some of our primary schools. Evert goes with them for a day of different adventures, including getting stuck in the mud. The work is going well, and we can see that the roof will be complete by noon tomorrow—our best time yet for putting a roof on—improving on the three days for Trigri.

We have become aware that there is a division within the Christian community, and almost half of the 40 families have Samuel Joseph from Talwandi as their pastor. Not only this, but spurred by Gulzar's example, they also are planning to build their own church on the other side of the village.

At the evening meal, a young man comes in, welcomes me like a long lost brother, and sits down beside me with his arm around my shoulder. Do I remember him? No, I do not, but there are many people I do not remember. He is disappointed. He is Buta. Do I not remember? He worked for me 14 years ago, and he did something wrong, and I forgave him. My mind is a blank, but the relationship is at least established. We are brothers.

There is a coolness from our hosts, and it is obvious that Buta is from the other faction in the village. They give him tea, but are anxious that I not go with Buta to see his 3-month-old son, Khurram.

Buta leads me up the short village lane where his friends are waiting, maybe a dozen or more, with two small oil lanterns. One of them speaks fluent English. They lead me to the pile of bricks. Standing in semi-darkness conversation goes on intermittently in three languages. They are anxious and insistent. You have helped them with their church, now you must help us with ours. We, too, need a church. The Full Gospel Assemblies have promised us a church if we join them—so have the Brethren Mission and the Roman Catholics, but we are 'Amreecan Mission' and are going to remain so. The English speaker tries to explain privately to me that the differences go back a very long time.

I talk to them of unity, of witness, and of the greater need for a school than a second church. They agree. They will cooperate together for a school, and they will have 100 children. At present, their children have to leave the village to go to the other villages to school where they learn Islamiyat instead of their own faith. That will come, but for now, their problem is the church. I assure them there is no likelihood that the 'Amreecan Mission' will roof two churches in the same village—*then help us individually yourself.* The discussions go on, good-natured, but intense and important. I promise to give them whatever drawings they need for the church, but that is the extent of the help I will give. *Then please come to our ground-breaking ceremony tomorrow for our own church*—this is important to them. I refuse, explaining my heart does not allow me to concur in division of worship in this way. *You come together for your betrothals and marriages, your funerals and sorrowings—use these bricks to build a school, not a church.*

There is no agreement; feelings run deep. *Salaam, may God give you blessings.*

Next day we see Evert walking across the fields from Talwandi. The Land Rover didn't get back to base at Gujranwala until 9 P.M., and at 6 A.M. this morning he has started out by bus to rejoin us. I throw him the keys of the Transit to see if he can get it push started. After much effort it eventually discharges billows of smoke, and our return is now imminent. We are almost finished as the ridge and side flashing is completed. The cross. With each church roof, we take out a steel cross to be affixed to an end of the ridge. A young man from the village is anxious to set this in place, so he sits astride the ridge assisting Mitch, one of our YWAMers, and bolts the cross tightly in place. As people walk across the fields from the main road at Talwandi, they will see not only the green roof but also the cross against the sky.

One further thing remains—a service of worship. All the villagers have been asked to come, but only Gulzar's faction is present. I preach the impromptu sermon. The people know the Bible verses I question them about. Our host has said that when electricity comes to the village, their lives will change. A few people may even have television. But the main thing will be that they will have light for their long, daily, after dark worship gatherings. I wonder whether electricity will be a blessing, but progress is progress.

The Transit won't start after we have loaded. Evert wants to tinker with the engine, but I restrain him. The people would like to give us a push start to get us on our way. Evert and I have been garlanded with rupee notes. Shouting and pushing the Transit roars into life and we are away.

A woman runs from the village with three boiled eggs as a parting gift.

Buta and several companions meet us further along the track. *Now you must come to us for a farewell meal.*

But we have already eaten and we need to reach Gujranwala before dark.

Then who will eat the food we have prepared?

I promise that next time I will certainly eat with him, and on our way home, we leave behind a cloud of dust and a cross in Manianwali.

Working His Purposes Out . . .

DHODHA

Easter 1988

David Lytle, a missionary of the United Presbyterian Church, U.S.A., kept a diary. In the month of November in 1883, the missionaries at Sialkot brought out their tents, hired camels (with many misadventures), and started out itinerating in the rural area. By mid-December, they had reached Dhodha, about 30 miles southeast of Sialkot. David wrote:

"Arrived at Dhodha, a large town south of Pasrur. Stayed over 'til Monday. Services Saturday evening and Sabbath morning in tent and Sabbath evening in the Chuhra portion of the town. Baptized two men, one woman and five children. These, added to the number of Christians already here, made 54."

Bill Hopper is the representative of the Presbyterian Church, U.S.A., in Pakistan. He writes from Lahore in desperation:

Ken,
Padri Nemat of Dhodha is about to drive us all crazy in this office and there may be a murder soon if he does not let us alone. He claims that he is the pastor of a congregation that built a church that was too long but that you have made a roof anyway that fits and that it is ready to be installed. His congregation insists that the roof be in place by Easter. Is this man a nut or am I going completely crazy? Please tell us what the situation is—we can't get anyone at your place to answer the phone!
Another man demanding a roof by Easter, much less vehemently, is Elder Barkat Khan of Chak 213 near Faisalabad. What is that story?
First, please, give us the answer to Padri Nemat!
Blessings, Bill

We are working our way through the list. Dhodha is number 155 on the 1988 list of 249 churches asking for help and the 28th on a list of 44 scheduled FitWeld roofs. So far we are at number 16, but if violence is to be averted
. . .

Nemat persuasively avers that Dhodha is merely three miles of well-surfaced road from Qila Soba Singh. I have long realized how circumstances color our perception of facts, so I go see. Nemat does not wear merely 'rose-colored' spectacles; they must be blood red!

Four and a half miles of horrible, narrow, rutted, brick-paved road and then four more miles of rutted dirt track just waiting for rain to make it a quagmire. But there indeed, at the end of it all, is a church waiting for a roof so I promise a roof before Easter if . . .

The rains came; they came late, but they came.

From Dhodha, the men to fetch the roof did not come; they couldn't. The road was a gooey mess.

Eventually, several days late, the trucks arrived in Gujranwala on Graduation Day.

76 boys, carpenters, machinists, fitters, electricians, draftsmen, and TV repairmen were about to graduate from the Building Trades Center and the Christian Technical Training Center. The shops were cleaned and displays organized for the Top Shop competition. Flags, bunting, streamers, and signs of WELCOME stretched across the road.

Everything was lifted to allow the trucks underneath.

Hurry! Hurry!

I was with the procession where the seventy-odd boys in the High School transferred to their new abode in what had been intended to be the Building Trades Center. Before that, there had been the graduation exercises of the primary school where 200 spic-and-span Christian children got their report cards, and 13 graduated into the new high school. Three of them are girls, the first girls in the High School.

Hurry! Hurry!

Evert supervised the loading. The trucks were to cost 500 rupees apiece.

They were away in double-quick time.

As the going towards Dhodha got stickier and stickier and the rain clouds massed again overhead, the price rose to a thousand rupees apiece.

The trucks still, after struggling, slipping, and grinding along the muddied track, could not get close to the church because of the pond now across the road and poor access beyond.

And the children of Dhodha gloriously took over!

There were no men in sight. They were in the fields and hurrying their work at the potters' kilns before the rain put their fires out. The burly drivers and their helpers stood amazed as the children came pouring from the village in their scores, little ones, big ones, girls, and boys. Imagine the children following the pied piper of Hamelin.

The kids perched the concrete blocks that weigh about 70 pounds on their heads, bent a little under the load, and staggered away in the direction of the church shouting, "Bachao, bachao, save yourselves." The 13 foot by 6 1/2 foot modules were swarmed over like ants after sugar. A score of the children, shuffling themselves without instructions into similar sizes, slid the steel sections onto their shoulders and hustled away, shouting like the others, "Bachao, bachao." More and more children came. The dumb boy who can only speak with a squeak was there squeaking and carrying. Some spots of early rain before the downpour came.

HURRY, HURRY!

The children hustled, running back to the trucks, dodging the others carrying the scaffolding and the roofing sheets. Underneath the roofing sheets, moving horizontally in the direction of the shell of the church, were a dozen bare feet scurrying along. They couldn't see where they were going. "Bachao, bachao!" The chicken scuttled for their lives, and the ducks climbed the piles of dung cakes and tried to fathom what was going on—now the ladders and scaffold planks.

The engines were already revving to move away as the last of the modules was slid out of the second truck. Now that the drivers knew how bad the road was, they were even more anxious to get out. They didn't wait for tea or wait to see the children jumping and dancing for joy because the roof of their church had come!

Saturday I have a court case hearing in Lahore—a totally false case of fraud, trumped up more than seven years ago that has been going on continuously and still hasn't reached the evidence stage.

There is heavy rain in the Sialkot area on Saturday night and next week is Easter week.

Monday morning the Land Rover and its trailer take off to see if it is possible to get to Dhodha. If it is not, there will be no roof by Easter.

By 11 o'clock, the loudspeaker is being assembled, and the people called to worship. The Land Rover is being unloaded, and work cannot start until there is worship.

There has been trouble over the loudspeaker. Electricity had come to Dhodha about three years previously. Dhodha is a large village, maybe a thousand families. Twenty-five of them are the Christians living on the north side and another ten families live on the west side. There are eight mosques. The village appears prosperous; the fields are full of the winter wheat just beginning to turn and three weeks away from harvest. They are harvesting lentils just now, and the cattle are treading out the plants to dislodge the seeds. There are several tractors. The scores of ox and buffalo carts have pneumatic tires, an advance on the old, steel-rimmed wooden ones. There are many potters making huqqa bowls and drinking and cooking pots by methods hundreds of years old. There are two or three television aerials and a couple of flour-grinding mills, but so far, the main benefit of electricity is light—and the loudspeaker.

When the Christians had obtained a loudspeaker and begun broadcasting their worship and prayers, the whole village was up in arms. It was disturbing the Call to Prayer at the mosque next door; it was hindering concentration on the Holy Q'ran. It was not possible—close it down was their demand. The Christians were just as adamant. They were going to have their loudspeaker too. There was life and leadership in the community.

Eventually, they hatched a plan that 'someone' would put a large padlock on the door of their roofless church and throw the key down the well just outside the front door. They would then accuse the users of the mosque next door and go in appeal up as far as was necessary, even to the President himself, to assert their rights as a minority.

Fortunately, it didn't come to this. A typically Punjabi compromise was sorted out. They could broadcast five minutes a day AFTER the Call to Prayer had been completed. This was agreed by all.

The first day the Christian worship was five minutes, the second day— 15 minutes, the third day—an hour and 40 minutes with a long sermon, and there had been no trouble since.

The boys from Gujranwala soon get into the swing and work moves faster than usual. They all want to be home for Easter. The scaffold towers are quickly assembled. The diagonals and the levels of the wall need no correcting action. The modules are sorted into the order of erection, and there are plenty of willing helpers, especially children. Their nimble fingers assemble bolts and steel and rubber washers and sort sizes and types. The smaller the children, the more adept. By nightfall on Monday, the whole of the roof structure, 47 feet long by 24 feet wide has been manhandled into place. The blocks of concrete set in the walls to hold the roof down in a windstorm are also in position.

Master Rafique's family has undertaken to provide the meals; the sleeping arrangements are in another house where the three school children and their grandmother have moved out into the courtyard to give the two rooms to their eight guests. After the evening meal, the invitation comes to drink warm and sweetened buffalo milk at Samuel's house. There the villagers talk of education, the new high school out on the west side, and their desire that their children be educated.

By Maundy Thursday morning, when the last ridge sheets are being put into place, the children, like children the world over, come happily home from school, hopping and skipping.

244 | WALKING THE WAY

It is 'grades' day, and they have been promoted to the next class. They are telling everyone they happen to meet, "Pass hogaya! (I have passed!)"

Now a problem—an invitation from Thatha Sirkari for the noon meal. It is only a mile (?) away. *Only I have promised to go, not all the others.* Yes, they have prepared food for us all, *but our work isn't finished . . .* but the food is ready!

Master Rafique and I walk across the fields to Thatha Sirkari. No servitude here in this village. Elder David has actually BOUGHT ten acres of land from earnings from his work as a labor contractor in a steel mill in Lahore. They now want a church roof, like at Dhodha. Yet they haven't even started! No matter. They have the land. This is where they will build it. They will build the walls in four months. There are 20 families and another six in the suburb village. Most of all, though, they want a school—their own school—where their children can daily learn about their own faith. When Master Rafique brings his son, Basharat (which means evangelist), to be enrolled in the Gujranwala High School, he will collect drawings for the Thatha Sirkari church, and we will build the church there.

Something important, something lively, and something promising is happening to this people who have spent so many years in poverty and subjection. They have hope, they have purpose, and they have direction, and they are beginning to acquire means. They are no longer afraid.

Working His Purposes Out . . .

ROOFS ON VILLAGE CHURCHES

These tales of small, Punjabi village congregations trying to get their churches built could cumulatively build a picture of a strife-ridden, discordant church. We acquire a picture of factions and divisions, but that is by no means the whole story. These are stories of vitality and determination, of sacrificial generosity allied to pettiness and to poverty. To me they are stories, all of them, of tremendous hope.

Village people the world over (and not only village people) have their feuds and enmities and gloss over their own unprincipled behavior in response to past hurts. These are real people we have been telling about. Most of them are Christians who were born into Christian families; it was their grandparents and their great-grandparents who made those first steps towards baptism into a different faith in a world very different and remote from their own.

The Presbyterian Church of Pakistan is still primarily a rural church, although it is affected by the worldwide trend to urbanization. Its young men go off to the cities to find work. Some train as artisans and find work, wealth, and prosperity in the Persian Gulf countries. The old economic balances are being shaken. The nurses and artisans working overseas are the nouveaux riche. Among the benefits flowing back home are some that reach beyond their immediate families.

A significant factor to the Christian community is the new ability to build a church in the village. Sometimes the land is donated by a friendly Muslim landowner; sometimes it is land on the edge of the village traditionally left for the use of the Christian peasants and their families.

The money flowing in from Abu Dhabi and Doha helps to buy bricks. Slowly, the walls rise. The window and door frames are made by the village carpenter—time for the doors and window shutters later. Long before the walls are at lintel height, the pastor or an elder is contacting Gujranwala for a roof. When news comes back that the village is listed for a roof and a tentative date for delivery is set, there is renewed activity.

Everything is on such a simple scale! Just four walls and a roof, earthen floors, a platform raised two bricks higher at one end, a door, and a few window shutters and, oh yes, a cross fixed at one end of the ridge, maybe even at both ends.

It isn't much—that cross painted with black enamel—just two steel bars welded together and a circle of similar steel strengthening the arms against the weight of the crows that will perch upon it.

Somehow, it is that cross that makes it all worth while. It is important because it belongs to them—just let anyone try to take it away!

BENEDICTION

He gave;
To the blind, sight,
Hearing to the deaf,
Walking to the lame,
Cleansing to the leper,
And, to the dead, life.
—yet to the poor
Who are with us always
not even bread,
Only the Gospel preached.
Who eats words?
What good the Kingdom
To a hungry man
Whose children cry for food?
—or is there something more
I do not understand?

Working His Purposes Out . . .

THE HEART OF THE POOR

Babu Khattu Mall was a beloved legend among the Christians in our part of the Punjab.

He never owned a bicycle and did all his evangelizing among the villages of the Punjab on foot. He must have walked thousands of miles. He loved us. When we were about to go on furlough, he brought a gift for Marie. She should buy something for herself that she wanted while she was on furlough. We should hurry back. He would be anxiously awaiting our return.

He brought out 100 rupees and offered it to her. Marie looked at me anxiously, hoping I would shake my head so that she didn't have to take it. One hundred rupees has represented variously over the years from two pounds to ten pounds. Much more significant was that it represented between two and three months income to Babu Khattu Mall. We knew he owned no home but that a kindly woman in a village near the center of his itinerating area had made a room available for him. We knew that because the roof of that little room collapsed in one of the monsoons, and we needed to get it fixed in a hurry so that he would have somewhere dry to sleep.

I nodded behind his back, and Marie took it and thanked him and poured him another cup of tea.

It was too precious a gift offered for us to refuse it, but later, Marie had the tailor make him a shalwar kamiz suit of white cotton cloth and found some quiet way to cause him to receive it without knowing its source.

One of my favorite portraits is Van Gogh's *Peasant*. The pain and experience of many generations speaks through his face. When you look at him, you look at history.

So it is with Babu Khattu Mall. He came today to say how glad he is that we are back. As the rain teems down, the 84-year-old evangelist talks to me of Amin Shah.

I know it well. It is where the railway line from Narowal passes over the canal. When I last went there, it was to check up on a small primary school the local congregation was wanting some help for. I refused the help because, although they had a dedicated young teacher, they didn't have the minimum 25 Christian children we look for in schools we assist.

I know that this little group dreamed of one day having a church of its own too.

"What has happened in the months we've been away?" I ask.

"Oh, God is blessing wonderfully. We have a girl who has finished her primary school and she is a very bright girl and she is teaching the other younger ones in the courtyard of her home. And the church—God is blessing us there too. We have obtained the land where you suggested it, on the edge of the village." (Probably a Muslim landowner has donated it, if it isn't land traditionally used by Christians.) "Yes, the land is too low, and we will have to bring in about five feet of dirt to raise it above flood level. I have told every wage earner, there are ten," (he counts up on his fingers and names them off) "and they have all agreed to give a whole month's salary for their church, half this month and half next month. We will then bring in the dirt and build our foundations, and then," he smiles at me as enjoying a great joke, "we shall come to you and ask if you will help us."

I think of the poverty of this people and the tenacity that drives them to wrest a living from a flood-prone land that is less than hospitable. I think of their readiness in all their debt and need to keep a school going for their children and to give a full month's salary to help build a little church—one that we probably wouldn't want to house a horse in, and I think about the resources of the church elsewhere and that wealth has many forms.

Khushi had been a tailor. He had quite possibly learned his trade at the Boys Industrial Home before we closed the tailor's school. Ed Carlson had been involved somehow in Khushi learning how to read and write. He had a thin, gaunt face, slender frame, and buck teeth, nothing much to look at. He had trouble walking as though in the earlier stages of his life he might have had polio. He also did not enunciate clearly.

Learning to read transformed his life. He could not only read his Bible now, but he could read it to others. Reading to others called for explanations of what was read, and his earnestness that others understand what they were hearing led him into simple parable-like explanations in terms that a Punjabi like himself could understand. He became an evangelist, a babu like Babu Khattu Mall, and then, although he was poorly educated, a pastor for a village congregation near Pasrur. This was a congregation that the seminary-trained graduates had trouble accepting as a suitable call.

He, too, rarely had any money and would usually arrange his visits to Gujranwala or Lahore or Sialkot to end up with a visit to a missionary or a Pakistani friend who could be relied upon to know his need and give him his bus fare to get back home.

I asked him on one of his visits to the technical center whether he tithed. He looked blankly at me and asked me to explain. "A tithe, Khushi, the word means 'a tenth part', is the share of our income that we give to God. We choose to live on nine tenths of our income and give the other tenth, the first tenth, not the last tenth, to God for His work in the world we live in. It can be used in any of a number of ways, but the important thing is that we set apart the first tenth of our income for His purposes."

Khushi was looking worried and uneasy. I had disturbed him with my question.

"Let me show you what I mean, Khushi. How much do you receive a month altogether, from the offerings, from the gifts your people give to you?"

He thought a while. "I might get as much as 40 rupees if I added everything in."

I was shocked at how little he received. How could any man live on that? I carried on, less certainly and less firmly. "Then, Khushi, one-tenth of that is four rupees. This means that your tithe is four rupees that you set aside for God's work and give to Him each month."

Slowly, he replied, "I haven't been doing that, Old Sah'b. I didn't know; no one explained it to me. I would have done it if I had known, but I didn't know."

A thought struck him. "Does helping the widows count, Old Sah'b?"

"What do you mean, Khushi?"

"There are two widows in the village, and they have no one to take care of them so I take care of them. Does that count?"

And I had nothing more to say.

Who was I to be trying to teach Khushi about tithing? Physician, examine thyself!

While I am in England, I receive a letter from Massachusetts in the United States. It is from someone at the high school in Quincy. My name has been given to them, and they write for advice on building a school in Pakistan. The story, as the letter unfolds, is deeply moving and raises emotions of both sadness and hope.

A young boy, Iqbal Masih, had come to Quincy. He represented the exploited children of the Third world. He was from Muridke, a town that lies on the road between Gujranwala and Lahore. He was a child carpet weaver. Iqbal's second name, Masih, told that he was a Christian child.

In many of our villages, I had come across these carpet-weaving communities. There were looms in most of the villages. The smaller the children, the more deft their fingers. In Shahabdeke, we had started a school for the children only to be forced to close it because the children were needed for carpet weaving and couldn't spare time for school. Local entrepreneurs most frequently owned the looms. They also supplied the woolen yarn and all the financial investment. Only the labor was supplied by the villagers against loans and wages. In Satiali Kalan, the children had started work before dawn by the dim light of a 40-watt electric light bulb.

In one village, I found women who worked 12 hours a day at the carpet looms with very limited breaks and for a pittance of payment. From that village, a part of the weaving community had broken away in desperation. They were squatting on land that had once been a brick-kiln beside the Sheikhupura road and were fighting litigation to evict them. Although every new home that they had built there had a loom, all were, again, owned by entrepreneurs who merely paid for the weaver's labor. However, their children were getting to school a mile or so down the road and weaving before school and when they got home from school. This community believed education might provide a way of escape for the next generation, although it wasn't very likely.

Iqbal Masih had been accompanied to Quincy by an adult who spoke English, and through this interpreter, he had spoken to the assembled school in the auditorium. He had told them simply about his life, his family, his day, and his hopes for the future. Even children like him had hopes and dreams.

When he had returned home to Muridke, he had been shot dead.

The children of Quincy High School were haunted by the thoughts of this winsome, brown-skinned young boy with the large brown eyes who had been recently among them. They decided that Iqbal Masih should not just be forgotten. With all the zest of a stirred-up American community, the kids began to raise money for a memorial to Iqbal. Initiatives to raise money were combined with truly sacrificial giving by the kids of their own money. Children in New Zealand came to hear of what Quincy was doing and decided to join in.

The letter said that the children had raised $100,000, and they wanted advice on how best to direct the money. They needed to build a memorial school in Muridke to Iqbal Masih.

Phew! $100,000!!! My village schools cost $20 a month and have no buildings! What could be done with $100,000?

Somehow, when things like this happen, you can still feel there is hope for the world.

Babu Khattu Mall and I are visiting a village in his area, not far from Muridke. It is a typical village mounded by centuries from the flat surrounding land that stretches to the horizons. There is only a small Christian community, two or three families. There used to be more, but the others have gone to the towns where work is available.

I take an opportunity to wander alone around the village, but I am soon joined by a young man maybe 18 years old.

He wants to show me his shop. It is a small corner room; its only light comes from the open door. My eyes adjust to the gloom. There is little sign of either stock or business activity other than a few sacks of peppers, potatoes, rice, country sugar, and small packets of tea. He explains apologetically that business is not good. He has exhausted his credit, and his customers find it hard to pay their bills.

We chat as we walk. We pause at the girls' school and look in through the gate. The school courtyard is full of neatly dressed girls of various ages sitting in rows on a thin rush covering on the ground, writing on slates. This is obviously a flourishing Government primary school. The lad, he tells me his name is Barkat Masih, asks if I would like to see his old school. The teachers, there are two of them, break off classes to welcome their foreign visitor, and the boys, again a full school, cluster round until shooed back into their places.

As we leave, I ask Barkat whether he enjoyed going to school there. I am surprised by his vehemence. "No! I hated every minute of it!" He goes on to explain. "I was the only Christian boy in the school, and I used to get beaten up every day. There wasn't a day someone didn't pick a fight with me, and the others were standing around to help if I was ever getting the upper hand."

This bullying was not, of course, for direct religious reasons but was the herd instinct of a gang or group against the outsider. I look at Barkat amazed. "Then why on earth did you continue?"

The boy's face is grim as he recollects those past days. "I was determined to escape from the village and I knew I had to be educated to do so. No matter what it cost, I was going to complete school and escape from the village." I marvel at the boy's tenacity.

Probed by further questions he goes on. After primary school, he goes for three years to middle school, pointing to a distant village on the horizon across the fields. I see him in my mind's eye walking with other boys and the red-shawled girls each day at least an hour's walk, probably nearer two, along the narrow, single-file tracks to the middle schools at Ghulampura to get the kind of rote learning that passes for education.

"Did you pass?"

"Oh, yes. I got my certificate."

"And then?"

He looks directly at me in a confrontation of remembered pain that still haunts my thoughts.

"And then I found it was all worth nothing!"

All worth nothing! Five years of bullied primary school, three years of walking long miles to and from school in all weathers, and all worth nothing! What kind of a world is this we live in? What childish hopes and gritted teeth and strength of character! All worth nothing! Surely children like Barkat deserve something better than this!

I offer to find him a scholarship to the Technical School where he can learn a trade. He is interested; his eyes have brightened . . . but no, he is needed here because he escorts his sister to school. She also wants to escape. I offer to find a scholarship for her also to go to boarding school or nursing school which will free him to come to Gujranwala. It is important to find some way to give back to this young man a sense of worth and values. We exchange addresses, but I hear no more of him, and I do not know what happened to him—though his words have echoed in my mind ever since I first heard them.

"I found it was all worth nothing."

We have taken with us visiting friends from the motor industry in Michigan. They push our old Land Rover out of the mud in bare feet and are glad their friends at home can't see them now. We visit one village where they bring out a sick man on his bed, possibly dying from tuberculosis, for us to pray for him. At Mandigarh the village lies within the Ravi river bund and is subject to frequent flooding. We discuss possibly rebuilding Clemmie's church at a higher level and using the old building as a school. Two little, bright-eyed girls, sparkling with mischief, catch Elaine's eye. I interpret for her and them. When they grow up, they want to be nurses. They will be into eighth class next year, and that will be the end of their educational options.

Elaine, a nurse herself, asks me to be sure to keep tabs on the two girls, and she will underwrite their education as nurses. I promise to do so.

Now years later, I am back in the village. We have progressed the girls all the way up to their applications for admission into nursing school at the Mission Hospital in Sialkot. I enquire after them; how are they doing in nursing school?

Ask them yourself, I am told, and a boy is sent running. Two young women, the sparkle now moderated by the gravity of their advancing years, salaam greetings. Our Punjabi girls are just so beautiful! I ask why they are not away in Sialkot at school. Alas, they cannot speak English, and so they could not be admitted into nursing school. English fluency is now a requirement for admission.

This is ridiculous! The two girls grow up speaking Punjabi. In their school years, they learn also the official language of the country, Urdu. No teacher in their village school can speak English nor is English part of the village school curriculum. These girls are effectively finding the doors of opportunity barred against them. I privately suspect, though I could be wrong, the English nursing advisor to the Government needed to find a way by which she could bring her own need to communicate into the Pakistani nursing environment. The best way was to require the use of English textbooks. We had met a similar problem in our early years at Gujranwala with technical education, but the answer was not to require the boys to speak English. It was to put the books into their language.

Two little girls among so many, but what happens to them—what *happened* to them—matters!

COMMUNION

Beyond prayer
And thoughts thrown out
Toward infinity
Lies something more
Where that within us,
Apprehending,
Is strangely part
Of infinity
Apprehended.

WALKING HIS PURPOSES OUT

*And thine ears shall hear
a word behind thee, saying,
This is the way, walk ye in it,
when ye turn to the right hand
and when ye turn to the left.*
Isaiah 30:21

The story doesn't end here although this book does. It is now the end of 2004 and there is much untold that deserves the telling. But enough has been said to tell the story of a God of the present day who loves us and wants us to prosper under His Hand, even though we may not be aware He is there.

So much of our Christian life calls for listening and then responding rather than just up, off, and out and doing. There are so many lessons we need to learn about the ultimate simplicity of our faith, if we are disposed to take the risk.

I recall the conversation in Lahore with my Muslim friend, the Director of Technical Education, more than 30 years ago.

"You are a Christian, Mr. Old. Do you have faith? Yes? Then start walking by it!"

Yes, that's all there is to it. We need to start walking.

*. . . prove me now herewith,
saith the Lord of hosts,
if I will not open you
the windows of heaven,
and pour you out a blessing,
that there shall not be
room enough to receive it!*
Malachi 3:10b

Contact author Kenneth Old
or order more copies of this book at

TATE PUBLISHING, LLC

127 East Trade Center Terrace
Mustang, Oklahoma 73064

(888) 361 - 9473

Tate Publishing, LLC

www.tatepublishing.com